Praise for "Delving into My Bitterroots: How I Resurrected My Enslaved Ancestor, Granvill, and So, Can You," by Donise Smith Lei

The book you now hold in your hands is a treasure. Amateur Genealogy has been one of America's favorite pastimes for decades, and the advent of DNA-based genealogy has only increased popular obsession with it. Yet there are very few guides in print, practical for enthusiasts at both the beginner and intermediate levels, that provide amateur genealogists with the tools to successfully tackle and solve many of the complicated barriers that arise for people engaged in serious family research.

Lei's entertaining and highly-informative book succeeds in two different ways: 1) It's a detailed, personal account of her journey to take as deep a dive as she possibly could into the life of an ancestor about whom she'd always been curious, but about whom she'd known precious little more than his name, and the tantalizing fragments of a couple of passed-down stories; 2) it's a detailed guide that lays out a blueprint other researchers can follow as they attempt to tackle challenging aspects of their own family research.

But beyond the world of amateur genealogy, the book will also be of keen interest to teachers of history who will find Lei's intensely personal story a useful addition to curriculum materials on the study of slavery - and to African American readers (and Americans of every stripe) who are curious about what it takes to do some serious family research but simply don't know where to begin.

African American history is American history. As we strive to move forward into whatever "more perfect union" we are able to create for ourselves as a nation, the strength and cohesiveness of the future we build will depend on our ability to understand and own up to a clear-eyed vision of our past. Books about personal encounters with the American past, not written by academics but by every-day citizens, are important and rare... and will always be an important part of what will get us there.

David Lawrence Grant
Writer

DELVING INTO MY BITTERROOTS

How I Resurrected My Enslaved Ancestor, Granvill, and So Can You

Donise Smith Lei

To Dale Jennings, who believed in me before I believed in myself.

Acknowledgements

The journey to write this book was both challenging and rewarding. I could not even have gotten started without the tireless efforts of my DNA cousins, Cheryl, William, James, Rashawn, Kerry, Chantal, and Julia. Not only were there at the beginning of this trek, but I could always count on them for help and support.

I am eternally grateful to my family members who provided stories and much needed feedback including my dad Cornell, my uncle Charles, my aunts Delores and Ollie plus my mom Gail, my sisters, Elaine, Jan, and Kelle, my niece, Vanessa along with my cousin Valerie.

A special thanks go to my beta readers, including my daughter, Shelley, my friend, Vicki, and my mentor, David, who spent hours reading and editing my book.

Writing a book is such a daunting task that can't get done without encouragement. I want to thank my huge group of teacher friends who keep me going. You know who you are, but I want to especially thank Ed, Gene, Christine, and Wendall, who provided me their unmatched expertise in their respective disciplines.

Finally, I can't give enough praise to my amazing husband, Weilin. He took me all over the country to gather research for this book. He patiently helped me to clarify every topic I couldn't make sense of. It's funny, but he often came to my rescue when I couldn't find the right English word to express my thoughts, and of course, his incredible knowledge of Chinese sayings added a unique twist to my narrative. Not only did he take care of all these things and more, but I appreciate that he was always there emotionally supporting me through it all.

CONTENTS

INTRODUCTION

I am sure, at some point, someone has asked you the question, "If you could meet any person or persons from the past, who would it be?" My answer typically might have been, George Washington, Martin Luther King, and maybe Queen Elizabeth I. What would yours be? In the past, I never would have answered with one of my ancestors. Now, I have changed. I have a better understand as to why we need to learn about our ancestors. In this busy, ever-changing world, your family history gives you an anchoring place where, no matter what, you will always belong. Your ancestry provides a source of pride in your ethnic identity to you and your family. Believe it or not, there is wisdom in your family history. They can tell you how others just like you had remarkable abilities to deal with life's struggles. Best of all, like adoptees reaching out to their biological parents, knowing who you are and where you come from makes you whole.

My newfound respect for my ancestors came after I had been seriously dabbling in genealogy and my family history for over two decades. I read books and magazines and went to genealogy and family history conferences. I built my family tree out six generations until I hit a wall due to a lack of records. Undaunted, I decided I wanted to find whatever I could about one of my enslaved 3rd great-grandfathers.

As I began the rudimentary research into my ancestor, I was fortunate that I have at least one document that lists my ancestor's first name, age, and skin pigmentation. Many people have ancestors with few records because they were poor. The records for the ancestors of most African Americans are very challenging to find, that is if they exist at all. With that one document, I began my quest to find out more about my ancestor and to eventually "resurrect" him, his life, and his world.

To "resurrect" my ancestor, I changed my mindset that history is about famous people. I switched my thinking to ordinary people are worthy of study. I researched history and other topics, intending to understand how my family interacted with major historical events. So, not only did I determine if my 3rd great-grandfather might have seen George Washington, but I explored a wide range of African American history.

I had spent years collecting genealogical data about my family. But when I used the structured format of a biography, it compelled me to think about topics beyond my data. For instance, my enslaved ancestor was born in Colonial Georgia. What was life like for him in Colonial Georgia? I did lots of research using books, articles, interviews, trips, and the internet. Sometimes I had so much information, I had to wrestle with selecting the parts that were pertinent to my ancestor. At other times, I had to squeeze insights out of limited facts. For example, the documents and correspondence of George Washington from his Mount Vernon Plantation illustrate the inside story of the lives of enslaved African Americans on tobacco plantations.

I did not realize that I would have to dust off those old high school English skills and knowledge. Remember when your teacher announced that all good literature has universal themes that provides insight into the human condition? It required a universal theme or two to guide me through my ancestor's world. My enslaved ancestor and his descendants faced the obstacles of prejudice and racism, and yet they persevered. How they responded to both helped me grasp some of their thinking. Other universal themes that might pertain to your family might be the ability to be persistent and survive immigration to a new place, combatting nature including natural disasters, the strain on relationships during economic downturns, and the consequences of war.

I had to be okay using words such as *most likely, possibly, no doubt* or *in all probability*. To give an example, at Mount Vernon, someone wondered what George Washington's favorite color was. Since he had his living room, dining room, and possibly a bedroom painted green, they concluded that he probably liked green. Since no written evidence that declares this favorite color was green, that is as close to the truth as we can get. This theory makes sense to me because my living room is painted my favorite color, but we will never know if green was Washington's favorite color for sure. When considering the past, you will have to be okay with having strong probabilities sometimes with little to no certainty.

Frankly, I found I needed a motivator to keep on track to "resurrect" my ancestor. If you are lucky, you can find someone like my friend, Dale Jennings. He sent me materials, gave me advice, and most importantly, he didn't let me quit. His passing drove me to finish this project as a tribute to his unselfish kindness. You will need to choose some motivator to help you to achieve your goal. For example, planning a family reunion with a firm date will push you to keep researching. Making a memory book for a significant birthday present for someone will keep you focused. Creating a PowerPoint presentation is an easy way to structure all your information. Another idea is to prepare for a visit to your ancestor's birthplace. Perhaps you want to make some kind of scrapbook for your family or children. Working with a partner or a club will keep you inspired. The choice is yours but try to at least pick something to keep you on your path.

This project was so rewarding. Not only did I strengthen my ethnic identity, but I explored a lot of history that is now much more meaningful to me. My enslaved ancestor provided me with a secret gift that I will always treasure and I uncovered my family's superpowers.

I hope you decide to take this worthwhile journey to discover your ancestors and find the joy that it brings. Don't worry if you're not sure of exactly how this adventure will work out. I certainly didn't know what I was doing or what I was going to find on the way. But the quest and the answers I found were amazing and worth the hard work I put into it.

Challenges

Think back to your childhood. Do you remember the exhilaration of going on a field trip back when you were in school? For years as a 6th grade teacher, on the day of a field trip, my antsy students seemed like they were ready to burst with anticipation waiting for their adventure to begin. Now it was my turn to gaze impatiently through the window of a small regional airliner. I was on the final leg of my journey from southern California to northwest Louisiana. As an avid family history researcher, this was a dream come true. I was going to visit Bossier Parish, Louisiana, the land where my grandfather, great-grandfather, and even my 2nd and 3rd great-grandparents had once lived. When I think of Louisiana, New Orleans comes to mind, but my people had lived about 400 miles to the north of the infamous city. My ancestors had resided in what is now known as the Deep South. What would I encounter there? By some luck, along with a lot of research, I was getting the rare opportunity to stand on the exact ground where my enslaved ancestors had once toiled on over a century and a half earlier. How would I feel setting foot on the same land where my people had been enslaved? I had been chasing my roots for over two decades. Would this trip live up to my years of eager anticipation?

As an African American, I counted it as a stroke of splendid fortune that I was able to find some of my ancestors beyond the usual roadblock of 1870. And even more unbelievable, I was thrilled to discover an ancestor whose birth in 1770 was before the founding of our nation. For the typical African American researching his or her family history, the year 1870 is farthest back they can find a record. Before that, enslaved people were only given a first name similarly to how you would name your pet. They were not in the census except on the Federal Slave Schedules, where they were listed them under the slaveholder's name as a number with no names. They were only distinguishable by age, sex, and color.

NAMES OF SLAVE OWNERS.	Number of Slaves.	DESCRIPTION.			Fugitives from the State.	Number manumitted.	Deaf & dumb, blind, insane, or idiotic.
		Age.	Sex.	Colour.			
1	2	3	4	5	6	7	8
J B Gilmer	1	18	F	B			
	1	16	F	B			
	1	16	F	B			
	1	12	F	B			
	1	12	F	B			
	1	6	F	B			

One of these enslaved African Americans may be related to me
1850 U.S. Federal Census – Slave Schedules, Louisiana, Bossier, Township 19 Ward 2, P.5

The 1870 Federal census following the end of slavery contained complete names, as well as other helpful information such as the age, place of birth and occupation. The lack of church records, marriage licenses, land records, and wills make finding documentation of enslaved ancestors very challenging. It requires that you find evidence of the last slaveholder.

Even though genealogy can be a daunting task, I've been hooked on the fascinating process of uncovering and piecing together my family history since the first time I went to the National Archives many years ago. That was before one could effortlessly type a query on an internet genealogy website. You had to find physical records, such as those on microfilm. While I was there, I could not contain my loud gasp when I dug up the names of my 2nd great grandparents on my mother's side. I looked up sheepishly at others in the formally quiet room, who were clapping for me. I must admit; not only do I love solving puzzles in my family history, but I feel a sense of wholeness when I get acquainted with my ancestors as people.

To understand the big picture in genealogy, I think the first place is to start with you. I began to collect records about myself, including my birth certificate. I asked myself five "W" questions - who, what, when, where and why? "Who" was my complete name. "What" were my relatives, of course, that's my father and mother. "When" gives the date and maybe time of my birth. "Where" provides the location of my birth. All of this information illuminates how I am a unique person in the world. I am the only one with that name, born to those parents, on that date, and in that location. I had to come up with a "why." Mine was "Why was I born in Texas?" The answer; my father was a soldier in the army. There was also something surprising. I hadn't noticed there was a place to designate me as "Legitimate." That referred to my legal status at birth because my mother was married to my father. That was my first introduction to an aspect of American culture, the rule of law. With this understanding of myself and my documents, I utilized this same technique over and over again as I gathered information and documents about my family, from my relatives and other records including the censuses. So, the more information I gathered and questions I could answer especially "why," the more I discovered about my family history.

After I had spent years doing all the prerequisites, such as gathering information from my family, building an online tree and making detailed timelines, I was finally going to Bossier Parish, Louisiana. My beloved grandfather, Lindsey Smith, always told us he was born in Plain Dealing, which is in Bossier Parish. Louisiana is divided into 64 parishes in the same way most other states are divided into counties. His father, Joseph P. Smith, was also born a free man in 1876 in the same northern part of the parish that became the town of Plain Dealing in 1887.

As a child, I remember hearing about the land our family still owned there, and there was a story about a man named Granville. The name Granville was captivating to me, I found it to be very sophisticated and regal sounding. When I researched the 1880 census records on the internet, I verified that Joseph's father was Sam Smith. I needed to use several censuses since the names were not consistent. Sometimes it was Sam and Joe while at other times it was Samuel and Joseph but there was no Granville. After that, I was stuck just after the Civil

War, like most other African Americans. Then, a few years ago, a game changer occurred when I took the AncestryDNA test. I received my ethnicity estimate which revealed the African portion of my roots was from many places including Cameroon/Congo, Nigeria, Senegal and Ivory Coast/ Ghana, as well as other regions in Africa. But more importantly, I found a person noted as my DNA match. (The DNA found in almost every cell in your body has information on your genetic heritage. A match is another person who has taken a DNA test from Ancestry that has DNA in common with you. The more shared DNA you have, the closer that person is related to you.) I excitedly sent him a message asking him to contact me, I told him I had more information about our family, and I asked him what his first name was. A few days later he replied. He suggested that I contact Cheryl Gaines, who had more original research on the Smith Family. At the end of the message, he wrote, "I am William Smith, the son of Granville Smith, Jr." It blew me away that the name Granville was in his message. This began my collaboration with my DNA "genetic cousins." William and Cheryl are both 2nd cousins 1x removed. They proved vital to helping me discover my roots. Together with another DNA cousin, James Austin Gray III, we unlocked many of the puzzles of the Smith family history. This trip to Bossier Parish was the next step in that process. I wasn't sure what I would find, but in the back of my mind, I was hoping that I would uncover a treasure trove of information both verifying what we already knew and exposing more about my ancestor's life and experiences.

I was glad to have my husband, Weilin, with me on this trip. I didn't want to travel here alone. We both had not been to a rural area in the South. As a Chinese born American citizen, his knowledge of the Deep South came from what he saw on the news and in the movies. He was afraid that the police would put him in jail with the smallest infraction of the law. We both shared some apprehension about what people would think of us; an interracial couple in the South. Nevertheless, he had promised to support me in whatever way he could to track down my family origins as my driver, assistant, confidant, and if need be, my protector.

Our first destination in the morning was the Bossier Parish Court House in Benton, the parish seat. There are all kinds of records found at courthouses including marriage and divorces, wills and probate packets, jury lists, land and property records, property maps, taxation maps and records, poorhouse, even lunacy records and more. Many of these records are primary sources because they were written very close to the time the event occurred, making them more reliable. Secondary sources were created after the fact, and could be less reliable, such as a birth date on a death certificate. From the FamilySearch Wiki on Bossier Parish, Louisiana Genealogy, I found that Parish Clerk Courthouse has marriage, divorce, probate, land and court records starting from 1830.

As we drove from Shreveport across the river to Bossier City, and then on Highway 3 to Benton, I had my first chance to catch a glimpse of the rural countryside. We were in northern Bossier Parish, which had been established in 1843. On this lovely sunny day, I could see the muddy red-colored Red River on my left. During the mid-19th century, I might have seen steamboats and ferries shuttling passengers and cargo destined for either New Orleans or up the river to St. Louis and beyond. The Red River, which is the western border of Bossier Parish, flows into the Mississippi River. On my right, I could see the flat wide, open spaces. The alluvial deposits over the eons made this some of the most fertile farmland around. For years, the Bossier Parish was the leading cotton producing area in northwest Louisiana. If I could hop back through time before the Civil War in the Antebellum Period, I would have very likely seen enslaved people, who had been laboring since sunrise on these lands.

Reaching the courthouse in Benton, we were set to consult with Clifton Cardin, designated "Official Historian of Bossier Parish." I planned to buy copies of his comprehensive cemetery inventory book, Bossier Parish Headstones, one each for William, Cheryl, and myself. He was a very friendly Santa Claus look-alike. His insider knowledge of the courthouse cut the time in half we would have needed to uncover the information I pursued. First, there was the original handwritten conveyance book from 1854 with the deed stating, in squiggly cursive, that, "Martha H. Gilmer gives and delivers to the said George E. Gilmer the following old Negroes, Granvill a man Dark aged 84 years…"

the Notary public — And further the said
Martha H. Gilmer, gives and delivers to the
said George E. Gilmer the following old Negroes
Vez, Granvill   a Man   Dark   aged   84 yrs,
" Eliza his Wife — Do Man —   —   —   56 "
" Abram   a Man   —   —   57,
" Lucy his Wife   Woman Yellow —   54
" Edmond   a Man   Dark "   53
" Patsey   Woman Yellow "   40
Which Negroes, I make this deed for the
last Named Six Negroes as a gift to have
his Care and attention, in old age —

Granvill in the Deed Book 3, Page 333

Only a few weeks before, William had seen this and other information about Sam in the book No Land...Only Slaves, Vol. 1, Bossier Parish Louisiana, Deed Book 3, Page 333, Registry no. 0792. He had speculated that Granvill might be Samuel's father. I quickly ordered a copy of the book. But now with my own eyes, I could see the "who;" my Granvill, the name that had mesmerized me for years. Unbelievably, this was my 3rd great-grandfather, known only as Granvill (Please note the first Granvill without an "e" was probably a misspelling of Granville, a name that would be carried down to many of his descendants.) There was another name, Gilmer. Now my evidence for the "what" was cemented, which was the relationship between my family and the Gilmer family, as being enslaved and slaveholder. This document was the most crucial step in recovering my family's history. Since in 1854 he was about 84, which put his birth in about 1770, I was able to find an answer to the "when." Later, Cheryl, an MD who always scrutinizes any of our group's new findings with the keen eagle-eye of a medical professional, demonstrated why looking at primary sources is crucial. She pointed out that this primary source document also gave us additional information that his wife was Eliza. On the page before, the names Marywether (26), William (22), Samuel (22), and Jane (17) are in a list separated from another family, thus adding more weight to the evidence of the "why," as they were members of our Samuel's family. Three of these names - Marywether, Sam, and Jane - were Smith's, and are listed near each other in both the 1870 and 1880 Federal Censuses of Bossier Parish, which gave me a clue to the "where," as they most likely lived next to each other.

Next, we inspected the old-looking original marriage license of Samuel Smith and Caroline Johnson. These are my 2nd great-grandparents, who were married in 1870. The "his mark" and "her mark" over their written-out names still was a poignant observation, but it became more of a painful realization when I first saw the copy that Cheryl uploaded online. It was like a kick in the guts when I saw the glaring evidence that slavery had deprived my ancestors of a simple act that elementary students today can to do with ease - writing their name. From my history classes, I remembered the "why" because enslaved people were not allowed to learn to read and write, but it hit me on a palpable emotional and personal level when it came to my own family.

After focusing on all the legal documents that pertained to my family members during and just after slavery, it was now time to locate the records for the land owned by my great-grandfather, Joseph P. Smith. We found the 1900 bill of sale to Granville Smith and Joe Smith. That Granville was Joseph or Joe's older brother, and he was the oldest of Samuel and Caroline's eight children. He had been named after his grandfather Granvill, who was also the grandfather of my DNA cousin, William. As the clerk was processing the information we needed to get copies, she calmly mentioned to us that there was some trouble with this property. There were some confusing legal terms about praying for a motion and judgments. The case was in the court system, and we could lose that land. Cliff then jumped into action to help us find all the documents related to the case. I was in shock. Suddenly, I was worried that we would have to surrender the land that had been in the family for well over a century. I knew I would have to take this back to show the elder generation, including my dad, my uncles, aunts and their cousins, who were the primary caretakers of the land. I originally had just wanted to see our property out of curiosity, but now I needed to know everything about the land before it would possibly be lost forever.

In the afternoon, we visited the Bossier Parish Historical Center located in Bossier City, which is just east of Shreveport. Genealogical and Historical Societies are actively engaged in the study of history, culture, society, and documentation in their area. One of the striking exhibits was a basket of picked but unginned cotton, so I snapped a photo of it. I should have taken a selfie. Wouldn't that be ironic? The second great-granddaughter of an enslaved person takes a selfie with cotton.

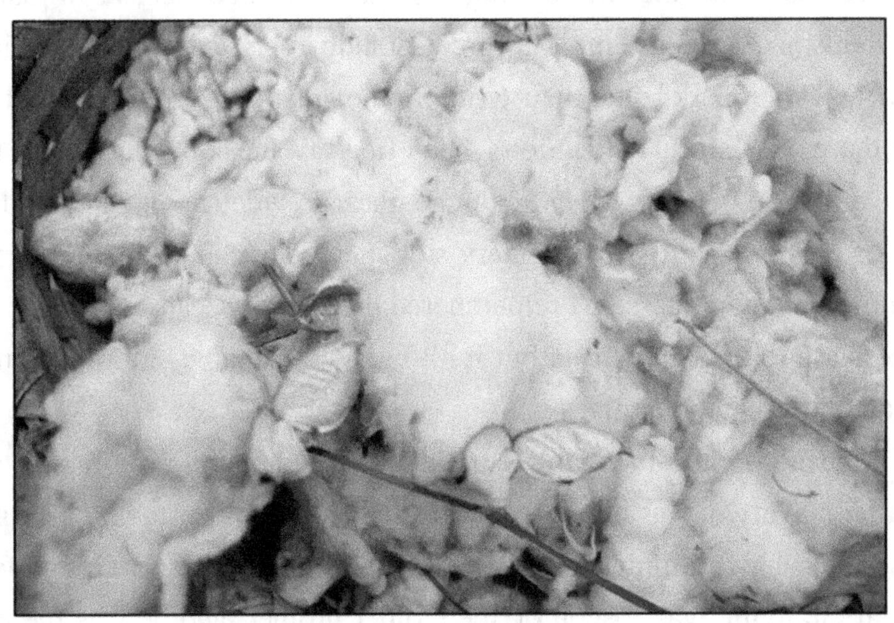

Unginned cotton that has not been put through a cotton gin

Getting down to business, Weilin and I split up the research. I researched anything I could find on the Gilmer family, the slaveholders of my ancestors, and anything I could understand about what life was like before and after slavery. Weilin researched the history of education in Bossier Parish, the timber industry, and how the railroads had affected the area. Everyone was most helpful in locating all kinds of information (including books, articles, photos, etc) about the Gilmer family, but the pickings for what life would have been like during and after slavery were slim. The director of the Historical Center suggested that I get in touch with Dale Jennings, who had written many articles about Bossier Parish. William had also spoken of recently emailing Dale. I was able to get in touch with Dale who proposed to go with us to Plain Dealing the next day.

Later, as Weilin and I were discussing our progress thus far, there was both a sense of satisfaction but apprehension. This place was more than names and places in history books. There was a disquieting fear of actually staring at the location where my ancestors had been enslaved. Slavery touches on just about all the scariest things that humans fear. Besides rape and separation anxiety, it involves many things on a recent list of the top 10 things Americans are afraid of like, "people I love dying, people I love becoming seriously ill and being a victim of terror." The slavery in my own family was never discussed or mentioned. I don't recall my parents or grandparents speaking about the enslaved members of my family. But now, everywhere we investigated and everything I laid my eyes on, kept bringing up this dark, depressingly painful history of slavery in my family. Then, there was the angst that we might lose the land that had been in the family for over one hundred years.

As I sat there slumped over, my husband understandably asked me what was wrong. I just sighed at my Chinese husband whom I thought could not possibly understand me, my fears, and how black people had endured, mostly in silence, the tortured legacy of slavery. "Well," he said, "the Chinese have an idea, if you are afraid of pointed objects, surround yourself with nails to train yourself to overcome your fear." He then explained what this meant. When you are facing unpleasant things, you should face it and overcome the fear. Through this process you can change a negative fear into a positive force that can help you to fight and win the battle. Weilin always amazes me with his ability to come up with Chinese sayings for almost any situation humans can find themselves in. He was right; I should find a way to cope with the "peculiar institution." Just like I forced myself to watch the disturbing movie, 12 Years a Slave, I should force myself to confront the personal tragedy of slavery in my own family. My new purpose was to train myself to face those horrors, to learn everything I could about the slavery in my family's history, and to unearth every fact I possibly could. One of my first steps was to change the language I used to describe slavery. Changing my use of the words slave to enslaved African American and slaveowner to slaveholder, reinforced the idea that my ancestors were not property, but capable human beings.

The next day, with my new resolve, we met up with Dale Jennings at his home outside of Benton on Vance Road. I wouldn't learn the full significance of the name of that street until months later. Dale was a kindly, older gentleman, who reminded me of a retired history professor. He knew story on top of story about this area with the exacting precision of dates and places. His wife, Larri, a very hospitable lady, explained her connections to this area as a descendant of the Vance family. With Dale as our knowledgeable guide, he directed us to the Plain Dealing Cemetery located on a high hill just northeast of the town of Plain Dealing. According to Clifton Cardin's book from 1997, the cemetery contained 1,420 white burials. Once through the gates, we walked past a huge tree to the earliest grave there, that of George O. Gilmer, who had died in 1849. Dale informed us that this cemetery had started as the family graveyard directly to the rear of where Gilmer had built his home. Of the 5,000 acres he had purchased to create his Plain Dealing Plantation, this was at a higher elevation. The house had rested on the southern brow of the hill overlooking his cotton fields in the Little Cypress Bayou Valley below. It's now populated by the town of Plain Dealing, and is mostly hidden by trees. The broken gray granite slabs marked the permanent resting places of George and his wife Martha, the slaveholders of my ancestors. The three of us were on our hands and knees, brushing away the dirt and leaves from the tombstones. Dale glanced up to notice a prim-looking lady who had stopped her car not far away on the cemetery drive though road. She was staring at us with a fixed disbelieving gaze, not comprehending what she was seeing. Dale later asked if I had seen her. I was so enthralled with the moment; I hadn't noticed her as I was desperately trying to wrap my head around this scene. Nearby was a monument for George and Martha's son, George E. Gilmer who had died in the Civil War, another slaveholder of my family. Among the many old Gilmer and Vance tombstones, was a headstone for JP Vance whom I would later learn was employed as the Gilmer's last overseer. Dale thought the slave quarters where my ancestors had lived back in the 1840s could have been in this spot or down below by the bayou next to where the fields would have been.

Giving the area more scrutiny, I stood quietly. The tall, slender trees jutting out in the distance along with small green bushes obscured the view of the town. Green surrounded me in every direction, with the sky being difficult to see without craning my neck straight up. How different did this look from the first time Granvill and his young son Sam saw this new place? If I stood very still, could I imagine what the plantation was like for them? Could I almost hear them working to clear the land to build the genteel home that once stood here? Could I taste the sweat from their brows as they wearily walked back from the fields during cotton picking time? My powers of imagination were not strong enough to faithfully transport me back to their time, but I can say that I walked the land that my ancestors once had walked. I had made the first incremental steps to confronting the challenges of my family's history.

Next, we traveled to the recently renamed Old Plain Dealing Cemetery. It was accepted to be a negro cemetery which was initially named Mt. Zion and had contained a Baptist church. It included the broken headstone of Jane Smith, Granvill's daughter. We also saw a headstone for Eliza V, wife of S. T. James, who was Jane's daughter and Granvill's granddaughter. Dale insisted that we noticed the V. He claimed that it was short for Vance. Dale's wife, Larri, was a Vance descendent. My research was not clear on this. It was something I would need to verify with census records when I got home. But all the same, I found the whole idea a startling coincidence that we Vance's and Smith's would cross paths in both the nineteenth and the twenty-first century!

Headstone of Eliza, the daughter of Jane Smith and granddaughter of Granvill

Next, we drove to view our family's land. I had an assessment map, but that turned out to be very impractical when we arrived in the area. We stopped at a little black country church to ask some people we saw for help with directions. There was a slight pause, as a black middle-aged woman looked at me, then the Asian guy driving and the elderly white guy in the back seat. After explaining my purpose, she gave us some directions and told us to go further down the road to see if another person she knew was more knowledgeable about the land. Judging from the map, I knew our property was not directly next to the road, so I decided to stop and take a photo of the general area. As I was walking to find the best shot, the same lady drove by and cautioned me to be careful because there were snakes.

It is an understatement to say that I hate snakes. As a small child, some medicine I was given caused me to "hear" snakes hissing all around me. Running and screaming through the house, my mother chased me trying to calm me down, and ever since then, I have a paralyzing fear of snakes. It's too bad I couldn't go to Ireland to find out how I got my Irish DNA, considering they interestingly don't have snakes in Ireland. Legend has it that St.

Patrick kicked out all the snakes, but scientist have found that there were never any fossils of snakes. But that doesn't help me here. Quickly, I hightailed back to the car. I decided I could see the property on Google maps later!

On the last day of our journey, we went to the Noel Memorial Library at Louisiana State University Shreveport (LSUS). With only a few hours before our flight home, we were barely able to scratch the surface of the available resources on Bossier Parish, the Civil War, Reconstruction, plantations, and even the Gilmer family. But there were few details about the lives of "colored people," even though in 1870 there were 3,505 Whites and 9,170 Coloreds. That meant 72% of the population in Bossier Parish was black right after the Civil War. From the scraps of information about the negroes, or "coloreds," to being only names in cemeteries, to almost no trace about the lives of my ancestors, it seemed that "the majority," which included my people, were almost invisible according to written history. My trip to Louisiana was very fruitful, yet it left gaping holes in understanding how slavery and its aftermath had affected my ancestors.

On the flight home, I contemplated my new-found purpose. I was committed to discovering more about the story of my family. I had this yearning to dig deep into the life and struggles of Granvill, my 3rd great-grandfather. I had to overcome the lack of documentation that African Americans face when they try to do genealogy.

Genealogy is the scholarly study of a family's line, heavily based on evidence gleaned from documents. Historically, in Western cultures, the legitimacy to claims of wealth and power by rulers and noble classes was demonstrated through their ancestry. It is a challenge to find out about our enslaved ancestors because they were stripped of their names, family ties, history, language, and culture. Plus, they were forbidden to write, marry, purchase property or anything else that would leave a record. I needed to find a new way.

Even though most people view me as mild mannered, I have a strong contrarian side. I decided to major in mathematics, even when "girls didn't do math!" As a teacher, when I couldn't find the curriculum I needed, I created my own. I am like one of my favorite TV characters, James T. Kirk. When faced with the no-win scenario of the Kobayashi Maru training exercise, he reprogrammed the program so he could win. Since doing genealogy research for my enslaved ancestors was becoming a no-win situation, I thought to myself, why not redefine the problem? I wanted to figuratively "resurrect" my enslaved ancestor,

Granvill. I knew I couldn't find details about what he would say or like, but I did think I could uncover a lot more about his life.

I decided I would try repurposing other methods of research. Historical research is usually meant for significant or famous people. I wanted to see if I could apply it to an ordinary person. All kinds of research are done on consumer behavior, which is typically employed to predict what people will buy. Why not look for patterns in the data from my family. I wanted to shed light on him by researching African culture. There is probably a lot of information to learn about African American history. Since trait characteristics are inherited, couldn't researching his descendants tell me something about him?

If I figured this out, I also wanted to explain to others how they can uncover the lives of their ancestors with just a few documents. Facing multiple challenges, I needed to continue to confront my emotions dealing with slavery, squeeze every ounce of information out of my limited records, and chart a new path to defeat all the roadblocks that lay ahead.

Bossier Parish in Louisiana

Culture

When we returned home, I felt a little letdown. It was like the day after a disappointing Christmas, but you still have to clean up everything. I realized I didn't have the same luck that Weilin had when we searched for his family history. On our first family history adventure, we traveled to Portland, Oregon, where we gathered lots of information on his paternal grandfather, Hugh Louie. He was born one year before my great-grandfather, Joseph P. Smith. By carefully scrutinizing every column in the 1900 Federal Census, we learned he had been in the United States for 16 years since arriving at the tender age of 8 from China. The most intriguing fact was that under occupation, it stated "preacher." I had previously learned that Hugh had graduated as a doctor from Oregon Science and Health University from family oral history, so I contacted the University Archivist.

Not only did he round up information on the classes that Hugh had taken, the admission requirements, samples of books he may have used, and his graduation photo, but he bought to my attention some new information. By placing the name Hugh Louie in quotation marks, an article turned up about Hugh and the First Christian Church. When I got in touch with the church, luckily for us, their regional minister had recently written an extensive article about the Chinese Christian Mission of Portland. He documented the work of Hugh Louie and others with the Chinese immigrants in the early twentieth century. Continuing this lucky streak, when we arrived at the church, on the previous day, they had just set up a special presentation on the 135 years of work in the community. The display included a section on the Chinese Mission and Hugh Louie. The Oregon Historical Society had ample information and articles in the newspaper about Hugh and members of his family. He had hit the jackpot. The information about my own family was puny in comparison. Pushing that thought aside, I decided that with the absence of luck, I would have to work harder.

Thinking that we could work together on our projects, I asked my husband if he was going to start writing the story down. He told me he was not ready yet. I wondered why, with all his information, why didn't he want to start? He felt that he needed more information to write a proper biography that hewed to Chinese sensibilities. I didn't understand why, but through our years of marriage, we have come to the realization that if something doesn't quite make sense, it must be cultural.

Our level of cultural competency had slowly improved over time. Cultural competence refers to how well people can negotiate cross-cultural differences. Since we married, obviously, we were not at the lower levels of cultural competency, which includes practices that try to eliminate other cultures. Examples are actions that seek to remove a person's culture, like the stripping of names, language, religion, cultural foods, and art from my African ancestors. Or, another instance was when Native American children were separated from their parents, forbidden to speak their language, and forced to live like the dominant culture. It also includes beliefs that the dominant group is inherently superior, such as the ideology of White Supremacy and hate groups.

We started at a level of some awareness in culture, mostly about material things that you would expect, such as food, language, celebrations, and maybe a little history. Our cultural competency level was tied to the notion that everyone is the same or, what is considered cultural blindness. We were becoming more culturally sensitive, which means we knew there were differences, but we didn't assign values of better or worse and right or wrong. But, at the end of the day, we were (and still are) a work in progress. Sometimes, it is hard not to judge. So, I know Weilin's reasons must have had to do with culture, but what specifically? I knew I would figure it out sooner or later, so I just started on my own work.

The land situation was still paramount in my mind. I needed to contact the older generation of the Smith family, which included my father, his siblings, and some of his cousins. The fate of our land was in the hands of the elders. My next problem was to organize the mountains of notes, papers, and documents we had hoisted back. I should have searched, "how do I organize my family history materials," which would have provided me with multiple options. I can't imagine what people do who inherit containers teeming with all kinds of materials. I categorized them by person, as well as chronologically. It would have been better if I thought about how I planned to organize everything from the start.

After I cataloged all my information, it became abundantly clear that my luck was even worse than I thought. Most of the information about my enslaved ancestors consisted of numbers and simple demographic data, even after emancipation. For example, the 1850 US Federal Census Slave Schedules included the name of the slave owners, the age, F or M for the sex, and B for black or M for mulatto under "colour." Thus, in 1850, for Martha H. Gilmer, the widow of George O. Gilmer, her first slave was an eighty-year-old black male, who was most likely my Granvill, because he was 84 in 1854. Another example was the education data listed for the year 1882, most likely the year that Joseph P. Smith began school. It states, "there were 563 whites and 758 colored pupils."

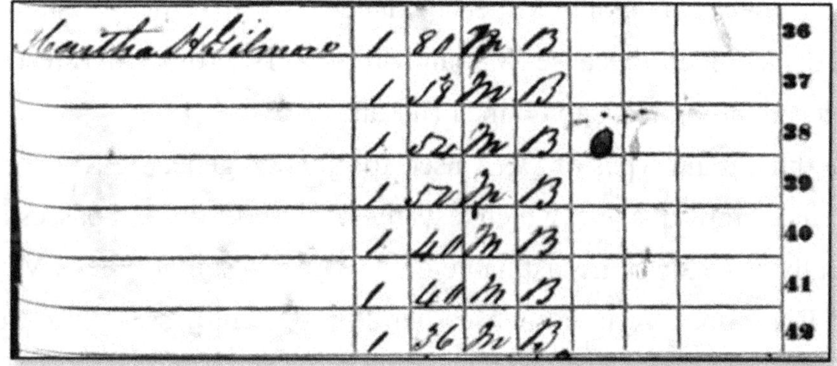

1850 U.S. Federal Census – Slave Schedules Township 19 Ward 2, Bossier Louisiana on Family Search

A little exasperated but not undaunted, I determined that I was going to have to "squeeze" my ancestors out of all these articles, letters, diaries, maps, and sketches of history about the Gilmers, our slaveholders. With careful analysis and "reading" between lines, along with lots of research, I needed to breathe life into the story of my ancestors, who were more than the number of slaves, negroes, or coloreds.

"Coloreds;" I had not heard or seen that term in a while. I vividly remember in the past, sitting in an auditorium of my small Christian college, when a man from England kept referring to the "coloreds." As an impressionable teenager, seeped in the language of the day, which was "black power," I was terribly offended. I scooted up to the front of my seat and glanced around to see if this bothered my classmates. It didn't seem to bother them, but it was true that I was the only black student in sight.

The names used to refer to us have changed over time. We are now either black or African American. Just what does African American mean to my family history? My husband is Chinese-American, which designates that he has Chinese roots. Others can say that they are German-American or Italian-American, which means their family came from Germany or Italy. What exactly does African American mean if there are fifty-four countries in Africa? Which country's culture do I study?

The answer would come from DNA. Several years ago, I was trying to find the slave owners of my great, great grandparents, Sam, and Caroline. I wrote to Cheryl, my DNA cousin, about my family's oral tradition. There was a story that Joseph's father, Sam, was the son of a European slaveholder. Cheryl emailed back that she was skeptical that Sam was the son of a slaveholder "because William Smith's Y-chromosome test, which goes from father to father to father, leads to Guinea Bissau."

There are three main types of DNA used for genetic genealogy. One is the Y-line DNA test. Only men can take this test, which tests the Y chromosome. It passes from father to son, and they usually have the same last name or surname. Another type is Mitochondrial DNA. This kind of DNA goes from mothers to her children but passes on to the next generation only through females. By using the company African Ancestry that specializes in Africa, one can find the ethnic group of your father's side through a Y-DNA test for men only. For your mother's side, the Mitochondrial DNA test can be used for either women or men. Another DNA test is the Autosomal DNA, which tests all the DNA provided by both parents on your 23 chromosomes. For example, AncestryDNA examined about 700,000 locations on my chromosomes, resulting in a list of cousins from both sides of my family. I have a list of many DNA cousins, including Cheryl, James, and William, on my Smith side, but it doesn't tell me my ancestor's tribe.

Contacting William, he told me he had taken a Y-line DNA test. He told me the male line in our Smith family traces back to the West African group, the Balanta people. That means I don't belong to the group of 30% of African Americans whose father's side traces back to European roots. That's how I learned the lesson to take oral traditions with a grain of salt. One aspect of genealogy is to find evidence for oral traditions or stories passed down from generation to generation. Almost everyone finds that some research doesn't correlate with oral traditions, so be a little skeptical until you can find the evidence. To be sure, I asked my uncle to take the African Ancestry test. Sure enough, it also came back to the Balanta people living in Guinea-Bissau.

African Ancestry Certificate on the Y-DNA of my uncle

Who are the Balanta, and what can I find out about them and their culture? I had heard of the Mandinka tribe from "Roots," and my brother-in-law is originally from the Igbo tribe in Africa, but I had never heard of the Balanta tribe. Before the transatlantic slave trade, the Balanta lived in West Africa along a strip of coast between the Senegal and Congo rivers. This vast region was home to a multitude of diverse cultures. I didn't know that for centuries, this region had contact with Arabs in North Africa and the Europeans, through scattered trading posts. There were cosmopolitan cities such as the fabulous Timbuktu. Leaders of large kingdoms such as the Ghana Kingdom, the Mali Kingdom, and the Songhai Empire dominated parts of this region as well as the mighty Benin Empire, who built extensive commercial trading networks. Others lived in small groups of villages ruled by tribal chieftains. The Balanta was among a group of stateless societies that made do without a chief or recognized leader.

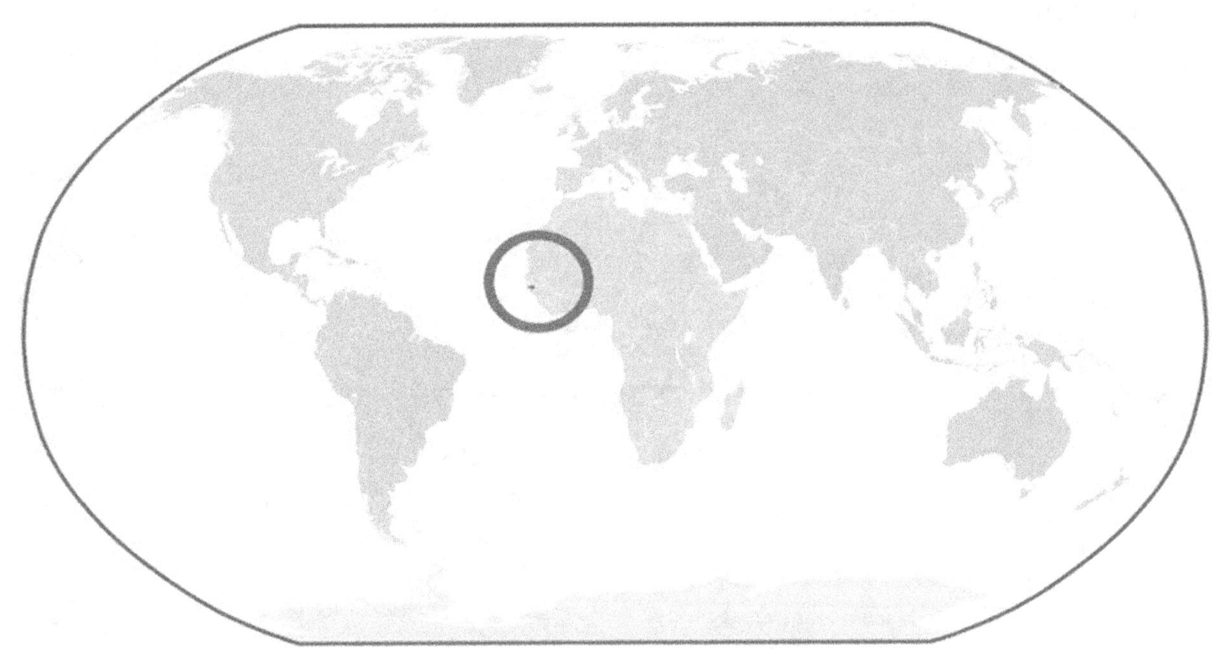

The Balanta live in present-day Guinea-Bissau in West Africa

The Balanta were farmers and herders whose heartland was near the Geba River. By the 1600s, they grew yams, beans, pumpkins, and maize, which had been imported from Mexico in 1500s. They also tended cattle, which, along with yams and salt, were their chief products traded at regional markets. The violent and unpredictable slave trade prodded the Balanta to adapt, innovate, and invent according to a book, *Planting Rice and Harvesting Slaves: Transformations along the Guinea-Bissau Coast, 1400-1900'* by Walter Hawthorne.

Hawthorne detailed how the Balanta tribe moved to coastal lowland communities. Previous to slavery, they had lived in spread out small clusters of homes knowns moranças. But to adapt to the threat of slave raids, they packed themselves into densely fortified villages known as tabancas. Living in difficult to access communities, they were better able to defend themselves against the powerful slave-raiding neighbors such as the Mandinka. Abandoning yams, they learned to grow the labor-intensive paddy rice. Since rice cultivation required iron tools, sometimes the Balanta would raid other villages to get slaves. They traded the captured slaves for iron used to make tools and weapons. By the time my fourth great-grandfather was born in the mid1700s, the Balanta had enhanced and developed sophisticated rice paddy techniques. The Balanta defied the stereotype that enslaved Africans were mere primitives that were victims of white slave raiders coming to capture them. My initial research on the Balanta gave me clear answers to the five "W" questions. But something was missing. The answers to the five "W" questions didn't tell me how they behaved, what their life was like, and what they believed, or more precise information about their culture.

What is culture? I define culture as the way a group of people follow similar ways of thinking and standards of behavior who share the same language, historical, and geographical place. If I am going to learn about my Granvill, my third great-grandfather, I think I need to know more about the culture of his father, my fourth great-grandfather.

I am African American, and my husband is a naturalized Chinese American. After living together for several decades, we are aware that culture sometimes affects the way we act and perceive the world. For example, not long after we were married, my husband's sister and family came to visit. Instead of home cooking, Chinese usually entertain their family or guests by taking them out to eat. We decided to take them for a new dining experience to a nearby Mexican restaurant. After we all found a seat at a long, wooden table, my husband turned to me and asked me to recommend what they should try. A little flustered by what I considered an odd request, I replied, "Well, whatever you like?" Whatever we ordered, they hated it. To this day, everyone chuckles about how they can't stand Mexican food. I didn't know it then, but this scenario aptly illustrates some of the fundamentals of culture. Weilin was thinking, since I had the most experience with Mexican food, whatever I liked, everyone else should like too. As I was busily looking over the menu to find just what I wanted, his request surprised me. This illustrates how two cultures act and think differently.

Cultures can be individualistic or collectivist. Individualistic cultures place the person at the center of bigger groups such as the family, then the community, which expands to the world. In an individualistic culture, people think in terms of "I," reaching toward individual goals, initiative, and achievements. Thus, from my more individualistic point of view, I think you should eat what you like. Often times, one has many options to customize their meal to fit exactly what they want. On the other hand, in collectivist cultures like my husband's family, the individual is just a small part of a larger group. People are born into an extended family or clan, which protects them in exchange for loyalty. As a member of the group, I should have known what they would like and "protect" them from awful food.

Another example of individualist vs. collectivist culture is the highest-grossing romantic comedy of all time, the movie My Big Fat Greek Wedding. It's about a 30-year-old single girl from a large collectivist Greek family who falls for a non-Greek guy raised in an individualistic small nuclear family. Much of the comedy revolves around the culture clashes that are caused by the collision of two kinds cultures. Those in North America, Western Europe, and Australia, which are individualistic, tend to value independence and the rights of individuals while emphasizing being unique. Cultures from Africa, Asia, Central, and South America that are collectivist. They tend to value cooperation, families, and communities while promoting selflessness and the needs of the group ahead of the self.

We don't usually pay attention to culture. It's like gravity, it's all around us, yet we hardly give it a thought. Ordinarily, we are not conscious of our own culture until we encounter another culture that has a different way of acting and thinking. It is similar to the way we never realized the rules in our native tongue until we studied another language. It's funny, but my husband has a much better grasp of English grammar than I do. He even taught

English grammar classes to remedial students. Those students were also amazed at his knowledge of grammar and his clear explanations.

Culture is learned at an early age, similar to grammar. Both are passed down unconsciously from generation to generation. Geert Hofstede, a foremost social scientist, defines culture as "the collective programming of the mind that distinguishes the members of one group or category of people from others." The first ten years of our lives are when we learn our culture's rules of behavior. That doesn't mean we are all the same, but we are like operating systems for computers. I remember those days in college, writing papers created on a Mac OS system, then, having to switch them so they could run in Microsoft Windows when I turned them in. We are compatible with our culture. We can perform lots of behaviors as long as we maneuver correctly in our culture.

Since culture is almost invisible to us, if we want to be more culturally proficient, the first thing that many experts suggest is to explore your own beliefs and values. I think I will try to understand the culture of my ancestor by comparing it to what I know about my life. How did I learn my culture? Using information gleaned from resources for professionals who interact with different cultures such as doctors, teachers, and employers, let me examine the process that I learned culture, starting with my birth into an individualistic culture and contrast with it with my ancestor from a collectivist culture.

I didn't realize that I was preparing to be a member of an individualistic culture from the day I was born. My birth was attended to by a doctor whose rank was First Lieutenant and a nurse who was a sergeant in a sterile military hospital. I asked my mother about the details of my birth. I learned that after being born, I was placed in a small crib next to her. In that room, there with six other mothers with their babies. She said it was difficult for both of us to sleep because the other babies were crying. All those red-faced babies with their eyes scrunched up, wailing loudly but without tears, which they would produce about six months later.

Consequently, I learned to sleep by myself on day one. When we got back home, I was put on a schedule. My dad said one of my exhausted parents had to wake up in the middle of the night to feed me. Although they fed me at first, one of my first milestones would be to feed myself. It was not always pretty, but I learned to get the food into my mouth by myself. Another achievement was learning to go to my little potty all by myself, thus building my path to independence.

On the contrary, in a collectivist culture like the West African Balanta, customarily, the mother of Granvill's father gave birth surrounded by sisters and female relatives with some functioning as midwives. He slept with his mother, where he was allowed to fall asleep naturally. His mother fed him much longer into his toddler years. She carried the baby on her back and learned to read the babies' cues for bowel movements, hence building the bond of interdependence. This explanation illustrates the first stage of our lives, where we each learned our culture from family.

Next comes the introduction to a group outside of the family. I went to school at age five. I remember kindergarten, where I learned to get along with other girls and boys, began learning the basics of reading, writing, and arithmetic. At home, I played with my sisters and the neighbor's kids. After elementary school, I went to junior high, where I interacted with more students and was taught by specialists in English, science, and - my favorite - mathematics, along with other subjects.

For my ancestor, at age five, he was put into his age grade. He began to learn how to do things like supervising the livestock. The age-grade was now his in-group. He was expected to listen to the older boys or be punished. There was no contact with girls, and in their free time, they would wrestle or have stick fights. At this stage, members of individualistic cultures learned that others were individuals that could choose to be friends with or not. In collectivist cultures, members learned to get along and maintain harmony because this was your group for the long term.

As a teenager, I went to a typical high school. All my classes, except physical education, had both girls and boys. I was "I" conscious because I needed to make decisions about my educational and career goals. In my government class, I learned about the importance of my individual rights. Graduation was a time to celebrate before I entered college.

By the time my ancestor's age-grade were teenagers, they could carry weapons and have contact with girls, but they were now the workhorses in the labor-intensive paddy rice cultivation. It was of utmost importance that they worked well with each other and cooperated. They were "we" conscious, as their contributions were vital to the survival of their tabanca or village. When they reached the end of their teens, their age-grade would be given a feast by the adults to show that they were now regarded as adults. In individualistic cultures, independence is valued, whereas, in collectivist cultures, the community is more important than the individual.

By the time I was an adult, I had exerted my independence by going to the college of my choice, choosing my major and career path to get the knowledge and certification to become a teacher. I was able to choose my mate and find a place to work and live separately from my parents.

Adulthood for Balanta males meant they passed the transition from youth to becoming men. They had to go through an elaborate initiation ceremony, which included circumcision. This commemorative occasion, which only occurred every four years, was announced by the deafening sound of an imposing talking drum beating all night long, which announce the coming ceremony. The initiation took several months to complete. Afterward, the initiates were eligible to marry. Since the young men depended on their fathers to provide the cattle they need to offer for a bride, they worked for their fathers until they could get their own land. Most living in an individualistic culture spend their lives trying to be unique individuals that focus on what they want, dream, and have the motivation to achieve. Those in collectivist cultures prize harmony, tradition, and family.

From my early years, my family and society pushed me toward being independent, self-reliant, and ready to achieve my potential. These values shaped my personality. My distant ancestor's family trained him to be obedient, dependable, and respectful. There is an African proverb that states, "A family is like a forest, when you are outside, it is very dense, when you are inside, you see each tree has its place." These principles most likely influenced his personality. That does not mean that everyone in either type of culture is the same, but when it comes to the milestones in our lives, we behave similarly.

I can only wonder what culture shock my fourth great-grandfather experienced when he came to the North American continent. Besides the horrific circumstances that he endured on his voyage to America, all I undeniably know about Granvill's father was that he lived, fathered a son, and that his DNA traces back to the West African Balanta people. The name Balanta means "those who resist." Not only did the Balanta resist efforts to be ruled by others, but they worked to evade apprehension. Contrary to our ideas about capturing of slaves, Granvill's father most likely was seized by Africans. He could have been a prisoner of war of the Mandinka of Kaabu Empire or a captive of other tribes. Since the 1600s in Africa, war captives had been used to supply slave labor for other tribes or, what is most likely in his case, exchanged for European goods and iron. He even could have been taken by another Balanta clan, because they sometimes captured slaves to trade for iron. This durable metal was very desirable to create weapons and farming tools.

If he were typical of other captives at the time, the father of Granvill was marched to the West African slave port of Bissau. He was confined there in iron shackles, perhaps for months waiting for the next Portuguese slave ship. The Portuguese were the first and number one slave transporting European country. They transported over 4.5 million slaves during 30,000 transatlantic voyages. Only 4.4% of African captives, such as Granvill's father, went to the British North American colonies, with most ended up in Brazil. Once on a ship, he would have been placed in a slave hold with up to 350 other captives. The space that held captive people was specially designed to hold them, while barely giving them enough food to keep them alive.

How appalling this must have been was made more vivid to me on a trip to Germany. We visited the Dachau Concentration Camp, which was the first Nazi camp opened in Germany by the infamous Heinrich Himmler in 1933. Seeing the bare wooden so-called "beds" where people were squeezed and stacked up to three levels high, reminded me so much of my ancestors squeezed under the deck of ships. Experiencing it person, I was so horrified, I hastily went to the end of the exhibit, so I could see where those people were finally liberated from this ghastly situation. I got back to the bus a little late, but no one said a word when I told them I had to behold the end of those horrors.

Inside the room at the Dachau Concentration Camp

Unfortunately, for three weeks or more, Granvill's father would have endured the unspeakable conditions of the infamous "Middle Passage." The Trans-Atlantic slave trade had three legs similar to the sides of a triangle. On the first leg, ships took European goods to Africa to trade for slaves. On the middle leg, European countries transported slaves to both North and South America. On the last leg of this triangular trip, raw materials such as tobacco, rice, cotton, and indigo were shipped back to Europe and turned into manufactured goods.

Granvill's father's voyage from West Africa across the Atlantic Ocean most likely occurred between April and September in order to acclimate he and his fellow captive Africans to the mild temperatures of spring and summer before the colder fall and winter came. He probably arrived in the New World at the slave port of Charleston, South Carolina, where he was quarantined on Sullivan Island.

While in Charleston, South Carolina, I shuddered to think of what that island meant to my fourth great-grandfather. It was familiar, motionless land without the constant ocean waves bobbing the ship. Possibly, it was fresher air and a larger space to move some of the cramped limbs of his body. It was uncertainty about what would happen next and if he would ever see his family again.

Sullivan Island near the port of Charleston

Then he was taken to the slave market. Traumatized by the horrors of the ocean crossing, if he were like most Africans, Granvill's father proceeded quietly to the marketplace. It was said that planters choose them "as they do Horses in a Market; the strongest, youthfullest, and the most beautiful, yield the greatest prices." Granvill's father was likely a slave who commanded the highest prices due to his knowledge of rice growing, but nevertheless, he and his descendants would not taste freedom again for over 100 years.

One small bit of fortune for Granvill's father was that his knowledge of rice cultivation would have given him a better chance to be with others that knew his culture and spoke his language. Between 1750 and 1775, Georgia's population of slaves increased from less than 500 to almost 18,000. Rice farming required intensive, coordinated human labor. In the low county of Georgia, large groups of enslaved Africans had to be able to work together on rice plantations. With eventually over 13,000 Africans brought to the Low Country in Georgia, they were able to retain some of their African identity and culture, leading to a unique Creole language and a Gullah culture. I saw vestiges of it still in existence to this day when I visited coastal South Carolina, including the beautiful Gullah baskets. Over the years, these enslaved Africans established deep kinship bonds and kept their tight-knit collectivist community. They retained their sophisticated agricultural techniques for growing rice. The enslaved people in the low country sustained part of their African culture, such as dietary preferences, some of their artistic expression, and they blended some of their African religious concepts with Christian beliefs and practices.

It is well established that the call and response in black churches have their roots in African traditions. Granvill's father, and other enslaved people during his time, may have been one of the first to blend African and Christian beliefs. He may have experienced one of the religious movements that swept through the American colonies. The Great Awakening was an evangelical and revitalization Protestant movement. Northern Baptist and Methodist preachers came down to the Low Country in Georgia to convert whites and blacks, enslaved and free. The sermons appealed to the African slaves because they were emotionally charged, which was similar to expressiveness in their West African religious practices. Also, baptism correlated well with the African belief that certain bodies of water were sacred. If Granvill's father did convert to Christianity, couldn't you imagine him using traditional expressive dance movements as he told his offspring about African animals in his telling of the story of Noah's ark?

Scholars have found that African customs exerted an influence on American culture. Even words such as bogus, phony, yam, tote, gumbo, jamboree, jazz, and funky have African roots. It stands to reason that Granvill's father embraced this blend of African and American culture. Did remnants of his African side and the Balanta culture survive in the Smith family? I thought about the similarities of my upbringing to that of my ancestor. Maybe, for example, instead of having a chief, a council of elders made the most significant decisions. Is my father's generation equivalent to the council of elders in my family, who will decide the fate of the family land?

Another example is that the Balanta had a system of age-grades, which clearly defined one's interaction within the clan. At each age-grade of life, from childhood to adulthood, both males and females had initiation rites which marked the entrance into a new social category. The age-group of young boys learned their roles and how to submit to the will of the older boys who, in turn, had appropriate responsibilities and obligations for their age group, which seems familiar to me. When I was a young girl, I remembered how my family operated on Thanksgiving. All the males got together at one place in the house. In the kitchen area, my grandmothers directed all the females in the kitchen area. When it was finally time to eat, the adult women served the food, at which point the males repeatedly complimented the cooks. Afterward, the teenage group that had to clean up and wash the dishes. Everyone sat in age groups, with the older adults sitting together at the big table with the formal place settings. Other age groups sat together wherever, down to the younger kids, who had to sit at the kid's table. I remember the secret joy I felt when I finally made it up to the ranks to the adult table. My grandparents' fiftieth wedding anniversary was another example of age-groups. Each age-group of females wore a different color of the same pink dress. This could just be what happens when you have large family celebrations, but still, it is comforting to hope that just possibly, some bits of African culture were not entirely obliterated by slavery.

The Balanta ate rice and fish with sauces made from palm oil or peanuts, tomatoes, and onions. Does this explain my grandfather's fondness for catfish? One of the last times I saw Deedee, as we called him, was not long after my husband and I were wed. He and my grandmother came over to our house for dinner. Knowing that he liked catfish, I prepared steamed catfish, which is the Chinese way of making it. Southern Fried catfish fillets are covered with a mixture of seasoned cornmeal and flour. With steamed catfish, you start with a whole fish covered with thinly sliced green onions and other garnishments. My husband remembered my grandfather saying, "I never had catfish like this before, but it tastes good too." My husband took that to mean that even though the catfish was steamed, it still was good, and even though he was Chinese, he still was good too.

I will never know for sure if Granvill's father came from Africa or if it was his grandfather who did. I know that one of my ancestors from Africa was a part of the 500,000 Africans imported to what is now the United States. Just like all those nameless Africans, I don't know his name. Our story begins with him. I am amazed that he and all others who have an African ancestor tenaciously survived. I hope I inherited their resilience. I thought everything about him was lost to time, but comparing my life in an individualistic culture to his in a collectivist culture helped me to know something about the way we both handled the milestones in our lives.

Understanding culture is something that many social scientists' study for their entire lives. As I researched and analyzed multiple dimensions of my life, it becomes easier to embrace the fact that one's culture affects the way we think and behave each day. I started keeping a journal so I could analyze the mundane approaches that my husband, who is from a collectivist culture, and I see things differently. Some were harmless, like he would've preferred to seek out the wisdom of experts or experience, while I liked to find what the data or the research says. Or when there was a problem, he was much more interested in getting started with something, then look at the result and reflect later. He always says, "Did you kill the mouse?" meaning was the problem solved. I, on the other hand, like to make a step by step pre-plan. We work well when we do both. But sometimes it is harder to understand the cultural differences, like why he wasn't getting started on his writing.

Finally, after reflecting on many instances of the collectivist and individualistic thinking differences, it began to make more sense. A biography for someone in Weilin's Chinese collectivist culture is not just about them. There are conventions that must be upheld. The Chinese have a saying, "Make your ancestor shine." It is not only about him but how he glorifies his group. To write a biography in the Chinese tradition, it has to be a lot more than information about his life. Weilin already has the names of twenty-five generations of all the males in his family line. To be worthy of having a biography written about you, one must be very significant and exhibit high morals. And importantly, the writer must be an expert in every aspect of that person's life. So, from my individualistic point of view, being interesting would be enough, but from my husband's collectivist viewpoint, he must honor and respect tradition.

Wow! Becoming more culturally proficient by learning to accept and respect the differences in other cultures not only helps me to "resurrect" the culture that influenced Granvill in his early life, but it turned out to also be a great tool to better my life.

When you take the time to investigate how culture influences someone's life, it's like a lightbulb turns on. You will see examples of culture everywhere. Think about how your family celebrates holidays as well as the stages of life from birth to death. If you are lucky, you have older relatives and photographs to illuminate your ancestor's first culture. You can research the "culture and values" of your ethnic group for a deeper understanding of your ancestor's culture. Thinking about your experiences through the lens of culture provides a more vivid comparison and contrast of you to your ancestor's life, especially when you don't have documents.

The Locale

What happy memories do you have of your home when you were growing up? One unforgettable image I have was peeking out my bedroom window with a sense of awe at our backyard, blanketed with a sheet of puffy white snow. Having snow was a great cause for celebration in sunny, Southern California. One reason was it had not snowed in almost two decades. We got to miss school and romp around in that magical snow. Thinking it must have been freezing, I reasoned that I should pile on almost every piece of clothing I could find. Bundled up, I finally made it outside. All the neighborhood kids were out running, laughing, and throwing snowballs. My younger sister and I tried and tried to erect a snowman but to no avail. Stopping for a moment, I realized I had to shed some of those layers of winter garments because I was sweating! The memories of that day bring back images of pure childhood bliss.

"Resurrecting" where Granvill lived, on the other hand, demanded I immerse myself in a very different type of imagery - the images associated with slavery. It's a subject that conjures up distressing, stereotypical images of enslaved people hunched over in punishing and back-straining positions, wailing spirituals. The features of that locale usually included a withering sun beating down on endless fields of cotton that they wearily picked. Or even worse, the towering slaveholder with a long whip posed to release a brutal, beating on a bare, bloodied back. My vow to at least confront slavery, after my trip to Plain Dealing, Louisiana, was forcing me to take the baby steps to wrestle with the inner demons of this disturbing topic. I had to deal with agonizingly dreadful emotions that are difficult to verbalize.

Psychologists tell us that to tackle something negative and painful, we need to understand it from the point of view of an intellectual, outside observer, and at the same time develop an awareness of our emotions. For me, it's easy to attack the subject of slavery from a research perspective, but I am not very good at expressing my feelings in words. My limitations are more pronounced living in a bilingual, bicultural family. Sometimes words and actions have different meanings in the two cultures. For example, the concept of being happy in American culture connotes delight, excitement, and pleasure. But, in Chinese culture, happiness is about cultivating a deep sense of peace, harmony, and working to keep problems at bay. To solve this problem, we came up with a way to convey our emotions, not using words, but numbers.

For example, Weilin thought it was cute to call me "Too Tall Jones." Being tall, people had picked on me all my life. I couldn't stand the fact that my husband would also pick on me. After many repeated attempts to explain to him that this nickname really bothered me, I came up with a number system. I asked him how much he thought it bothered me using a scale 1 to 5, the number 1 representing "not much" to 5, meaning "unbearable." He thought maybe a 2. He was shocked when I revealed it irritated me 4+. Of course, he immediately quit. Similarly, I think I can utilize our number system to deal with the emotional powder keg of the treatment of my enslaved ancestors.

It was uncomfortable to force my mind to think about slavery. So, to get a different culture's slant on slavery, I queried Weilin on what he had seen or heard about it in his schooling in Taiwan. He noted that it was barely covered. The scant facts he had been taught were the black slaves were captured and enslaved by a stronger adversary, just like prisoners of war were made slaves in Chinese history. Also, Abraham Lincoln saved the slaves, and that was the end of that. When he came to the United States right during the height of the Civil Rights movement, he was surprised there were continuing racial tensions. Weilin's knowledge later increased to include the whipping of slaves after viewing "Gone with The Wind" [1939]. And the most memorable character to him in "Roots" (1977) "Chicken George," helped him to understand that some slaves were raped.

Sadly, my instruction on slavery was not much better than Weilin's. I dug out an intriguing textbook that I had saved from my early teaching years. The name of the book was Negro American Heritage. It was an old book published back when I was in elementary school. In the first chapter, that quickly introduces Africa and slavery, it has one paragraph about the transatlantic slave trade. It states,

It was the Negro of West Africa that became the victim. Without adequate weapons, the natives were an easy prey for the European slave traders. Captured or lured into ships, they were chained and taken to countries of Europe and to America to be sold.

I now know that almost every fact in this paragraph is false. First, technically, there were no "Negroes" in Africa. There were Africans. Second, the African slave traders were a varied group. The most successful were organized societies with strong rulers who enslaved prisoners during perpetual wars with their neighbors. Others, like the Luso-Africans traders who lived near the Balanta people, were astute businessmen. And as stated before, stateless societies sent raiding parties to secure people to trade for essential and other items. Whichever way, the Africans were captured, they ended up at the slaving ports on the West African coast. Eventually, the European slave traders loaded the African captives onto their ships after someone else captured them. The majority of enslaved captives ending up in Central and South America.

Nearly 85% of people who survived and settled in the Western Hemisphere between 1492 until 1776 were African. Most of them worked on sugar plantations, feeding the Europeans craving for sugar, in Central and South America. Only a tiny proportion, less than 5%, were shipped to North America. Although very few enslaved Africans ended up in Europe, the profits produced by the transatlantic trade provided the staggering amount of money needed to fuel the Industrial Revolution in Britain. How can an official state-sanctioned history book be so full of lies and inaccuracies?

Furthermore, at the bottom of the page is a wood engraving from the Frank Leslies' Weekly, published from 1855 to 1922. It depicts a line of men, women, and children chained together in a slave coffle. Illustrating the definition of a coffle, which means a line of animals, prisoners, or slaves chained and driven together, there were women with babies wrapped in bundles on their backs. There also were small children and men with wooden fork-like braces around their necks. I located the original picture in a book by David and Charles Livingstone, who were missionaries and abolitionists. Was this supposed image of slavery really abolitionist propaganda? Unquestionably, this demonstrates that whatever I learned in school was quite biased and inaccurate.

With newer movies such as "Django Unchained" [2012] and "12 Years a Slave" [2013], the general impression is that slavery is about cotton fields. And all enslaved people were backward simpletons who had nothing to offer but brute labor. These stereotypic images are as painful as the aftermath of a terrorist act and gruesome as a mass shooting. I tend to bury these visuals way back in the furthest corner of my mind. When I allow some emotions to bubble up, there are vague feelings of fear, helplessness, guilt, and anger. James, my DNA cousin, told me when he first researched his ancestors, he felt shame. With my goal to face this tragedy, how can I move beyond what Hollywood and my schooling has taught me?

With so much confusing information and inaccurate images about what actually happened during slave times, I needed to get first-hand knowledge for myself. So, Weilin and I traveled to the Lowcountry in South Carolina. We went to Charleston (formally known as Charles Town), where I visited the Caw Caw Interpretive Center. It's a county park located in the Lowcountry that includes former rice fields. Toni Carrier, a resource I found on the Lowcountry Africana Research Community Facebook page, recommended it. Enslaved people, like Granvill's parents, transformed a swampy landscape into acres and acres of rice fields hundreds of years ago. Looking down into the flooded areas, the straight lines of miles of canals are still visible. We gazed at rice on the stalk, imagining that it took bunches of them to make one bowl of rice. How did this place affect Granvill and his parents when he was growing up in Colonial Georgia in the Lowcountry?

Rice on the stalk   Unfinished rice grains

Researchers have found that the place a person lives shapes them at a fundamental level. This concept doesn't mean that everyone gets shaped the same, at the risk of overgeneralizing. However, there is a consensus that environmental, economic, and social factors affect one's health, well-being, and thinking. Outside factors such as access to technology, laws, and politics affect your ability to thrive. If where you are born plays a role in shaping you, I wondered what I could learn about Granvill from where he lived? Granvill began his life on a different locale than a cotton plantation. He was born in Colonial Georgia, very likely, on a rice plantation. How did geography and climate play a part in his life? What specific technological innovations shaped Granvill and his family's lives? And which particular local history and economic factors influenced his life? How was the society different on a rice plantation than images from Antebellum times in the Deep South?

I can imagine Granvill's father being herded, like a sheep, from the port in Charles Town, in Colonial South Carolina. His treatment like an animal is a fact I hate. Unfortunately, it is what it is. If I were to use my negative emotion number rating system, I think that's a number 4 on the scale of 1 to 5. After the roughly 100-mile trek south to the coastal counties in the region known as the Lowcountry in Colonial Georgia, he encountered some familiar geography.

He saw a place that was similar to the home of his ancestors, the Balanta in West Africa. The Balanta people lived along the coastal region in an area known at that time as Senegambia. Both locales were freshwater tidal marshes along rivers. Though the tides influenced the water level in both, the water in the marshes remained fresh. The semi-tropical climate in Georgia (Savannah) is slightly cooler, with an average temperature of a few degrees under 80°F and fluctuates over the year. Guinea-Bissau's (Cacheu) 80°F is a tropical climate with an average calculated from a much narrower range. The rainy season is June to October in both places. But Guinea-Bissau gets most of its average of 60 inches of rainfall during those months while Georgia gets its average of 48 inches mostly during the summer and fall but at other times in the year too. In both places, the trees, the cypress in Colonial Georgia and the mangrove in West Africa, had unusual adaptations, which allowed them to grow in swamps. In both places, the first task to begin rice cultivation was to clear those trees. It gives me a small solace that Granvill's father arrived in an area with many similarities to back home. No doubt, this allowed him to at least adapt to his new environment faster, but the expectations of this place, I'm sure, made life miserable.

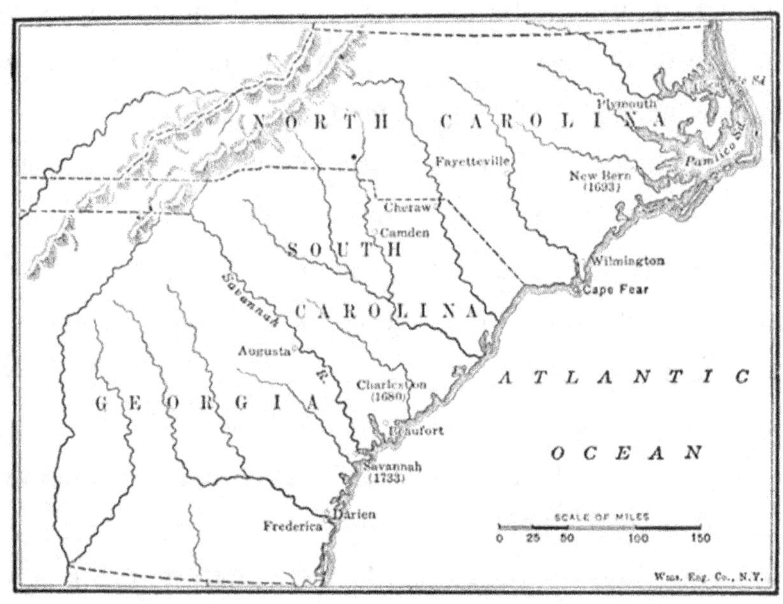

Colonia Georgia was the southernmost colony

My research about the colony of Georgia revealed two surprising facts. First, it was the last of the Original Thirteen Colonies. Second, the initial plan for Colonial Georgia was to prohibit slavery. But the colonists saw their northern neighbor, South Carolina, making hefty profits from rice cultivation. So, the colony of Georgia repealed the original plan of the prohibition of slavery in 1752. Georgians envisioned themselves also profiting from the cultivation of rice. They needed skilled laborers, like Granvill's parents, who had expertise in rice cultivation. All along the Savannah River in the Lowcountry, rice plantations sprang up in the freshwater swamps in the coastal counties. The rush by wealthy planters to start rice plantations led to an economic boom in Colonial Georgia, all made possible by the enslaved people like Granvill's parents. For example, articles I found using the keyword "Savannah," from the 1770s at Newpapers.com, were mostly about rice, plantations, and Negros for sale. On one page, the governor of the province of Georgia offered a reward to catch the "wicked and malicious white perfon or perfons" [sic] who tried to burn his barrels of packed rice and a barn filled with rough rice.

While at the South Carolina Historical Society in the College of Charleston, I came across some eye-opening but disturbing letters from 1773. Reading one letter, which was the prevalent form of communication at that time, showed why everyone who had the means, tried to start a rice plantation in Colonial Georgia. It is hard to believe, but George Whitefield, a foremost evangelist of the Great Awakening in the 1700s, also fell prey to seeking the profits made feasible by exploiting the enslaved Africans. Whitefield dedicated his life's work to building Bethesda an orphanage, college, and library just outside of Savannah, Georgia, in the mid-1700s. He became convinced of the need for enslaved people to work at a rice plantation to fund his project. Since slavery had been banned in the colony when it began in 1735, Whitefield became one of the leading proponents to legalize slavery. It was a betrayal of trust that such a great evangelist would use his gift for persuasion to plead for slavery in Colonial Georgia, where it did not exist before. I guess great people can be simultaneously high-minded and small-minded. It feels like the letdown of finding out that Alex Haley, the author of Roots, stole parts of the story of Kunta Kente, while still knowing he inspired the movement to find one's roots. Giving a score using my rating system can be tricky in this situation.

Whitehead got his rice plantation, then started the Bethesda Orphan House, and then a College. After his death in 1770, Lady Huntingdon, one of his followers back in England, took them over. Rev. William Piercy wrote this letter to her to detail the financial problems and his ideas to boast the profits from the plantation. The plans on improving the plantation, revealed a lot about the economics of this locale. He suggested that spending 2,000 sterling pounds to purchase more enslaved people would allow her to clear 100 more acres of land. Local wealthy planters had assured him that investment would be recouped in three years. With that being over $300,000 today, that means that these acres (plus however many acres already in the plantation) could make $100,000 of today's dollars for every 100 acres. It demonstrates the economic forces driving the economy. In actuality, just before the Revolutionary War, the South held about 46% of the wealth of the colonies. This reminds me that a wise person once said, "Nothing destroys one's respect in the hearts of others more than greed."

It stands to reason that Granvill's parents most likely labored on the rice plantation of a large slaveholder. Even though it was a moneymaker, growing rice was a challenging endeavor in the mosquito and poisonous snake-infested swamps of the Lowcountry. I witnessed the remnants of canals and dikes etched into the ground. I was amazed to learn how much of this kind of technological know-how came from West Africa. Just like in West Africa, swamps had to be properly drained, cleared of the cypress trees, and flattened to make them suitable for growing rice. Next, knowledgeable enslaved Africans knew how to create an elaborate system of irrigation that allocated the precise amount of water required to cultivate rice. The whole process could take one to two years to ready a working rice plantation. Before he was born, Granvill's parents were, no doubt, involved in these challenging and demanding tasks.

Being a city gal, I am sure I will never truly understand this agricultural wonder. The museum at the Caw Caw Interpretive Center had a quote stating the amount dirt excavated for the rice fields in the South Carolina region was almost three times the volume of Cheops, the world's largest pyramid. In 1936, David Boar, believing that the European planters were responsible for the "intelligence these men of old exhibited," wrote:

What skill they displayed and engineering ability they showed when they laid out these thousands of fields and ditches ...the "check" banks, which divided field from field, are as straight as mathematical exactness could make them...

He was unable to believe that the "hands of intractable negro men and women… bought from the jungles of Africa" were the brains behind this feat.

A former rice paddy

Laying my eyes over the vast area filled with shallow water as well as examining the how-to illustrations on various boards, I could tell that growing rice required precise irrigation and a large, coordinated workforce. Typically, 50 to 100 slaves, like Granvill's parents, began the process of growing rice in January. Each enslaved person, male and female, was given a task. The driver, a respected enslaved man who was knowledgeable about rice cultivation and appointed to supervise the daily work, assigned the task. Over several months, an elaborate system of levees, trenches, canals, ditches, and floodgates had to be constructed.

Afterward, typically, the women planted the seeds by trampling the seeds into straight rows of trenches in the swampy soil with their bare feet. Next, for eight to nine days, the fields were flooded, after which the men emptied the water while the fields dried for ten days. After the seeds began to sprout, the area needed to be flooded and drained repeatedly for six months. Whenever the water was removed from the rice, there had to be a good deal of hoeing. Additionally, since rice required freshwater, the whole intricate system had to be calibrated to the rise and fall of the tides.

After the final flooding in September, the mature rice was harvested with a sickle. Enslaved men grabbed the rice stalk with one hand, cut the rice, and continued in a rhythmic fashion. Next, the women threshed the rice to remove the rice from the stems. After the harvesting, the rice is removed from the hull. The hulls on rice are akin to those on peanuts. The enslaved Africans created unique tools to accomplish this feat. A huge mortar and pestle were used to pound the rice for hours. It was both a strenuous task but required the exact amount of pressure to keep from breaking the rice. I tried to get the "press and twist movement," but had little success. Next, the hulls were separated from the rice by shifting in a winnowing basket, which was another tool from West Africa. Finally, they put the rice back into the mortar and pestle to be polished. It was gut-wrenching number 5 on a scale of 1 to 5, to see first-hand what Granvill's parents endured.

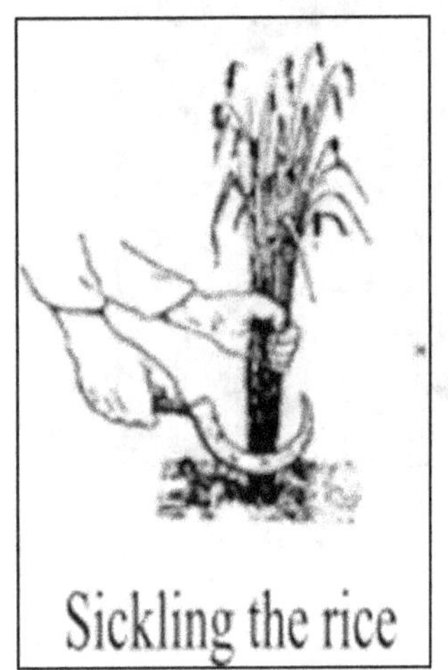

Sickling the rice

The pestle and mortar

the winnowing basket

Finally, it was packed in barrels and, using the dominant form of transportation of those times, it was shipped for export. During the colonial period, the knowledge and expertise of enslaved people like Granvill's parents helped to make rice one of the top ten exports to England from Georgia and South Carolina. This innovative technique of tidewater production, perfected by West African women farmers, significantly increased the level of rice production in the southern colonies. In economics, productivity is a measure of technological progress; unfortunately, the only people to benefit from this progress were the wealthy planters.

The Colonial Slave Law of 1755 defined the "power of the owners of slaves," so they could keep them "in due subjection and obedience." While they were not allowed to be too cruel, such as maiming or disabling them, they could work them up to 16 hours per day. Every owner of a plantation with twenty-five slaves over the age of 16 had to have a white man capable of bearing arms. Slaves were restricted from reading and writing, beating drums, playing horns, or travel on the high roads in groups of more than eight without a white person. They also could not leave the plantation without a letter or a ticket from a white person. These laws demanded that the enslaved parents of Granvill work incredibly hard, with almost no benefit from their efforts. It's like the story of the Little Red Hen in reverse. She does all the work and the other animals get to eat the bread.

When I think of all the times I worked hard in my life, I realize that there was always a payoff. If I spent a lot of time designing a lesson, usually more students learned. I really can't imagine what it must have felt like to finish shipping the rice and know it will not help your family, but make someone else get rich. The wealthy planters fancied themselves aristocrats who mostly resided in the heart of Charles Town. We saw the opulent Heyward-Washington House built about the same time that Granvill was born. The stately rooms, polished furniture, and formal gardens dramatized the vast difference in lifestyle between the wealthy and the enslaved people - whose sweat made it all possible. This injustice makes me angry, definitely a 4+.

And yet, despite all the hardships faced by Granvill's parents in this place, they were resilient enough to find a way to start a family. How could enslaved Africans like Granvill's parents typically begin a family on a rice plantation? What were the social factors that influenced this decision? In Colonial Georgia, at this time, there were three men for every two women. If I translate this mathematical fact in human terms, I believe that Granvill's father must have had some advantage to beat out his other male competitors. I wonder, was she also from the Balanta tribe? Perhaps she was from another tribe in Senegambia.

Once she was pregnant, Granvill's mother faced multiple issues when bringing another human being into the world. The lure of huge profits pushed slaveholders in this region to tax the physical endurance of everyone, including pregnant mothers. Slaveholders typically were not sympathetic to losing the high level of labor expected from Granvill's mother, even during her pregnancy. Since the importation of slaves had not ended, there was no incentive for him to see babies as an investment in the future. Whereas the slaveholder may have seen the pregnancy as a hindrance to his profits, Granvill's enslaved African parents, like any other expecting parents, no doubt tried their best to get ready for their child. Enslaved women worked in the task system, where she was supposed to complete a given amount of work in a day. Granvill's father most likely tried to find a way to lessen her burden. He, perhaps friends and other members of their team, assisted in completing her tasks during her pregnancy. It is comforting to know that they did whatever needed to be done to ensure a healthy birth.

Granvill was born around 1770 in Colonial Georgia. When Granvill's mother was about to have the baby, a midwife was most likely was summoned, since medical treatment was only provided by other enslaved African American women. Midwives were highly respected and played an essential role in the community. The midwife handled not only the experience of childbirth but the emotional needs and the practical knowledge of caring for the baby. Granvill's mother would have typically been allowed four weeks in recovery before having to report back to work. With the flexibility of the task system, she could have decided when to breastfeed him. During the day, on large plantations, the babies were taken care of by a caretaker and the younger children. I saw an advertisement in the 1779 newspaper selling a young Negro girl who knew how to take care of children. The caretaker also had other responsibilities such as spinning, sewing, or cooking. If either of Granvill's parents were able to find a way to get their tasks done quicker, they had more time to spend with their offspring.

Since the Georgian rice plantation owners were fairly new at rice cultivation in the mid-1700s, they were very dependent on their enslaved Africans, such as Granvill's parents. Fearful of contracting malaria, the plantation owners often lived in Savannah to escape the unhealthy swamplands. They employed white overseers who set the tasks which were assigned and supervised by the black drivers. When they finished their tasks, the enslaved had time to tend to their own needs. Armed with some bargaining power due to the plantation owners' dependency on the slave's cooperation, this may have benefited the young children of the enslaved Africans, such as Granvill. One benefit to Granvill was the moist climate and landscape of Georgia resembled the homeland of his parents in West Africa. This resemblance made it easy for enslaved Africans, like his parents, to adapt to the conditions. Recent excavations in Georgia suggest that the enslaved Africans constructed their own homes that closely resembled West African dwellings. They were roundhouses composed of clay and sticks built around a center chimney with thatched roofs and dirt floors.

The enslaved Africans worked together to organize a market system to sell fresh vegetables and hand-made crafts. With the benefit of less harsh working conditions, many of their cultural traditions could be maintained. It is reasonable to think the children were raised during this time more closely to how they would have been brought up back in Africa. Accounts from the times comment on how "slaves love their family dearly." I also found it interesting that doing colonial times; the planters regarded splitting of the families as "unnatural and barbaric."

While in the Lowcountry, we came in contact with a distinct Gullah group of African Americans that still live in close-knit communities in the coastal areas. Many Gullah arts and crafts such as baskets, rice implements, mortar and pestles, and clay pots, which closely resembled ones from West Africa. The Gullah's religious beliefs are a mixture of African and Christian traditions. People come from all over to see and buy wares derived from the rice cultivation culture begun by the enslaved West Africans long ago.

My husband, Weilin, found it fascinating the way they grew rice in Africa was similar to how it was done in China. The Chinese not only grew rice in the lowlands, but they also produced it in terraces carved into the slopes of hills and mountains. They used water buffalo to plow the water-soaked fields, thus the name. The cultivation of rice in China led to an agricultural society revolved around rice culture, with plowing in the spring, weeding in the summer, harvesting in autumn, and hoarding in the winter. And rice was so crucial that it played an integral part in traditional Chinese festivals, including the Spring Festival or Lunar New year and the Double Nine cakes made from the fresh new rice in the fall. He also told me a funny fact that rice is related to the plants that include grass, bamboo, and marijuana. Such rhythms probably governed life on the rice plantation in the Georgia colony, too, but then history got in the way.

Lots of research has documented the earliest historical influences in places and continue to shape and define it for generations. Young Granvill's routine childhood became a casualty of the first monumental historical influence in American History, the Revolutionary War. A few years after the Americans declared their independence in 1776, the British decided to try to get the upper hand in the war by focusing on the South. In the South, there was a bitter division between the Patriots and the Loyalists. The Patriots were the colonists who rebelled against British control. The Loyalists wanted to stay part of Britain. Built upon enslaved labor, the southern colonies had the most significant share of the colonies' wealth. The British hoped that scores of these wealthy Loyalists in the South would flock to the King's cause. Not known is whether the slaveholder of Granvill's family was a Loyalists or a Patriot.

The British chose to start at Georgia, which had a small population of 3,000 white men of military age along with its 18,000 enslaved people. On December 29, 1778, the colonial capital of Savannah fell to the British troops. It only took a few months to restore Georgia to British control, and in September of 1779, the Siege of Savannah began.

It was a turbulent time. Granvill's family must have done what they could to survive. Both Loyalists and Patriot slaveholders fled their plantations, and in this confusion, perhaps as many as 5,000 of Georgia's 18,000 enslaved inhabitants escaped bondage. Throughout the occupation, some enslaved people were used as pawns. When captured, they were given to the soldiers as part of the payment for their services. Both the Loyalists and Patriot forces seized and moved many hundreds of them to distances far from their original plantations. Some enslaved people were killed. Outside of Savannah, plantations were ransacked. After two years, the British were finally defeated with the aid of the French. When the Siege of Savannah ended, the British evacuated, taking many of the Loyalists with them.

During this time, what happened to Granvill and his family? Patriots returned to find their plantations in disarray in 1783, with most of the enslaved laborers gone. Over the next few years, runaway enslaved people were captured and dispersed, some to their former slaveholders, and some to new ones. These events are the most plausible explanation for why Granvill may have ended up in a different part of Georgia. On the other hand, he could have been brought to the interior by the Gilmer's or another slaveholder. At some point in time, the Gilmer family purchased Granvill. It seems more likely that the father, John Blair Gilmer, would have bought him as a young slave of 17 years old. If the son, George, bought Granvill when he moved out, Granvill would have been 44 years old. Whenever Granvill arrived in Upper Georgia, he entered upon a new phase of his life, not on a rice plantation.

Granvill's birth and survival show how much he overcame. He didn't fall victim to the high infant mortality rate on rice plantations nor the considerable health risks and environmental hazards, like malaria, alligators, and water moccasin - the only venomous snake in North America. I wonder how this locale might have shaped Granvill's life? It seems reasonable to assume that Granvill, as a child, grew up in a collectivist culture. His parents nurtured him to work within the group. Rice cultivation required a great deal of cooperation and teamwork. He could have had the job to shoo away birds from the rice in the fields. With extra time at the end of the day, Granvill's father may have had time to teach him skills like fishing and hunting. The laws in Colonial Georgia stipulated that enslaved people on the plantation had Sunday's off. Did the clergy's effort to "preach to slaves" include Granvill and his family? The laws also forbade the teaching of reading and writing to enslaved people, so any education would have come from his parents through the use of stories. It seems to me that Granvill's childhood coincided with the least restrictive form of slavery. The slaveholders rarely interacted with their enslaved workers. Black drivers supervised. If someone did something wrong, they would be punished, but the time of rapes and ghastly whippings would be in the future.

The rice plantation that Granvill's family most likely lived on provided me with new images of slavery. This image was very different from the one thrust at me by the media and my education. It is an informative image of the ingenious enslaved Africans from the Rice Coast and their descendants, who bought their rice cultivation innovations to America. Growing rice was both demanding and required a great deal of sophisticated knowledge and skill. There was also an image of families, with loving mothers and fathers, and raising their children with African traditions and culture that had to reflect American realities. Confronting the old images of slavery in my mind, I was able to move past the old stereotypes and misinformation of the past. I could move on with an enlightened vision of how my African roots were essential to the building of America, not just as laborers but as providers of valuable expertise and innovators of African American culture. Knowing that my ancestors were part of this legacy of bringing the agricultural skills to the New World makes me feel proud. There are many painful and tragic aspects of the experience of Granvill's parents and Granvill's early life, mainly because they lived on a plantation, but there are a few pleasant aspects too. Can I dare say I score an emotion of 2.5 on a scale of 1 to 5? Something must have changed after the Revolutionary War. What happened? What else could I use to "resurrect" Granvill's life?

Understanding the struggles your ancestor dealt with living in a particular locale, both illuminate the constraints that shaped his or her life, as well as provides images of what life was like. A great place to collect real-life images from the place your ancestor lived is <Pinterest.com> Pinterest is like a virtual bulletin board of images; the more you click on a certain topic, the more this social media site will find for you. Although the newspapers found at <chroniclingamerica.loc.gov> and the fee-based <Newsaper.com> usually won't have images, they can provide a vivid glimpse into life at the specific time your ancestor was there. Local histories often provide geography as well as social information, such as demographics and religion in an area.

Nothing can replace going to the place(s) your ancestor lived. When we traveled to the locales in China where Weilin's grandfather had been, my husband realized something important about the timeline he had reluctantly made. He needed to pay careful attention not only to the place, but to the intersection of that place at a specific time. On multiple occasions, we had to refer to that timeline, which helped us place his grandfather in the correct "when and where." The more information you can find, the clearer you understanding will be of the reality of the place and time your ancestor lived and how that environment shaped his or her life.

History

Most people don't have fond memories of their teenage years. I would be rich if I made a dollar every time someone said, "Bless you," after I told them I teach middle school. The teen years are a time of intense growth as one transitions from childhood to adulthood. Granvill was changing as he had just entered into what we now call adolescence. In 1784, the country was changing from colony to country, after an eight-year war for independence in which 50,000 Continental troops were killed or wounded. Both he and the brand-spanking-new nation of the United States of America were beginning new phases in their existence. Granvill, no longer a child, had reached the age of around 13 or 14 years old when enslaved African Americans typically were assigned the same full day's work as an adult. At the same time, during the period after the Revolutionary War known as the Early Republic, the new country was engaged in the challenging work of building a new type of nation that had never existed before. My ancestor, Granvill, and the new republic were about to endure trying times.

Unfortunately, as I tried to analyze Granvill's life as a teenager, I have no documented evidence of his precise location. From his birth to the birth of his son, Jack, in 1814 in Georgia, I have no census data, no marriage licenses, bills of sale, tax records, or even wills to provide direct information on his life and whereabouts. Additionally, the Georgia census from 1790, 1800, and 1810 was destroyed by the British. The White House, the Capitol and other government buildings were set ablaze by the British army in the War of 1812. Our national anthem, the Star-Spangled Banner, was written just after this tragic event. Regardless, without any records, how could I restore Granvill's life? I supposed I would need to use indirect strategies. One of my fellow middle school colleagues Ed Hoffman, a history teacher, impressed me with his mantra... First, think about the story of yours or your families' life, and then find the history.

That is the opposite of what I had unconsciously thought of history. To me, history was comprised of a bunch of dates and famous people that didn't relate to me. I was sure there was no history in my life until it suddenly dawned on me that I would have never met my husband, Weilin, without the Vietnam War. At the beginning of my career, I taught refugee children, known as the "boat people," who were ethnically Chinese. My students and their families were pushed out of Vietnam when our military left that country. Not only did I enroll in Chinese language and culture classes, but I also traveled with a group of teachers to learn about China up close and personally. It so happened that my future husband, Weilin, was our fearless leader for the six-week study tour during the summer. Thus, history profoundly influenced the story of my life. That moment of discovery forever gave credence to the idea that history should be linked together with people's lives. Naturally, applying this to Granvill, I decided to mull over his life to find connections to history.

If Granvill was indeed in Upper Georgia, there were differences from where he was born in the southern coastal part of Georgia. Northwestern Georgia was a combination of vivid colors. First, there were greens created by the dense forest of different types of oak and hickory trees blanketing the hills. Upon first witnessing the Georgia red clay soil, he may have wondered about why the clumpy earth was reddish. Nearby, the sometimes-muddy Broad River did not reflect the blue sky like the ocean in the Lowcountry.

Additionally, the climate was bit chillier and not quite as toasty as the Lowcountry, but much muggier. This area was on the edge of the very young country of the United States. It was a rugged place with no sizable cities like Savannah or Charleston. This region had wild turkeys, deer, and raccoons, which were familiar animals to him, but was he leery of running into the Creek Indians who lurked nearby.

I wondered, did Granvill understand that no one knew how this experiment of people trying to govern themselves would turn out? Did he react the same way I did after moving to a brand-new place to teach at a new middle school? The area was experiencing rapid growth with new homes springing up everywhere. I found it mildly amusing that after the installation of the first electric stoplight, it was cosmic news in the local newspaper. On the one hand, I thought this was exciting that one could chart a new path, but, on the other hand, I learned that without norms and traditions to follow, it was chaotic. Did Granvill and his fellow enslaved blacks experience this kind of uncertainty?

The period in history known as the Early Republic was a time of nation-building and plantation start-ups. How did Granvill feel about his new circumstances? Was he a moody teenager that kept his feelings to himself, or did he act out with non-verbal gestures such as pinched lips, squinting eyebrows and rolling of the eyes that drove all of the adults crazy? For sure, he was disappointed, like all the slaves, that the rumors of freedom had not come to pass. During the Revolutionary War, the British had implored the slaves to take up arms and fight against the rebels. In 1775, Lord Dunmore, the last royal governor of Colonial Virginia, drafted a proclamation which in part stated,

I hereby further declare all indentured servants, Negroes and others
(appertaining to Rebels) free that they are willing and able to bear Arms, they joining
His MAJESTY'S Troops as soon as may be, for the more speedily reducing this Colony
to a proper Sense of their Duty, to His MAJESTY'S Crown and Dignity.

Since communication was slow in those days, it took a while for the contents of this message to reach the Lowcountry, but soon an estimate of up to 100,000 enslaved people escaped to British lines throughout the thirteen colonies. Did everyone in Granvill's family agree on whether they should leave or stay? Granvill's parents, more than likely, had known freedom in their lives. It must have been a gut-wrenching decision. After the British left to return to Britain, all hopes of liberation were dashed. The drudgery of slavery was the only future in Granvill's sight. Having been around teenagers most of my teaching career, I would love to know how he, as a teenager, handled this slump back into slavery.

When did Granvill first meet the Gilmer family? The most likely time was when he was a strapping young man. John Blair Gilmer was born in Williamsburg, Virginia. Talk about finding history in your family's life, I was extremely interested to discover that John's father was the personal doctor of Thomas Jefferson's family. John Blair Gilmer's nephew, George R. Gilmer, wrote about the first settlers in Upper Georgia after he retired as governor of Georgia. I found this book searching for county histories. In his book, Sketches of Some of the First Settlers of Upper Georgia, of the Cherokees, and the Author, he described John as a handsome lady's man who indulged himself with pretty girls and European upper society. The Revolutionary War dramatically changed his life as duty called. In return for his service as a lieutenant where he served under the Marquis de Lafayette. He received a land bounty of 1,000 acres in Upper Georgia. The bounty land system was set up by the new country during the war to encourage at least three years of military service and keep the soldiers motivated to defeat the British to claim their promised land.

STATE of GEORGIA.

To the Honourable the _President_ and Members of Council, now fitting in Augusta for the Purpose of granting Lands in the two new Counties of Franklin and Washington.

The PETITION of _John Gilmer_, a Citizen of the State aforesaid,

SHEWETH,

THAT your Petitioner is entitled to _One thousand_ Acres of Land, on the Head Rights of _Himself and Family_ as appears by Affidavit annexed, for which he hath never had any Lands granted him in this State.

May it therefore please your Honourable Board to grant your Petitioner _One thousand_ Acres of Land in the County of _Washington_ on the Right aforesaid, and on his complying with the Terms mentioned in the late Land Act; and your Petitioner will pray.

John Gilmer

Georgia Headright and Bounty Land records for service in the Revolutionary War,1783-1909

This land was former Creek and Cherokee native land opened for settlement in the early 1780s. John Blair Gilmer was part of a wealthy group of emigrating Virginians, who had fought in the Revolutionary War. The Founding Fathers were well known to them because they were their relatives and neighbors. They introduced the large-scale practice of slavery to this frontier area. Since in 1783, John Gilmer only had 20 blacks, it was highly probable that he needed more enslaved people like Granvill to handle a 1000-acre plantation in what would be later known as Oglethorpe. To put that in perspective, that's larger than Central Park in New York and about the same size as the four theme parks - the Magic Kingdom, the Animal Kingdom, Epcot and the Disney Hollywood Studio in Disney World!

Oglethorpe County, formerly the home of the Goose Pond community along the Broad River

Granvill's probable slaveholder, the Gilmer's, and his prominent neighbors bonded together to form a tight-knit community on the Broad River. Among the old high-society Virginia emigrants of this community, known as Goose Pond, were members of the Marks,

Meriwether, Taliaferro, Lewis, Harvie, McGehee, and the Johnson families. They formed deep ties through intertwining marriages and business dealings. As an illustration of these convoluted connections, John Blair Gilmer's neighbor was a Marks, his father-in-law was a Meriwether, his wife's mother was a Taliaferro, and his brother-in-law was a Lewis. Additionally, his daughters would marry members of the Harvie, McGehee, and Johnson family. In fact, one of the areas more famous inhabitant was Meriwether Lewis of Lewis and Clark fame, was also related to John Gilmer's wife. Being well educated, these men often gazed with contempt on the lower classes. They were frequently at odds with the transplanted North Carolinians and the white yeoman or small farmers. In Gov. Gilmer's book, he describes twenty family histories sprinkled with his observations. Comments about the males often distinguish whether or not they were educated, wealthy, industrious, or sometimes he would describe their looks and their drinking habits. I am curious about what Granvill's comments would be about Gilmer and his neighbors.

Gilmer and his like were among the 2% wealthiest in the county. Although they most certainly viewed themselves as superior to my enslaved ancestor, Granvill, in reality, one could say they too were slaves to tobacco. This cash crop controlled every aspect of their lives. These wealthy planters were in a perpetual hunt for new land. Growing this crop wore out the soil by exhausting the minerals and nutrients in it. After the Revolutionary War, almost like runaway slaves, this small elite group moved to Upper Georgia to seek new lands in hopes of regaining their former lifestyle. Gov. Gilmer, in his writing, implied that life was rough after the Revolution because the new Americans were "penniless in purse and restless in spirit" without the luxuries they had once enjoyed during Colonial times. This hilly land in Upper Georgia, which had recently been purchased or ceded from the Creek and Cherokee Indians, offered fertile soil, wooded areas with large trees and luxuriant grasses. Lured by the fertile soil required by tobacco, Gilmer and the other transplanted Virginians established scores of plantations along the Broad River. Over time, through the hard work of their enslaved labor force whom they referred to as "their negroes" and attention to the "almighty" tobacco, they would bring a highly profitable tobacco economy to the Goose Pond community.

Using the date of birth of Gilmer's seventh child, who was born in Virginia in 1785, as well as his eighth child, George, born in 1787 in Georgia, I can estimate John Gilmer's location. Enslaved African Americans, perhaps even Granvill, must have worked on the preparations for new tobacco plantations sometime between 1784 and 1786. Before cultivation could begin, wooded areas were cleared. First, medium-sized trees were chopped down, and small stumps were left, which caused the stumps to rot more quickly. A portion of the wood was hauled away, burned, or left to decay to enrich the soil. The area between the stumps was broken up with a hoe very similar to the ones we use today.

The governor relayed a humorous story about those stumps and a wealthy neighbor, Mr. McGehee, described as "knowing nothing of books but industrious." The McGehee's were the first in the area to plant a peach orchard. Using the money earned by making and selling peach brandy, they were the first to buy a carriage known as a stick-backed gig. On the second day after receiving it, "old man" McGehee turned his carriage over due to the numerous stumps in the road.

If this was Granvill's induction to being enslaved on a tobacco plantation, the older enslaved workers brought from Virginia, probably educated him in the art of working under bondage. Granvill had to adapt to his work by finding the delicate balance of doing enough to keep from being punished. The enslaved worker had to acclimate to working hard, but there was a line between hard and too hard that could not be crossed if the slaveholder wanted work completed.

In some ways, but certainly not all, I can understand this situation because it is similar to running a middle school classroom. In both circumstances, it was an institution with seemingly invisible hands that kept everything in order. My students followed an established routine reinforced by bells. A loud signal or other noise announced the beginning of the work routine for enslaved African Americans. Both Granvill and my students didn't get paid, but hopefully, my students received a valuable education. The overseer and I wanted things to work efficiently. We both pushed hard, but we both knew that if we went too far, we invited pushback. If a group of enslaved workers felt that they were unjustly treated, they stepped up their resistance level by slowing down the pace, breaking things, or pretending to be sick. Not wanting this, many slaveholders were concerned with how their enslaved workers felt because they believed that their emotional state directly linked to their labor output. This concept is understandable as a middle school teacher or even a parent. You know you can't push too hard, or you will face defiance.

But, there was an inescapable difference in punishment. I could send misbehaving students to the principal's office, but enslaved people could face whippings or worse. In the summer of 1787, the leader of a group of escaped enslaved blacks in a maroon community was first beheaded and then hung to make the gruesome point that enslaved people should have no illusion that freedom and liberty applied to them. In his book about the first settlers who lived in the Goose Pond community, the former Georgia governor suggested that the slaveholders employed a carrot-and-stick approach in dealing with their enslaved workers. He recounted that Gilmer's next-door neighbor and future father-in-law, Col. Nicolas Johnson, would "send into the fields for his negroes and treat them to an exhibition whenever a monkey or other show passed by."

Unfortunately, my enslaved ancestors had few of the rights my students had; their movements were severely restricted and were always under the threat of cruel treatment. This exercise in trying to fathom Granvill's world help me to get a glimpse of how much slavery was an institution just like education. Although there were layers behind the scene of rules, regulations, and people that kept them functioning, the execution of how they worked were on opposite ends on the spectrum of compassion. When it came to planting tobacco, Granvill had to adapt to a crop that was very different from rice. Growing tobacco was labor-intensive, but not as much as rice cultivation. The process of cultivating this plant required year-round attention from both enslaved males and females. Very tiny tobacco seeds started in seedbeds of soil with extremely fine particles. The transplanting of seedlings to the fields occurred in late spring. After planting, the tobacco plants were hoed once a week to keep the ground loose and to get rid of the weeds. When the plant began to bloom after about a month and a half, enslaved workers pinched the tops off with their thumb and fingernails. During the growing season, sprouts or suckers had to continuously removed, which improved the quality and profitability of the tobacco.

Experienced planters, like John Blair Gilmer, knew when the plants were ready to be harvested. After collecting the leaves, they had to be air cured for six weeks. The leaves were stripped from their stem and finally packed in wooden containers called hogheads for shipment. At other times in the year, Granvill, in all likelihood, learned a skill that contributed to running the self-sufficient plantation. Enslaved blacks were allowed to be blacksmiths, brick masons, and carpenters. On George Washington's Mount Vernon plantation, about 25% of his enslaved Africans Americans were in skilled positions, which helped to augment Washington's income from tobacco.

The first time I saw tobacco leaves for myself was with my husband, Weilin, on a trip to Taiwan, of all places. We were at a museum that showcased the history of Taiwan during its occupation by colonial Japan at the start of the twentieth century. Under this oppressive Japanese government, tobacco was grown as a profitable export by the subjugated Taiwanese farmers. This situation fascinated me that other colonial powers such as Japan forced their subjects to grow tobacco 40 years after the end of the Civil War. This nicotine-laced plant, from its humble beginnings in the Americas, became the foundation for the growth of the American economy. Later, other countries made it the drug of choice for governments wanting to add to their coiffeurs all over the world. How sad that others faced oppression in service to the "almighty" tobacco.

Tobacco gown in Taiwan

As I collected more and more research on various topics here and there, it only gave me a fleeting glimpse of Granvill's world because it was so random and disorganized. One way I increased my understanding of his life was using the website <HistoryLines.com>. The site, which bills itself as the "Stories of Your Ancestors," provides a timeline of what occurred historically in the life of one's ancestor. Either you furnish some details, or as I did, upload a GECOM file of my tree from Ancestry. It presented a clear, cohesive story of many aspects of Granvill's life. There was extensive information about the state of Georgia. I was impressed it included material about enslaved African Americans as well as Native Americans. I personalized their research by adding details from other sources.

During the late 1700s, this website suggested that plantations did not have dwellings we associate with the Antebellum South. These weren't neat rows of wood-frame cabins, which were probably later created to deflect the abolitionist claims that slaveholders showed callousness toward the welfare of their slaves. Poor Georgians and enslaved blacks lived in simple houses. Recent archaeological evidence shows evidence that during this time, some enslaved African Americans lived in earthen structures with mud walls, and thatched roofs and others lived in a room of a multi-roomed log cabin. Furthermore, the wealthy planters in the Goose Pond community lived in homes that provided basic shelter but were nothing like the grand, imposing and columned southern mansions we think of now. The largest houses were two stories with ten to fifteen rooms. The lower floor included an area with a parlor and dining room to entertain guests and perhaps a library. The kitchen was a separate building to minimize the heat and protect against fires. The upstairs was the private area for bedrooms. More concerned about getting back to profitability, these transplanted Virginians built homes that were unappealing large wooden structures crafted from local lumber.

From the unlikely source of slave runaway notices, I learned the usual dress of a male "working negro" like Granvill included knee-length breeches made from hemp, a small jacket, maybe a shirt of course material and a hat made from linen or felt. The females typically wore petticoats, and button-up jackets or blouses also made from an inexpensive, durable cloth - often imported from a place in present-day Germany. Local Native American tribes fashioned their clothing from animal skins and feathers. Besides providing warmth, many tribes believed that by wearing animal skins, they might imbibe the qualities of that animal. I wonder, did the enslaved African Americans trade with the Native Americans living nearby?

Granvill found a wife and started a family during his seasons on the frontier. There were few luxuries afforded to the slaveholders and probably even fewer to their enslaved blacks. Thus, simple weddings normally held at night, so others from the surrounding plantations could have the opportunity to attend. Starting a family marked a new stage in one's life. Like many women today, Granvill's wife probably had to work outside the home all day and then come back to do all the work inside of their dwellings, such as cooking, washing, and cleaning. Enslaved African Americans grew peppers, okra, peanuts, and watermelon and often integrated traditional African cuisine with what was available locally. Alcoholic beverages were commonplace; indeed, Gov. Gilmer commented on the abundance of peach brandy and the local minister's vigilant opposition to the drunkenness in the community.

Granvill's pregnant wife received medical advice and support from the midwives in the enslaved African American community. Once weaned, her small children most likely had to spend their days being cared for by older children and elderly slaves. Since Granvill was almost two decades older than John Blair Gilmer's two youngest boys, it was likely that Granvill's children played with George O. and David Gilmer when they were children. Gov. Gilmer would later state in defense of slavery, "as infants, the negroes were fond nurses, in our childhoods our playmates and later in life, our obedient and willing servants."

The workweek for the enslaved blacks was Monday through Saturday with Sundays off. The renowned founder of the Methodism, George Whitefield, and his follower, the Countess of Huntingdon, sought to improve the fate of those enslaved by allowing them to go to church on Sundays. Yet, they saw no contradiction between understanding Christianity and the ownership of slaves. They promoted an egalitarian approach with both black and white preachers and literacy among believers, including those who were enslaved. Moreover, Lady Huntingdon, a follower of Whitefield, supported and encouraged the publishing of religious poems by the first published African American poet, Phillis Wheatley. During 1809, Gov. Gilmer proclaimed that there was a great Methodist revival of religion on the Broad River. Granvill and his family may have begun the path to possibly developing literacy, as well as a robust Christian ethic that would last for generations.

In the summer of 1793, it is possible that Granvill and the other slaves would face one of the most dreaded and fearful situations for slaves. John Blair Gilmer died at the age of 45. Gov. George R. Gilmer claimed in his book that his uncle had been a handsome playboy in his youth, but his marriage to the industrious Mildred Meriwether and "the hard realities of frontier life" transformed him into a "pious" man. The death of the slaveholder was a time of uncertainty and fear of being separated from their families. In his will, Gilmer "lent" the plantation, its stock, and the household furniture to his wife so she could bring up his young children. Gilmer also desired that "the whole of my negroes be kept" to work on the plantation. He also wanted the proceeds from selling his land, and the slaves, be equally proportioned to each of his nine children when they became of age. Maybe this was another way that as a slaveholder, he thought his kinder treatment led to improved yield from his slaves.

For Granvill and his family, the Gilmer family kept this tradition of keeping its slaves together in families, until the end of slavery. Was Granvill one of the slaves mentioned in the will? There are no records to say for sure. It was possible surmising from the fact that Martha, the wife of George O. Gilmer, felt compelled to take care of Granvill in his old age. All of Granvill's children reported that he was born in Georgia as well as Jack, the oldest known son. And he named one of his sons Marywether, very likely after the mistress of the house, Mildred Meriwether Gilmer. Even though Mildred was not allowed to own the property, I found her name listed as the one responsible for paying the taxes in the Oglethorpe County Tax Digest for 1794. It also stated 26 in the Slaves column. If Granvill were indeed part of that number of 26, he would spend about two dozen more years on the tobacco plantation.

After considering the story of Granvill's life, I wondered if I could tell when major historical events impacted someone's life. I came up with a test for looking for the connections to history that seemed to work. First, find the significant historical events and determine if one's life was changed in some way by them. A list of events in the Early Republic from 1783 – 1815 includes the ratification of the Constitution, the first president George Washington, the invention of the cotton gin, and the Louisiana Purchase. George Washington does not seem to matter to the life of Granvill, but the other events had significant ramifications.

Since the ratification of the Constitution in 1787, historians still argue as to whether the Constitution was pro-slavery or not. Even though the words "slave" and "slavery" are not in the document, the three-fifths compromise and the fugitive-slave law affected Granvill and as well as other enslaved blacks. The three-fifths clause gave the South increased representation in the House of Representatives, thereby ensuring that slavery would be protected. Years later, the clause also was the rationale in a forgotten case that would be humorous, if not for its tragic consequences. In an incident in Alabama, in 1840 a clever enslaved African American argued he could not be arrested for a crime because "a slave is not a person," but merely considered property. The court ruled that since three-fifths of the slave population is represented as persons in Congress, thus enslaved people were "a mixed character of persons and property." And even more dreadful, the fugitive-slave provision in the constitution made it much harder to run away, because the law required captured enslaved people to be returned. This all means the inhumane blot of slavery was sewn into the fabric of our country from the start.

In the year 1793, several events would occur that had major significance for Granvill and his family. The first began in 1791 with the Haitian Revolution, the largest and most successful show of slave resistance in history. Slaveholders all over the South were extremely apprehensive upon hearing of this slave rebellion inspired by the 1789 French Revolution. It was especially frightening since tens of thousands of enslaved blacks in Haiti violently revolted against slavery. They burned fields, killed slave owners, and smashed the machinery used to produce sugar.

Thomas Jefferson, who was president at the time, found himself in a personal paradox. He was in favor of the ideals of liberty and natural rights proclaimed in the French Revolution, but as a Virginian slaveholder, he feared the possibility of a Haitian inspired slave revolt on American soil. The specter of slave rebellions always loomed for the white slaveholders who feared the possibility of "another Haiti" in their own backyard. Enslaved African Americans such as Granvill accounted for 35% of Georgia's population in 1790. Paranoia over the unrest led to some places in Georgia passing an ordinance that forbade slaves to have religious services without a white preacher present. Although resistance to slavery continued in covert ways throughout the history of slavery, dramatic revolts like Haiti did not occur. A few overt armed, organized slave rebellions did happen in New

Orleans in 1811 and the most famous Nat Turner's rebellion in 1831. Even though the rhetoric of rights had its advent in the United States, freedom for the slaves in the United States would not come to fruition for several more generations. But the seeds had been planted by the emancipation of the enslaved populations in Haiti. Ultimately, the end of the Civil War would eventually give Granvill's children a taste of freedom.

Additionally, in 1793, something happened that would transform the lives of enslaved blacks, the slaveholders, and even alter the history of the young nation. Near Savannah, Georgia, Eli Whitney built a machine that would effectively intensify the demand for more enslaved African Americans. After graduating from Yale, Whitney headed south, looking for a job as a private tutor. Instead, he found work on the plantation of Catherine Greene, the widow of a Revolutionary War general. After learning about the problem of having to remove the seeds from cotton painstakingly by hand, he invented a machine that could separate the seeds from the cotton. Nowadays, historians are debating whether Catherine Greene or perhaps even some of her enslaved African Americans actually invented the cotton gin. Nevertheless, Whitney received a patent for his invention called the cotton gin in 1794. Soon the success of the cotton gin helped to expand slavery all over the South. With cheap labor provided by enslaved African Americans and an easy way to remove the seeds, cotton became the leading export of the United States by the mid-19th century. Machinery spurred by the Industrial Revolution allowed manufacturers to churn out affordable cotton clothing. This fact, in turn, increased demand for cotton, which boosted the requirement for more enslaved blacks, like Granvill's offspring.

Another hugely historical event was the Louisiana Purchase in 1803, which increased the size of the expanding country. It was paradoxical that one of the few slave rebellions that succeeded in Haiti so rattled Napoleon that he sold the Louisiana Territory to the budding young country of the United States. But this action would radically increase the land devoted to the use of slavery. John Gilmer's son, George O. Gilmer, followed the cotton bandwagon. Granvill and his family would soon have to adapt to cotton.

Searching for Granvill's life through the point of view of finding the history in his life and then examining history to see what influenced him, has provided some insights. After the Revolutionary War, a disappointed Granvill was not freed, but very likely was moved to a different locale and type of plantation. It was an agrarian society, the Goose Pond community of wealthy Virginia emigrants, which revolved around the tobacco plantations that barely changed for decades. As to whether or not Granvill might have seen George Washington, the answer is it is highly unlikely. George Washington did visit Georgia, but only the urban areas. The interior, where the Goose Pond community was, would have been considered the frontier at the time. When I tell people about our slaveholder's mother, they are impressed. Mildred Meriwether, very likely Granvill's slaveholder for several decades, had a father-in-law that was the doctor to Thomas Jefferson, a nephew who would become Governor of Georgia, and she was also related to Meriwether Clark of Lewis and Clark fame. I was left with a vexing question; did these famous people in history have anything to do with my ancestor's livelihood? My husband jokingly chimed in, "Maybe that place had excellent Feng shui!" He explained that the Chinese traditionally believed that harmony and prosperity would come their way if they located a place where all the elements are aligned. The idea was if it was not blocked, the positive chi would collect in that place. Chi is something like the Force in the popular Star Wars saga.

All joking aside, studying the life of Granvill through the lens of history allowed me to take a more rational and detached point of view. Even though he was just an ordinary person, I learned that his life was worthy of study. If I stuck with the facts and logic, I could somewhat deal with the uncomfortable emotions surrounding slavery. Granvill's life was still not quite like the typical images of enslaved blacks toiling away on a cotton plantation as they sang Christian gospel music to assuage their sorrow. He continued to be enslaved on a plantation, albeit most likely on a tobacco plantation, instead of a rice plantation. But Granvill had moved closer to that standard image because of the likelihood that he and his family had become Christians. I can also use moments in my life to gain insights into his, which somehow makes his life relatable, more human. As I continued my pursuit to resurrect his life, what more would I discover?

You will probably find that it's easy to unearth the history which occurred during your ancestor's life. Actually, you may find too many historical events. Test whether an event affected your ancestor's life by thinking about whether or not it impacted any part of your ancestor's daily life, especially making a living. Sometimes big things influenced their lives, and sometimes it was smaller, more local events. Hopefully, you will experience the Aha! moment of learning more about the connections to your ancestor's life in history.

Economics

It was an ordinary day as I was trying to drown out the racket of my husband singing and the whirling sound of his electric shaver. Unexpectedly, a thought fired up the neurons in my brain. Did Granvill shave? I squinted my eyes as if that could help me to find a satisfactory answer. Alas, this was one more of many essentials of daily life details that I just didn't know about Granvill's life. Using census records, the bill of sale, and DNA matches, we thought we knew the family of Granvill and Eliza. So, it came as a complete surprise when Chery, my DNA cousin, divulged that she had discovered a brand-new branch on Granvill's tree.

By new branch, I mean a new offspring of his. With almost 500 4th cousins listed on my AncestryDNA page, it is a bit frustrating that I have thousands of people who are related to me through a labyrinthine web of connections that I may never be able to fully sort out. It's like having a bunch of puzzle pieces without a picture of what the final product will look like. The Shared Matches tool, which is available from all the major DNA companies, shows a list of people that share DNA with you and one other match. Cheryl and I have at least 66 shared DNA matches. With painstaking effort, Cheryl discovered that one of them led her to another daughter of Granvill. Not only was she born in Georgia in 1809, but she later named her youngest son, Granville. Lucy was also on the same bill of sale where we first unearthed Granvill, his wife Eliza, and six of his other children. Since Eliza was too young to be Lucy's mother, it was reasonable to deduce that her mother was a first spouse, which I had always presumed that Granvill had. Her birth in 1809 may not have been a sheer coincidence but quite possibly a result of the economic forces of the times.

1808 was a consequential year for African Americans. Granvill, at 38 years old, had already lived longer than the average life expectancy in the 1800s of 37 years. On January 1st of this same year, the United States Congress passed legislation, agreed upon by the founders in the Constitution, to end the transatlantic trade slave. In the previous year, the British had decisively declared an end to the Atlantic Slave Trade. Historians continue to debate why the Atlantic slave trade was discontinued; some think it was for ideological reasons and others think it was for primarily for economic reasons. Some Americans questioned the irony of slaveholders, proclaiming their own "natural rights of freedom" while withholding these same rights from the enslaved African Americans in their midst. Throughout the revolutionary era, "Slavery" had been used as a battle call against the unfair rule of the British. George Washington admonished his men, "You are free men, fighting for the blessings of Liberty—that slavery will be your portion, and that of your posterity, if you do not acquit yourselves like men." Taking these revolutionary ideals seriously, many of the Northern states set themselves on the path to eliminating slavery.

Not only did the Southern states resist any attempts to cast off the bonds of slavery, they chose to tighten their grip on their "peculiar institution." Three decades after the ink dried on the Declaration of Independence, that institution was becoming entrenched. The Northern states called for abolishing slavery in twenty years as part of the compromise to approve the Constitution in 1787. For this concession, Southern states could count each enslaved black as three-fifths of a person, giving the South more representation. Twenty years later, most of the almost 900,000 enslaved Americans in 1808 were in the Southern states. Having an estimated worth of over a quarter billion in today's dollars, with their slaves' worth that money, economic fundamentals overshadowed moral considerations.

Table 1 - Average Price of a Slave Over Time
Current dollars

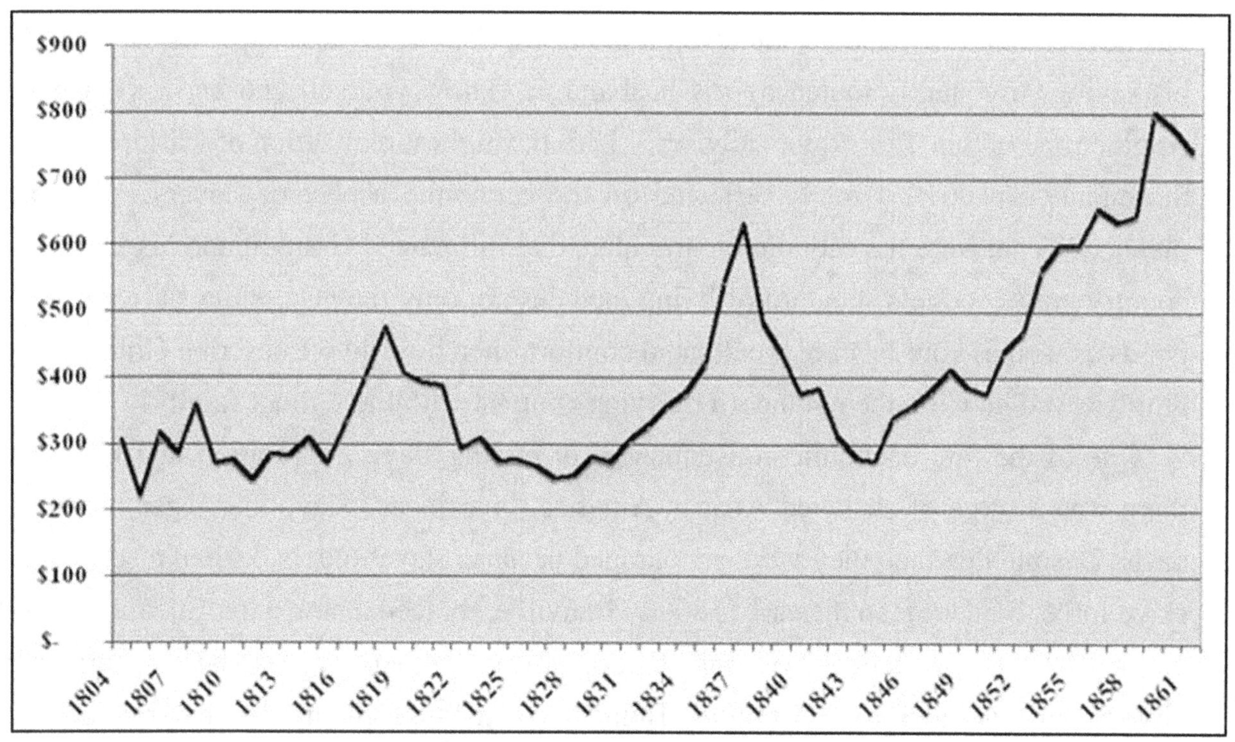

Source: Historical Statistics, Table Bb212. Average Slave Price.

This graph of Average Price of Slaves Over Time indicates a bump in price around 1808. Now that there would no longer be possible to purchase slaves from Africa, did the Gilmer family offer some incentive to Granvill to have more children? It seems highly plausible. Economic necessity was changing the Southerner's beliefs about slavery. I wondered, in what other areas did economics impact Granvill's life daily as well as the country? Using the lens of economics to examine the microeconomic level of one's personal standard of living, as well as the macroeconomic level of national events, what can it reveal about Granvill's life?

73

I supposed I was ready to take the next steps, since I was making progress on coming to terms with the emotional land mines that go off when I ponder slavery. I was obliged, at the very least, to push up my sleeves and understand this heinous system of oppression. As often happens, Weilin prodded me to take the advice of one of China's most brilliant minds, Sun Tzu. He is considered China's most celebrated war leader and strategist. Even today, many business and military leaders, and even football coaches' study and apply his advice. One of his sayings, frequently touted by my husband, is "know yourself and know your enemy." Another one of Sun Tzu's quote advises, "Thus the highest realization of warfare is to attack the enemy's plan…" I never reflected on the economic aspect of slavery. Was slavery planned? What were the economic particulars that influenced Granvill and his family as the country grew? If one's standard of living includes not only the necessities but your material goods as well as your level of wealth and comfort, then how do we describe Granvill and his family? And how did their standard of living contrast with the Gilmer family?

One of the first economic consequences of ending slave importation in 1808 was that there was a surge of enslaved African American marriages. Slave marriages had no legal basis. Despite this fact, they were encouraged because slaveholders desired a self-renewing slave force. Sometime in the early 1800s, Granvill embraced a new wife, Eliza. Her children all stated that she was born in Georgia. Our only record of her suggests she was born in 1798, almost three decades after Granvill. Being on a tobacco plantation that required fewer enslaved African Americans than either rice or cotton plantations, Granvill and Eliza were possibly "married abroad," meaning they had different owners.

Whatever the exact situation, working together as a couple provided a remedy to lessen the burden of slavery. Not only did slaveholders not pay wages, but to maximize profits for themselves, some only supplied a bare minimum weekly food allowance of pork and corn. Some other planters suggested providing "plenty of meat and vegetables to discourage pilfering." Whatever they received, Granvill could supplement their diet with hunting, especially 'possum, and fishing. Eliza could gather wild food and herbs for medicine along with tending a garden plot, which hopefully included a favorite of mine, watermelon. Whenever they were together, they could make a life that was separate from the prying eyes of their slaveholder or their overseer. They could tell stories, sing, and find some comfort.

Thus, marriage increased the amount of necessities they had, as well as provided spiritual and emotional support to each other, as well as their family, as it grew.

In the spring of 1812, the eighth child of John Blair Gilmer was about to wed. It was a young twenty-four-year-old George Oglethorpe Gilmer. His portrait revealed he had a medium build, light eyes, sandy brown hair, a bumpy nose, and thin lips that barely smiled. On Friday, May 8th, he legally wed the fifteen-year-old Martha Harvie Johnson. She was a plain-looking girl with dark hair. In all likelihood, it was her membership in the elite planter class and not her looks, which pressed her to follow the typical path of females marrying early within the small inclusive group of wealthy families. The newlyweds were practically next-door neighbors, living on plantations near each other on the Broad River in the Goose Pond community. No doubt, their wedding would have been a premier social event. Marriages were usually spectacular affairs with the extended family and local elite in attendance. Nicholas Johnson, the father of the bride, proclaimed that he gave to the husbands of his daughters $500 (almost $10,000 in today's economy) because it would "mortify him to see his children laboring hard for a pittance" or slave wages.

This statement provided a clue into the socioeconomic structure and beliefs of the Old South. The wealthy slaveholding males, such as George O. Gilmer, were at the apex of Southern society. Consequently, the bride's father gave the money to his son-in-law, since women were supported financially and legally by their husbands. Slave ownership was a way to elevate a woman's status in society. White women, rich and poor, accepted the institution of slavery because they all strove toward the idealized Southern plantation mistress. She barely lifted a finger to do manual labor, which of course, was reserved for the lowly enslaved blacks. Considering themselves to be superior, this supported their mindset that the natural order was the master ruling over those that were inferior. I lament the fact that in their day, the "American dream" was to be a land-owning slaveholder with an ever-increasing number of enslaved African Americans.

Sometime after their marriage, George and Martha traveled to Christian, Kentucky. I have a hunch that they hightailed there to come to the aid of John Thornton Gilmer, George's brother, after one of the most massive earthquakes in American history. Known as the New Madrid earthquakes, they were a series of thousands of smaller tremors, along with three massive earthquakes ranging from a magnitude of 7.8 to 8.8 on the Richter scale. During the second earthquake, the first steamboat to travel on the Ohio River was chased by Native Americans who speculated that the "fire cannon" had caused the quake. After the last one on Feb. 7, 1812, some claimed that the Mississippi ran backward for a few hours. Although the earthquakes' epicenters were in Missouri, places nearby Kentucky, Tennessee, and Arkansas would have felt the violent shaking of these powerful earthquakes. No doubt, Granvill, and Eliza felt the tremors as well as President Madison and his wife Dolly in Washington DC. Life goes on, and while in Kentucky, the Gilmer's first offspring, James Blair, was born on Wednesday, May 4, 1814.

Granvill's family also increased with the addition of a son named Jack. Although there is no mention of his name in the census records, all of his children concurred he was born in Georgia. Born into bondage, Jack could look forward to the status of being the property of the Gilmer family. His standard of living included only the barest of necessities, few materials goods, and even scant comforts. Jack could consider himself lucky if he lived with just the members of his family in one room of a multi-roomed structure. If he had any clothes, they were durable but extremely uncomfortable. Day in and day out, Jack consumed a carbon copy of yesterday's meal, with occasional interruptions provided by hunting, fishing, and seasonal delights from the garden.

When Jack was a small child, he probably played with home-made toys, including marbles and hobby horses. He might have run races or had jumping contests. By virtue of being enslaved, Jack was denied a formal education, ensuring his place at the bottom of the economic ladder. His schooling would come from on the job training for whatever job he performed on the plantation and at home with his parents.

As part of his upbringing, for all one knows, his parents told him stories. Perhaps he heard some of the Brer Rabbit stories which originated in Georgia. Possibly he listened to the story of Brer Rabbit and Sis Cow. In that story, Brer Rabbit asks Sis Cow for milk, but she refuses to give him any. Knowing that Sis Cow was stronger and bigger than him, Brer Rabbit came up with a clever plan. He asked Sis Cow to knock some fruit down from a tree by hitting it with her horns. Sis Cow hit the tree so hard, her horns got stuck in the tree, which allowed Brer Rabbit and his family to get a generous amount of milk from her. After freeing herself, Sis Cow chased Brer Rabbit into a briar patch. Disguising his voice, Brer Rabbit fooled Sis Cow into looking for him somewhere else and then got away. This story and other similar ones, with West African roots, pointed to a way that one could outwit more powerful adversaries. Many enslaved people passed down stories, skills, and ideas that helped them to endure slavery. Many children like Jack learned to hide their feelings to escape punishment, to assist the family in any way they could, and that blacks were superior to white people, who were lazy and incapable of running things well.

As Jack grew up, the expectation was for him to gradually do more and more work until he was able to work as an adult. As an adult, Jack married and took his place in the slave quarters on a cotton plantation. Typical slave cabins were one-room log cabins with a dirt floor and chimney. Many slaves, and possibly Jack, worked hard to transform their quarters into homes. Their homes were as comfortable as possible as a way to defy their subservient status conferred upon them by the institution of slavery.

On the other hand, James, the son of George and Martha, was born into privilege. His standard of living included all the comforts and material goods that the wealth of his family could provide. At the time of his birth, the homes of the wealthy were large cabin-like structures with multiple rooms, one of which contained his bed. As a boy, typically, he would wear dresses until about age six. His meals would include a variety of the best of the meat, vegetables, and other dishes grown on the plantations.

James could look forward to a high socio-economic status in Southern society built upon wealth produced by his myriad of unpaid enslaved workers. Growing up, James may have been subject to new ideas about childrearing in the young nation, which called for play and education as essential in raising healthy, intelligent children. James most likely had a tutor or was sent away for his schooling, because even though the northern states were pursuing the new idea of public education, the South lagged far behind.

As James grew older, notions of slavery changed from the founding father's idea of an evil necessity to defending slavery as vital, to maintaining the superior Southern lifestyle, which emphasized good manners, honor, and graciousness. Southerners also employed pseudoscientific theories that blacks, and for that matter, all nonwhites, were racially inferior.

As an adult, James would take his place among the wealthy elite, owning multiple cotton plantations. His cousin, George R. Gilmer, a former Governor of Georgia, called James "enterprising to recklessness, and very determined in his purposes." His home would be one of the showplaces of North Louisiana. An authentic Southern mansion called the Orchard Place, with wooden columns and doorknobs made of silver, all advertising his socioeconomic status as a millionaire. His divorce from his second wife would rival today's tabloid filled stories of the rich and famous, with the Supreme Court of Louisiana ruling on how to divide the couple's slaves and land.

Land ownership was encouraged by the founding fathers, especially Thomas Jefferson. In line with his commonly held white supremacy views, he believed that owning land encouraged men to become civilized. That led credence to the notion that land-owning societies were superior to others, such as the Native Americans and Africans that were not permitted to legally hold title to land. With this frame of thought, after the War of 1812, to promote agriculture and land ownership, the federal government sold land in northern Alabama that had previously been the hunting grounds of the Cherokee, Creek, and Chickasaw Indians.

How could a nation establish on the motto that "all men are created equal," and then treat enslaved African Americans and Native Americans so poorly? The answer is to first thoroughly dehumanized them, and then exploit them for economic advantage. David Livingstone Smith, after surveying atrocities such as the Holocaust, the genocides in Rwanda and Armenia and slavery, wrote a book titled *Less than Human.*' In it, he theorizes that in order for a group of people or a race to be harmed, they first have to be dehumanized. This dehumanization imagines others as disgusting non-human creatures disguised in a human form. George Washington provides an example with his ineloquent proclamation, "Indians and wolves are both beasts of prey, tho' they differ in shape." Another founding father, James Madison, describes, "… the slave may appear to be degraded from a human rank, and classed with those irrational animals which fall under the legal denomination of property." Once the majority of Americans subscribed to these beliefs, it didn't bother people when blacks were deprived of their freedom while being forced to work, or to see Native American's ancestral lands yanked from them. It's also worth noting that economics blinded their vision.

In 1818, embodying the youthful population spreading across the country, George O. Gilmer purchased property in Madison County, part of the fertile Tennessee Valley. Did he acquire the deed on the land by perhaps buying it on credit with the collateral of enslaved African Americans such as Granvill, his family, or others on the plantation in Georgia?

Meanwhile, 1819, the records at the Bureau of Land Management (< blm.gov>) show he purchased nearby public land released by the government. Between May 1800 and mid-1820, over thirteen million acres of public land were purchased in the United States. Landownership was one of the most defining factors, besides race, in the socio-economic class structure of Southern society in the nineteenth century. Granvill and other enslaved blacks were considered the very bottom, below the landless whites, while perched at the top were the wealthy slaveholding families like the Gilmer family. He and the wealthy sons of the group of planters who had transplanted themselves from Virginia to Georgia, flocked to Alabama's black belt, named for its dark, fertile soil. Known as the "Georgia faction," they entrenched themselves into the political structure of the new frontier state, making sure that the slave-based economy built on cotton cultivation treated them favorably.

For instance, the 1819 Constitution of Alabama forbade the government from making laws that would emancipate slaves. With the elite grabbing the most productive plots for themselves, this uneven distribution of land laid the seeds for the underdevelopment of the South. All the same, cotton, land prices, and as noted in Table 1, the average cost of slaves soared as small farmers and wealthy planters alike rushed in with visions of making massive amounts of money.

Madison County, Alabama

As often happens after a boom, the next year, like the landing of the ill-fated airship, the Hindenburg, the economy came crashing down. The Panic of 1819 began a depression that hit the cotton economy with low cotton prices and land foreclosures. As seen in Table 1, slave prices also fell. Gilmer most likely weathered the storm because deeds recorded in the Madison County showed that he bought more land in 1824 and 1825. Granvill and his family would have been part of the over 100% increase of the county's slave population from 4,200 in 1816 to 9,255 in 1820. Enslaved African Americans also increased from 30% of the total population to 47%. Gilmer cemented his status as a member of the most powerful class in the antebellum Southern hierarchy, conferred to him by slave and land ownership.

In 1824, Granville and Eliza had a son, Austin, while George and Martha had a daughter, Mary Ann. Both families had a similar sizable gap between this birth and their last child. Was this the first occurrence of a drop in fertility rates during economic tough times? Is this indicative of time spent carving cotton plantations out of this frontier land? Or did some type of disease wipe out other children who had been born to them? Without records, we can only guess.

I wonder if Granvill and the other enslaved blacks could fathom that their work of stripping the forest and clearing the land to plant more cotton was changing the world. The state of Alabama quadrupled its production of cotton. The first governor of Alabama, also a former Broad River resident, quipped, "the haunts of the savage will become the dwelling place of civilized men and the forest of the wilderness will become fruitful fields." The finished product of their efforts, raw cotton, was transported by the technical innovation of the steamship. Did they know that perhaps some of the soft, fluffy fiber they picked was exported far away to Great Britain?

The insatiable demand for cotton cloth fueled huge profits for planters like Gilmer and Great Britain. These profits helped to finance technical innovations in the machinery of cotton textile mills, as well as other advances in the Industrial Revolution. Gilmer used some of his substantial profits to purchase corn and pork from Western states and clothing for his enslaved labors. Some he used to enhance his standard of living with luxurious items such as the latest clothing, art, furniture, silver, and china from the Northern states and Europe.

As it so happened, oil paintings of George and Martha from the early 1840s show them dressed to the tee in the latest fashions from the high society of Europe.

Another son, Marywether, was born to Granvill sometime between 1825 and 1828. I was always curious if that name had a connection to George Gilmer's mother. Her name was Mildred Thornton Meriwether. I possibly found the answer in the 1795 Georgia Property Tax records. Her brother, Francis Meriwether, and her husband's cousin, Thomas Meriwether, were the males that ran the plantation. They were also in her late husband, John Gilmer's will, which I obtained from Oglethorpe County. Mildred died in 1826. Since, in all likelihood, they had spent 37 years together, did Granvill name his son as a tribute to her or the others? It's also possible that George Gilmer wanted the baby named after his mother. Unfortunately, names listed on records can't reveal to us what happened, but many times African Americans used names to convey their history.

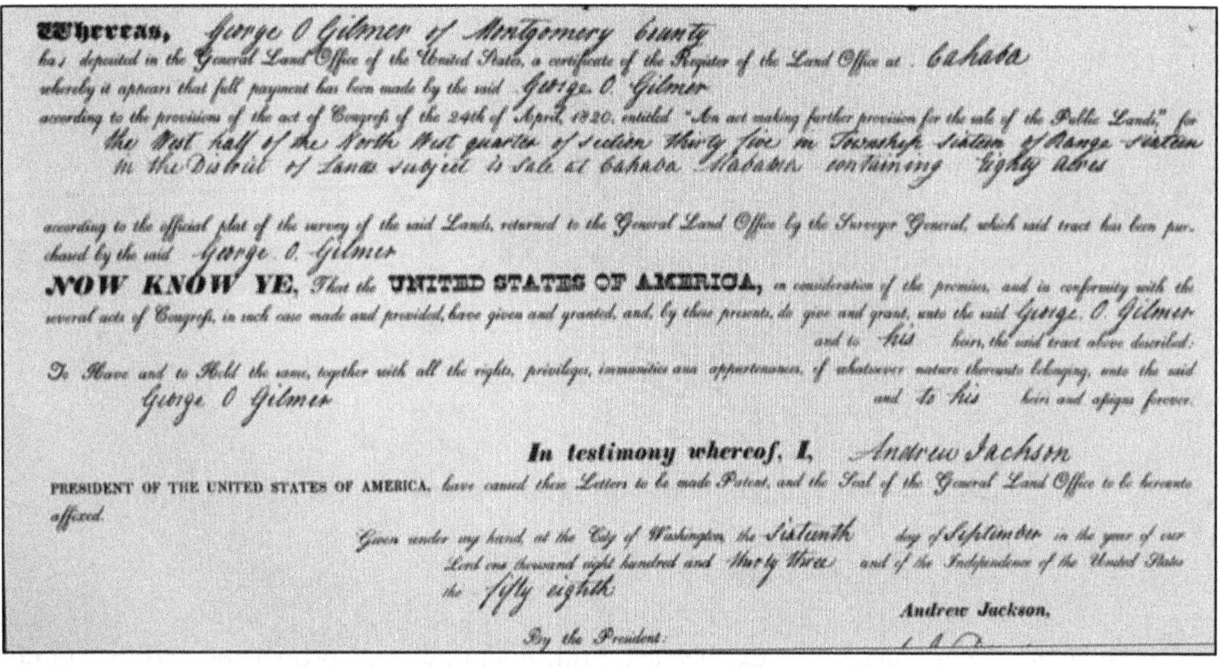

Land Patent for George O. Gilmer in 1833 from the Bureau of Land Management

Some records do illustrate a clear-cut story. The land patent record above shows the land Gilmer purchased in Montgomery, Alabama, apparently after selling his property in Madison, Alabama. Near the bottom of the document, the signature of President Andrew Jackson (he's on the twenty-dollar bill) belies the fact that his brutal defeat of the Native Americans as General Jackson made this document possible. After the Indian Removal Act of 1830, he confiscated 23 million acres of land. No doubt, Granvill, teenaged Jack, and the kids, Austin and Marywether labored to clear this and other properties bought from the government. The 1830 United States Federal Census for Gilmer, indicated his growing wealth with twenty enslaved African Americans over the age of 10 years old and eleven under 10.

Montgomery County, Alabama

Over the decade until the next census, both his number of properties and the number of enslaved blacks more than doubled. This increase was right in line with the sale of over 57 million acres of public land between 1830 and 1837, which also coincided with a significant increase in the economic measure of the United States Gross Domestic Product (GDP).

In the early 1830s, the twins, Samuel and William, were born. The twins, which include my second great-grandfather, Samuel, experienced many of the transformations to the institution of slavery. These were due to the watershed event, the Nat Turner Rebellion in 1831. After a fiery preacher rose a group using knives, hatchets, and axes to brutally slay between 55 to 65 people in Virginia, slaveholders demanded stricter slave codes. The South made it unlawful to teach blacks - enslaved or free - to read and write. The implementation of slave patrols was a precursor to modern policing methods. Slaveholders were terrified of losing their golden goose of staggering profits from cotton production.

Furthermore, George kept expanding his holdings by purchasing more and more land. So, he may or may not have moved his family and business to Montgomery, Alabama, when the twins, my second great-grandfather and his brother, were born. When he moved, it was probably to a new plantation that had a fashionable "big house" and slave quarters with rows of cabins.

If you think of economics as studying how those in society take care of their needs, then Granvill and Eliza had the basics of food and shelter, including a sparsely furnished cabin with a bed. The wooden framed house had holes to run home-made cords, crisscrossed to support a mattress stuffed with cotton or straw. I found it interesting that to remind people to check the tautness of the ropes on a routine basis, the expression "sleep tight" was coined. Thus, the standard of living for enslaved African Americans, such as Granvill and his family, increased ever so slightly over time. There was more food to eat because it was purchased rather than grown. There were more holidays, such as Christmas, Easter, and New Year's to take the day off. Eliza could sell eggs, and possibly milk, to generate money to buy some fancier clothes, especially for going to church. Whatever the peanut-sized progress in their standard of living, the Gilmer's were, comparatively, on their way to becoming millionaires.

Jack, dressed in the coarse clothing provided by the Gilmer's, was now old enough to labor in the cotton fields full time. Cultivating cotton was a time consuming, back-breaking endeavor done by a gang of hands, as the enslaved workforce was known. After all the old cotton stalks were gathered and burned, the ground was prepared into beds. The seeds were planted in March and April after the planting of the corn in February. After the cotton plants sprouted, they needed to be hoed frequently to remove the weeds and grass. The hoeing season was from April until July.

In the latter part of August, the bolls began to open, and the cotton-picking season began. Jack, his mother Eliza, his father Granvill and all the other hands, as they were known, were given large baskets to fill to the brim with cotton. This most dreaded time of year was probably the busiest, as everyone worked from daybreak until it was too dark to see. Picking took a few months steadily through the fall months into winter. During this time, the cotton was put through the cotton gin to remove the seeds. Every planter of importance had his own gin house, which probably included Gilmer. It was then pressed into bales of about 350 pounds before being shipped down the Tennessee River to New Orleans.

The most valid argument that the defenders of slavery often made was that ending slavery would have a profound economic effect on the South, one that relied on enforced slave labor as the foundation of their economy. They argued that a continuation of the status quo provided affluence and stability for the slaveholding class and all free people who relished in the bounty of the slave society. The unfortunate tale of George Gilmer's brother-in-law exemplifies this affluence. With plenty of leisure time, going deer hunting was a pleasant past-time echoing the aristocracy of their European past.

One day, a group on horseback slowly plodded their horses through the field toward the green forest just beyond the fencing. Edward, the youngest son of Col. Johnson, was at the back of a line. Someone opened the gate, and the men passed through on their way to embark on the hunt. Suddenly there was a deafening noise; everyone stopped. Spinning around to check for the cause, they witnessed Edward slumped over his horse. He had carelessly shot himself when he tried to shut the gate with his gun. Even so, I can only imagine the uproar this caused for Granvill, his family, and the other enslaved African Americans in the slave quarters. No doubt they were all abuzz about that event at the next opportunity everyone could get together, perhaps in a quilting party or a dance session called a frolic.

Large scale cotton plantations were extremely profitable for their owners like George Gilmer, who was able to purchase at least 360 acres of land in Montgomery, Alabama, in the 1830s. That was a portion of the millions of acres sold by the government between 1830 and 1837. Alabama exported goods, mostly cotton valued at 2.2 million dollars in 1830, and before the Civil War, would be one of the ten wealthiest states in the nation. The wealth, made possible by the work of enslaved people like Granvill and his growing family, made cotton the king. George O. Gilmer even persuaded his nephew to give up being a lawyer and become a planter. Not only did the South thrive, but so did the young nation, which was just the beginning of the US economy's ride to the top of the world.

But as noted in Table 1, the third spike in slave price indicates that something went awry near the end of the 1830s. A crisis in the financial and economic conditions, known as the Panic of 1837, was a national economic event that caused the nation to dive into a seven-year depression. Multiple factors triggered it. One included President Andrew Jackson's attempt to end runaway land speculation prices by demanding that purchases be made with precious metals, which dried up credit and growth. Another was a wheat crop failure in the Northern States.

And further, as a consequence of being connected to the global economy, a depression in Great Britain dramatically lowered revenues from cotton sales. Unemployment soared when factories, mills, and mines closed. Foreclosures, bankruptcies, and bank closures came next. People lost their entire life savings when the banks closed. Bread riots broke out, mobs broke into warehouses searching for food, while churches established soup kitchens. Somehow George and his now-grown son, James, managed to obtain many land lots during this Depression. I wondered, had they sold before the market collapse?

I contacted the Montgomery County Archivist and obtained copies of the deeds of four transactions listed in 1839. Oddly, some of the paperwork consisted of transferring properties back and forth between George O Gilmer and his oldest son, James B. Gilmer. Another document laid out a list of multiple lot tracts and parcels of land that he had sold. By the next year in 1840, Gilmer was on both the state of Alabama's Census, with 31 enslaved black adults, and 10 more in the Louisiana Census, working in agriculture. That left 10 in some other capacity. With Granvill being about 70 years old at the time, had he earned his right to be one of the elders caring for up to 27 children under the age of 10, including four of his own?

Gilmer's insatiable appetite for land had impacted Granvill's life. The ability to be a landowner was a recent development in history. Centuries before, King Henry VIII started this trend. As part of his bid to make himself the head of the church instead of the pope, he confiscated monasteries and sold their land to bring in money for his government. Slowly but surely, anyone with enough money could buy land where British law prevailed. In the new nation of the United States, after forcibly removing the Native Americans, millions of acres were made available.

From the land, the American economy grew. In the northern and midwestern states, farmer's created wealth by producing crops on their improved land. In the South, Gilmer and other slaveholder's wealth grew as cotton became king. Cotton directly or indirectly touched much of the country through the textile mills, insurance brokers, and bankers in the Northeast, the steamboats on the mighty Mississippi, and ships headed to Europe, while the Midwest produced pork and beef. My third great-grandfather, the rest of my family, and the other enslaved African Americans were the engine that made it all possible. From the dominance of cotton exports in the South, the growth of financial institutions and textile mills in the North, and the production of meat products in the Midwest, the unsparing exploitation of Granvill and other enslaved African Americans was the foundation of economic development of the United States.

I thought I was ready to deal with my emotional flare-ups as I reflected on slavery. Staring at the economics of slavery, I was blindsided. My husband is fond of popping up with Chinese sayings for almost anything you might run into in life. "Know your enemy," Sun Tzu's quote is bantered around so frequently that it is now a part of my repertoire. No one - not in my family, not in the media, and not at school - ever made me understand that the United States was built on slavery. Some slaveholders defended slavery with economic justifications. What would Gilmer's life be like without the labor from his enslaved workforce? How can we ever defeat the enemy of racism in this country without coming to terms with these facts?

From the microeconomic to the national level, it is plain to see that every fabric of society was woven together to reinforce the economic gains made possible by the institution of slavery. It was challenging to use the lens of economics to examine Granvill's life. To determine his standard of living, I individually researched what necessities, material goods, and items of comfort he had, starting with "Life on a cotton plantation" and "What was Life like Under Slavery." Using a list of the worst recessions, panics, and depression, I uncovered pertinent economic information. As I wove the economic facts with the history, Granvill's life became very apparent. If you are willing to dive in, examining your ancestor's life from an economic perspective, it's very revealing. Who knows, it might even reveal the answer to the shaving question. Sources from the 1830s describe how enslaved African American men shaved on Sundays to get ready for church. What economic forces may have impacted your ancestor at the personal, local, and national levels?

Politics

When is the last time you got into a political debate? Most people are very careful when it comes to discussing politics. As a rule, we avoid political discussions except with those that agree with us. Political conversations can make us stressed, especially when dealing with divisive issues. Throughout the history of the United States, there has always been daunting and controversial issues. During the latter half of Granvill's life in the century, that issue was slavery. It was like an insidiously creeping cancer, touching almost every aspect of American society. The South enthusiastically supported the spread of slavery into each new addition to the country, while the North diametrically opposed it. Living in the South, no doubt, the politics of slavery affected Granvill's life.

Today's bone of contention, the politics of how to handle climate change, only hints at how contentious things can be. Although most agree that climate change is occurring, there are fierce political debates about how to respond to it at the national, state, and local levels. At the national level, should there be legislation that promotes decreasing fossil fuel usage? Should people bear the cost of these disasters, or should the government be responsible? Should state governments force local action with stricter building codes? Although we often take them for granted, political issues affect much of our lives, even keeping us safe. Matters such as government control, taxation, states' rights, legal status, rules, and regulations are bound into most political issues. Climate change, which affects us today, is no different. The political issues of each period in history dictate what dominates the spoken and written discussions of that day. By examining the political affairs of his day and how they affected him, it can help to understand Granvill's life.

How would I research the politics in Granvill's life? When I thought about politics, the next thing that came to my mind was presidential politics. So, I had googled, "politics and Louisiana in the 1840s." That gave me information about the election in 1840. It was intriguing, but it had little to do with my ancestor. Next, I had tried to narrow down the topic. What would be in the newspapers back in that time? Of course, I knew slavery was a hot topic, so I tried "slavery and Louisiana in the 1840s." That search produced a slew of information on which I spent hours delving into aspects of slavery in Louisiana.

Sitting in my black chair, kissing the computer, as my husband claims I do when I'm intensely focused, I felt a throbbing pain creeping up my right leg. My body was fighting my desire to keep researching. I kept going and somehow, and I happened onto an animation of maps depicting the slave states and free states from 1789-1861. My jaw dropped, which caused my gum to fall out of my mouth. My eyes were locked on the map for 1789, when Granvill was a mere child. Eight red states were slave states, while five blue states were free. I grabbed my calculator to calculate that 60% of the colonies were slave states. Was that right? I hastily rechecked my math; it was.

Furthermore, the total amount of area dedicated to slavery was even higher. My rough estimate was about three-quarters of the young nation was devoted to slavery. I couldn't believe my eyes. How could I have not known this? I called Weilin over to ask what he thought. He told me he didn't know that there were slaves here before the United States was a country. Yes, I knew George Washington had slaves. But the 13 Colonies were always depicted as places of religious freedom, where one could escape religious persecution. I felt like I could scream at the top of my lungs, "I've been deceived!"

This map made it plain to see; the United States was founded with a majority of slave states. That just bolsters the fact that Granvill was born into a country that was a slave nation from the beginning. Over time, the ratio of slave to free states lowered to 50/50. As states requested admission into the Union, several politically expedient compromises were hammered out to try to keep this balance of free and slave states. By 1837, Louisiana, along with Alabama, Mississippi, and Arkansas, joined the nation as slave states. Formerly, French

Louisiana already had sugar cane plantations, but after the Louisiana Purchase in 1803, Americans rushed in to establish cotton plantations. With the attraction of huge profits built on the unpaid labor of enslaved African Americans, the Louisiana population of slaves increased from about 10,000 in 1810 to 45,000 in 1830. New Orleans became the slave shipping capital of the nation, dispatching slaves to anxiously waiting plantation owners all up and down the vast Mississippi River. Gradually creeping westward, the institution of slavery invaded new areas of the country. As it did, it changed Granvill's life as he, other enslaved blacks, and slaveholders were forced to alter their physical, social, economic, and even political lives to grapple with this abhorrent money-making affliction.

As Granvill approached the seventh decade of his life, his legal status of enslaved manifested itself in the dreadful fact that he did not have the freedom to determine his family's home. His slaveholder, George O. Gilmer, had chosen a new place over 400 miles away in northern Louisiana. In that state, slavery was such an important issue, unlike in Alabama, the Civil Code of Louisiana from 1825 defined, in shameful details, precisely what a slave is,

A slave is one who is in the power of a master to whom he belongs. The master may sell him, dispose of his person, his industry, and his labor; he can do nothing, possess nothing, nor acquire anything, but what must belong to his master.

This Civil Code piqued my interest when I googled the Code of Law of Louisiana in 1840. These new laws expanded the earlier law. The comprehensive 1806 Black Code was primarily concerned with the discipline and regulation of enslaved blacks. The 1825 Civil Codes paid attention to the issue of the emancipation of those formally enslaved blacks. I presume this must have been a political question for the slaveholders in the state because Louisiana had many free blacks. The newspapers routinely reported on the new 1840 laws and amendments to the Civil Codes voted on in the Louisiana Legislature, which were still greater in detail. Those codes offered a glimpse into what was happening at that time.

As slavery moved westward, George Oglethorpe Gilmer was usually among the pioneering settlers. As he did in both Madison and Montgomery, Alabama, he utilized his knowledge of soils, keen business sense, and the local politics to seek the best opportunities ahead of the crowds. Somehow, possibly using his web of relationships within the Georgia faction in Alabama, he was ready to pounce on the new land that opened up in Northern Louisiana. After Captain Henry Shreve removed the 165-mile-long log jam on the Red River, the government proceeded with federal land auctions in 1839.

A seasoned Gilmer and his newly widowed young adult son, James, each legally purchased about 5,000 acres of land in tracts of varying sizes and along with several locations along the Red River. Taken together, the expansive Gilmer empire of 10,000 acres, was equivalent to over 15 square miles. To get an idea of how large that was, Jersey City, one of the 100 most populated cities in the US today, has a population of over a quarter-million people, with a land area of about 14.8 square miles. With a forward-looking entrepreneurial vision, he and his family began to build an empire of multiple plantations, each full of enslaved African Americans. After beginning the process of purchasing the land in 1839, the Gilmers went back to Alabama to gather their families, their belongings, and the enslaved African Americans to prepare for the arduous journey to their new home. Gilmer's name, along with President Tyler's, were affixed to certificates for 17 different properties by 1843, made possible by laws approved by Congress to sell them as public lands. This illustrates how some laws suppressed the rights of enslaved African Americans, while others encouraged and benefited the slaveholders.

Moving to Louisiana followed a long process, but Granvill and his family had already possibly endured a move from Georgia to Madison, Alabama, then to Montgomery, Alabama. According to the 1840 census, ten enslaved African Americans, belonging to Gilmer, labored in northern Louisiana in Claiborne Parish. They may have been Granvill's sons, Jack, Austin, Marywether, or a friend John, who later married into the family. Presumably, they were preparing for the eventual arrival of the rest of his enslaved blacks and the Gilmer family. It was paramount that this pristine land was cleared of its clusters of tall trees and fenced.

Trees in present-day Bossier Parish

Unquestionably, they were preparing for the eventual arrival of the rest of his 71 enslaved African Americans listed on the 1840 Census in Montgomery, Alabama. Using the political lens to analyze this situation, I asked myself why Gilmer's enslaved African Americans were listed in both the states of Alabama and Louisiana in 1840. I had an inkling that it might have to do with taxes. Researching "taxes and slavery in Alabama," the answer popped up. In Alabama, the state's slave tax was a vital revenue source for the state government. Gilmer had to pay 25 cents for every enslaved Black younger than 10, a dollar for those ten and up. The property tax was set at a very low level, so most of the state's tax receipts came from taxes on slaves. The average non-slaveholding farmer barely had to pay taxes, which made them more inclined to support slavery. Louisiana also had its own state tax on slaves, so neither state could afford to lose that tax revenue source.

Forcing myself to think about the politics, policies, and laws of Granvill's time was something I would not ordinarily do. Yet, the more I peered into the everyday political aspects of slavery, the more I clenched my teeth in disgust. Without pushing myself to consider Granvill's life from a political perspective, I probably would not have figured out how tightly the institution of slavery was woven into every part of society.

Granvill and his family were uprooted from Alabama to start the 475-mile westward trek to northwest Louisiana. They were part of the group of roughly one million enslaved African Americans forcibly relocated from the Upper South to the Lower South. It is known as the Second Middle Passage or the Domestic Slave trade. About one-third were moved by their slaveholders, like Granvill and the others. The other two-thirds were sold to slave traders, who then marched them hundreds of miles. The expression "sold down the river" occurred with increasing regularity from the 1830s to 1860s, as families were ripped apart and put on the auction block. This forced migration was greater than the combined number of Native Americans forced to migrate in the Trail of Tears and the number of willing settlers who migrated to the West. It's possible that along the well-traveled route, Granvill and his family might have seen a coffle of mournful African Americans chained together. With a painful glance, they could have seen the anguished faces of those suffering from the inconsolable grief of being separated from their families.

By the 1840s, transportation had improved in the North with many roads, canals, and steamboats, but the South was not as developed. The trip from Montgomery, Alabama, to Claiborne Parish, was slow and tedious. There were few established roads, especially after they crossed the mighty Mississippi River into Louisiana. In the front of the group, typically enslaved blacks drove the herds of cattle and hogs, others walked with their families, with the Gilmer's pulling up the rear in covered wagons. I found it curious that there was a black code prohibiting enslaved African Americans from being "found on horseback" under penalty of 25 lashes if they didn't have permission. So, in all likelihood, the elderly Granvill walked, which is a small illustration of how the laws influenced his life.

As the whole group lumbered along their journey from Mississippi into Louisiana, did they encounter free people of color? Because of his dark skin, Granvill, according to the law, was assumed to be a slave unless proven contrary. In Louisiana, this had to be spelled out, because legislators were tightening the grip on the state's sizable group of free people of color. It's possible his children had never seen a free person of color because the Slave Code in Alabama prohibited free persons of color from settling in Alabama.

After checking everyone's age in 1843, I could imagine their journey. A forty-five-year-old Eliza had to keep an eye on her energetic 5-year old daughter Jane, her son Handy, and the growing twins, Samuel and William, who were about 8-years old. Wherever they were, Jack would have been about 23, while Austin and Marywether were teenagers of 16 and 17. Granvill's older daughter, Lucy Ann, in her early thirties, had to tend to her two babies, but perhaps she helped out.

They had to traverse through clearings in forest and streams without bridges. Hopefully, there was a crude ferry if they had to cross a broader stream. Finding a place to stop each night was a headache because it had to accommodate about 70 slaves, the livestock, and the Gilmer family. Martha Gilmer and her teenage daughter, Mary Ann, must have had their hands full, making sure the slaves took care of her 6-year-old George and perhaps, the two young children of her eldest son, James, who was a widower. Depending on how fast they moved, it could have taken the band anywhere from a month to two months to plod along to northwest Louisiana.

Once they all arrived, the undeveloped fertile land began the transformation into fields bulging with lucrative white bolls of cotton, no doubt by members of Granvill's family. In this newly cultivated area, everything had to brought in or made. Gilmer named his plantation in the "hills" the Plain Dealing Plantation. According to the officially adopted story of the "Early History of Plain Dealing," tradition asserts the named stood for integrity, honesty, and the Virginia plantation of his ancestors. Drawn by an insatiable appetite for more land, Gilmer continually expanded his landholdings. He and other wealthy planters also bought large river plantations along the Red River that contained rich alluvial river soil, which significantly increased their cotton yield.

Additionally, slaves-quarters were essential. Tradition, handed down about the founding of this area, states that once finished, they were "substantially built and comfortable log houses, spaced at equal distances apart, with streets between, fashioned somewhat like our modern towns." The construction of a temporary home for the Gilmer family was also required. A fortunate side effect of the difference in the legal system in Louisiana than other states, was the requirement of the recording of private agreements in conveyance books, which sheds some light on this situation. A Bill of Sale of 68 slaves, dated Dec 1842, interestingly, included two smiths and a carpenter acquired from a company back in the county of George O. Gilmer's birth, Oglethorpe, Georgia. At some level, Granvill and his family readjusted to whatever the circumstances afforded them, including the construction and manufacturing all around them.

Before long, George Gilmer built a splendid mansion painted white with green blinds. Eventually, the Gilmer family plantations would grow even more extensive and become a vast self-sufficient enterprise. The headquarters had a wagon yard, a brickyard, a blacksmith shop to build and repair all the tools and other needed items. There was a wood yard, a gin house, a sawmill, and a tan yard to tan hides for making leather goods. Pottery, cloth from their herd of sheep, and of course, cotton was manufactured on the plantation. There was a church for the enslaved to attend on Sundays, which was in line with the 1806 Black Code of Louisiana dictating that "Slaves shall have free enjoyment of Sunday." They would also bring in a famous doctor from Ireland, Dr. Walker, to run a clinic mainly for the slaves.

With enough new inhabitants, including Gilmer's family and all their enslaved African Americans, the state saw fit to carve out a new parish from the western part of Claiborne Parish. Bossier Parish was formed in 1843 and named after Pierre Bossier, a well-known flamboyant politician from a prominent French family who resided in the region for generations. He was also famous for surviving a duel.

In the Old South, duels of honor were frequent, especially in Louisiana, which was known as a place where gentlemen were easily offended in deference to their personal honor. Dueling was adopted from the aristocracy in Europe. Since many men had not been born into the upper classes but arrived by way of the slave economy, Southern culture developed around being a gentleman. A gentlemen's honor was jealously guarded in the absence of a family pedigree.

Not only did the elites invent traditions, but the enslaved African Americans also developed a strong culture that helped them to be resilient in the face of adversity created by the policies enacted to maintain slavery. Through the internal migration, sometimes called the Second Middle Passage, slavery spread throughout the South. Extended kinship groups enabled enslaved African American families to cope with the grim realities of slavery. One of the most heinous phenomena of being enslaved was the perpetual fear of the family being separated. Many families were separated as husbands, wives, teenagers, and even small children were sold as surplus slaves from the Upper South to meet the needs of the expanding cotton fields in the Deep South or when the slaveholder died.

About half of all US enslaved children grew up cut off from their father because he had been sold, lived on a different plantation, or was white. With little power to stop the outside circumstances that ripped their families apart, enslaved parents like Granvill and Eliza tried to protect their children by instilling into them a sense of loyalty to the family and the slave community. They named their children after family members, especially boys, who were often named after their father or grandfathers. (Unbeknownst to him at the time, Granvill would eventually have 17 males, including family and friends, named after him.) Children were taught to be very polite in hopes of sparing them from the whip. Children were also instructed to respect the elders and call everyone older than them auntie and uncle. Tragically, but hopefully, if they were sold, unrelated people, whom they called auntie and uncle, would take care of them. Enslaved African Americans actually heeded the words of the famous Chinese philosopher, Confucius. He urged people to treat each other well to build a morally, ideal society. Every day, my husband passed by this quote on a scroll on his father's office, it translates "to honor old people as we do our own aged parents, and care for other's children as one's own." Isn't it ironic that oppressed enslaved blacks behaved at such a high moral level spurred by evil laws that made their survival depend on it?

In 1844, Granvill and Eliza extended their kinship group as they became proud grandparents. Jack had taken Barbary as his wife. I presume that consent was given by Gilmer if they followed the state's Civil Codes. If they were not enslaved, I could find a record for this marriage in FamilySearch. Their daughter, Mary Ann, was born. A few months later, Austin and his wife Caroline gave birth to their daughter, Emmeline. Being in the more fortunate half of enslaved children, these babies were born into a large slave community, which included grandparents, uncles, and aunts who helped them, and shared whatever resources they had.

A few years later, Austin, Caroline, Emmeline (or Emily), and their next baby son, Granville, were given by George Gilmer to his daughter, Sarah, wife of Leonidas Spyker as a Deed of Gift. That meant that they were moved to the nearby Hard Times Plantation, perhaps making it harder for Granvill and Eliza to see some of their grandchildren. In time, many other grandchildren would be born, including Charity, Isaac, Matilda, Tom, Elizabeth, and George.

George O and Martha Gilmer

LSUS Archives and Special Collection, Noel Memorial Library

With one eye on evading inheritance taxes and the other on his family, old George Gilmer gave much of his land to his children before he died. Gilmer's anti-tax views were in line with the slaveholding elites of his time. They enjoyed all the benefits of slavery, but then they tried to skirt policies that required them to pay their fair share. Always trying to increase their advantages was part of the constitution, including the clause that counted the slaves as three-fifths a person, thereby increasing their political clout in the government. Because the Electoral College elects the president, the extra presidential electors in 1800 allowed Thomas Jefferson to be elected, a result that wouldn't have occurred with a strict direct popular vote. The political benefits of the three-fifths clause provided the additional proslavery representation to get beneficial legislation passed, and to avoid any hint of taxes at the federal level. Southern politicians rallied voters to stop the power of the "government to oppress the people," in this way discouraging taxes. They were afraid that non-slaveholders would tax their lucrative profits; thus, the strong anti-tax sentiments of today may have had its roots in slave politics.

George Gilmer devised his way to avoid the federal inheritance tax, which was a federal tax on wills in probate, by giving away most of his holdings. He probably thought his eldest son, James, was set because the widower had married another wealthy widow, Paulina Degraffenreid Pickett, in 1843. As one of the wealthiest couples in North Louisiana, they resided in an opulent showcase home, the Orchard Place. So, George gave his three younger children river plantations complete with slaves and farm implements. His two sons-in-law, John Sandidge and Leonidas Spyker, managed their wives' portions as well as the part for young George E. Gilmer until he came of age at 21 years old.

Before all these transactions were recorded in the Louisiana Deed books, a 61-year-old George O. Gilmer died of cholera. An infectious disease, cholera is caused by eating food or drinking water that is contaminated by a bacterium. There were national epidemics outbreaks of cholera in 1832 and in 1849, which killed Gilmer, and another just after the Civil War in 1866. Gilmer died in November. Notably, former President James Polk also died of cholera earlier that year, and some believe he contracted it while in New Orleans, Louisiana. This particular pandemic first arrived from Europe in New York. Shipping brought it to New Orleans, where early in 1849, on average, more than 100 people a day died. It moved up the Mississippi to be carried all the way to California by adventurous forty-niners seeking gold. Seventeen slaves also died in December, according to the 1850 US Federal Mortality Schedule in Bossier Parish, along with 10,000 slaves across the South, leading to higher prices. In the remarks on Gilmer's death in the Mortality Schedule, they had concluded cholera was contracted by traveling on or living near the Red River.

My DNA cousin, Cheryl, a doctor, explained to me that without an understanding of modern germ theory, most doctors at the time thought one contracted cholera due to bad air. In a few years, they would come to understand that it was the contaminated water. Searching for the political angle of health in the Antebellum Era, I found out it didn't exist. There was no government intrusion into one's life for the benefit of the common good. Everyone was free to get sick and die with few remedies available and nonexistent health codes to protect them.

Similar to what happened when George Gilmer's father died, his wife Martha was left to manage the estate until her son George E. Gilmer was old enough to take over. In George Gilmer's will, he stated that his debts be paid by money owed to him, very likely to pay any taxes owed. He willed the use of his property and "one family of negroes" to his wife Martha until her death. Records show that family was my second great uncle, Marywether's in-laws. Before Martha died in 1857, she sold the farm equipment, livestock, and slaves to her son, which again avoided the inheritance tax. Without this tactic, I would have never known the name of my third great grandfather. Isn't it opportune that I was able to travel halfway across the country to see the conveyance with the name of my 3rd great-grandfather because of a tax avoidance scheme!

George O. Gilmer's tombstone

The search results of "Slavery Laws in America in the 1800s" revealed most of the legislation governing slaves were left to the states. For the time while Granvill was in

Louisiana, there was a very long list of Slavery Statutes. An amusing instance in 1852 was an Act that made it an offense for a white person to gamble or bet with free negroes, mulattoes, or slaves. Even though there were few laws at the Federal level, one of the most controversial and consequential laws was the Fugitive Slave Law of 1850. This update of previous fugitive laws required all escaped slaves returned to their masters and, even more importantly, the citizens of the free states to cooperate. The law had several consequences for enslaved African Americans in states that bordered free states. One was that those trying to flee on the Underground Railroad were forced to continue to Canada. Another result was that free men were kidnapped and shipped to the Deep South. For example, Solomon Northrop, a musician, was snatched from New York and spent twelve years in southern Louisiana. The book 12 Years a Slave recounted the experience with such passion and clarity, it became a bestseller that furthered the abolitionists' cause. Yet another consequence was the rise in abolitionist sentiment.

In my mind, this law and the increased abolitionist voices probably barely touched the rurally isolated community where Granvill lived, but I was wrong. The local newspaper, at the time emanating from Shreveport, stated in 1855 that they considered the new black code so significant to their readers, especially the planters, that they published "its substance for their benefit." The first ten sections detailed how any slave will suffer death upon conviction of murder, drowning, striking his master, raping anyone, shooting to kill, poisoning, maliciously burning down a building, causing any insurrection, or forcibly taking goods. The other sections, up to 100, all dealt with regulations for multiple situations dealing with slaves, including not removing a slave from the state, if the slave was mortgaged. Section 31 requires anyone aiding and counseling a runaway slave to be imprisoned. No doubt, they were trying to curb those with abolitionist leanings.

When I decided to use a political lens to examine the life of Granvill, I had no idea what I would find. Like most people, I never thought about how laws directly influenced people's lives both in negative and positive ways. As I discovered many examples of how laws affected enslaved people's lives, my awareness increased. Weilin was also very skeptical that laws affected ordinary people's lives at first. I shared with him several situations, including Solomon Northrop and the Fugitive Law, which were definitely harmful. Looking at Weilin's life, we found a positive consequence of changes in immigration policy that allowed him to immigrate to this country. Also, there was legislation that promoted bilingual education, providing a new avenue for his employment. That prompted me to hunt for a positive effect of any law in Granvill's life. I discovered the first section of the Black Code of Louisiana of 1806 provided for Sundays off, food, clothing, time to eat, medical care, and maintenance in old age, which allowed Granvill to live, to some extent, a long life.

But most consequences of the black codes were negative, like what happened not too far from Granvill on Hard Times Plantation. Late in 1856, Leonidas Spyker, the son-in-law of the Gilmer's, began a diary that survived until today. Each day, he included the weather, other information about who happened to stop by, and what the "hands," as enslaved African Americans were referred to at the time, accomplished that day. Near the end of 1856, it describes how Spyker pushed his enslaved blacks to pick cotton in damp, freezing weather. He described awful working conditions, such as his enslaved blacks being forced to work all day and then late into the night. The law was on his side. Articles 631 of the Civil Codes states,

He who has the use of one or more slaves or animals had the right to enjoy their service for his wants and those of his family.

So, this is a vivid description of how the Civil Codes reached into the daily lives of not only enslaved blacks, but specifically some of Granvill's kin.

Spyker pushed so hard because in January of 1857, he planned to leave Bossier Parish and set up a new plantation in Bastrop, Louisiana. The Sunday, January 11, 1857, before they left, he wrote a poignant account of the day, "The old lady's negroes all are here to tell us good bye." No doubt those negroes were from the next plantation, the Plain Dealing Plantation. That likely included my third great grandparents, Granvill, and his wife, Eliza. Austin, their son, and my second great uncle was leaving with his family never to see them again. Isn't it heartbreaking that the only known record with a precise date for Granvill, is the day he was separated from his son, daughter-in-law, and grandchildren, Emmeline and Granville? This cut-off a branch of the Smith tree grew and eventually prospered. It took over 150 years, but it brings me such joy to know that spurred on by DNA technology,

Granvill's family would be reunited with my match to DNA cousin James Gray, a descendant of Emmeline. The first message he wrote to me on December 19th, said,

The DNA says we cousins. Looking at your tree, the North Louisiana Smiths show the greatest promise. I am related to Smiths from Bastrop, Louisiana. The names Granville and Meriweather appear in both trees. My first Smith was Austin.

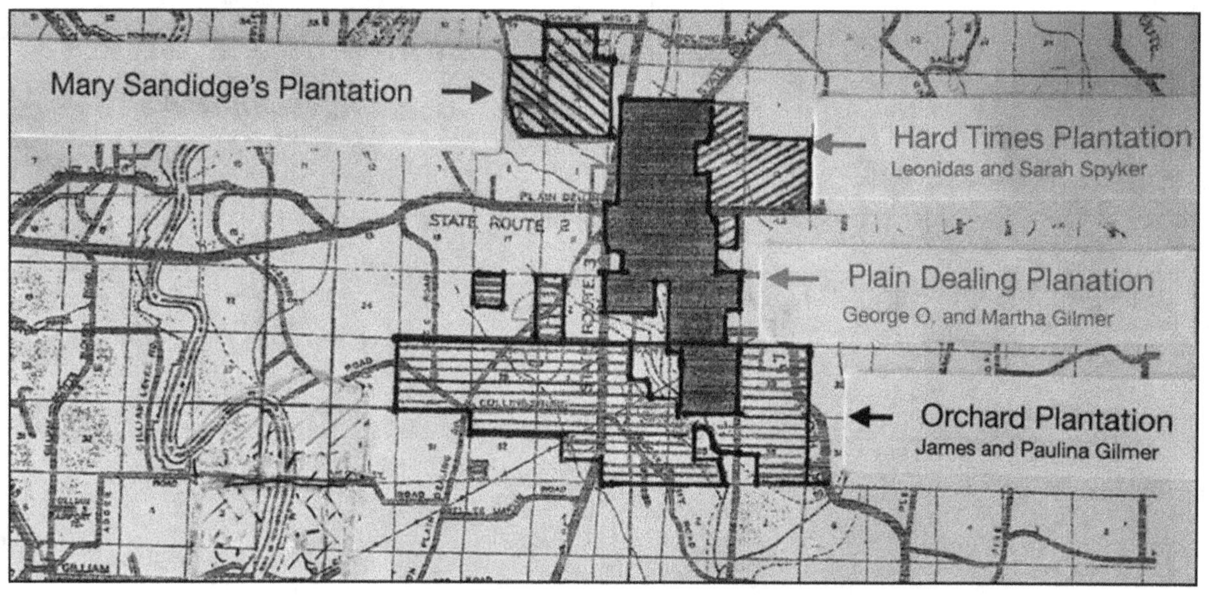

The Gilmer Family Plantations in the hills created by Dale Jennings

Granvill's life, which spanned over eight decades, was quite unusual for that time. Henry Louis Gates, Jr citing number about the slave population in 1860, "only 3.5 percent was over 60." in 1860. Martha H. Gilmer had given her son "six negroes to have his care and attention in old age" as a gift, which included the 84-year-old Granvill in 1854. She followed one of the few codes designed to protect enslaved blacks who were "disabled by old age, sickness, or any other cause." Since I didn't find him in her son's list of slaves in 1864, I presume he died sometime in the early 1860s.

Year	Lucy	Jack	Austin	Marywether	William	Samuel	Handy	Jane
1800-1809	*Georgia* 09 Born							
1810-1819		*Georgia* 17 Born						
1820-1829			*Alabama* 24 Born	*Alabama* 25 Born				
1830-1839					*Alabama* 32 Born	*Alabama* 32 Born	*Alabama* 34 Born	*Alabama* 36 Born
1840-	*Alabama* 40 Robert							
1849	*Bossier, LA* 42 Almeda 44 Rebecca	*Bossier* 44 Mary Ann 47 Charity	*Bossier* 44 Emmerline 49 Granville					
1850-1859	52 Isaac 54 Jenny 56 Granville	51 Isaac 53 Matilda 54 Tom 56 Eliz. Eliza 58 George W	*Morehouse, LA* 53 Meriweather 54 Austin 57 Leander 59 Pauline	*Bossier* 57 Laura 58 Louann	*Bossier* 58 Granville	*Bossier* 55 Mariah 57 Jeff		*Bossier* 58 Francis

Granvill and Eliza's Family Timeline Just Before the Civil War

Granvill's children above, with each column listed their children and the shading representing where everyone was born

Born into slavery, Granvill would only taste the freedom brought by his death. Granvill had been a witness to the institution of slavery on rice, tobacco, and cotton plantations. He experienced the results of many of the political debates which came up as slaveholders and the politicians beholden to them tried to maintain the peculiar institution. The young Granvill lived through the birth of the young country as compromises over slavery affected the constitution. Inventions such the Eli Whitney's cotton gin and John Deere's steel plow caused states to upgrade their slave codes to embrace slavery even further.

I wonder if Granvill ever saw life beyond the plantation and cotton fields. Did he see Samuel Moore's telegraph or Isaac Singer's sewing machine? Did anti-slavery rhetoric reach his ears? What kind of person was he? Was he stern or patient, opinionated or easy-going, or was he quiet or talkative? Did he have a knack for mathematics like me? How much English did he speak? How did he look? I guess I will never know because Granvill was forbidden by the law to read, write, and have records created about his life.

By the time of his passing, his homegoing - as it was called then - was a distinctly African American cultural feature of slave life that was tradition, not the law. When an enslaved black died, everyone usually got the rest of the day off to prepare for the somewhat elaborate funeral. In keeping with West African traditions, funerals were held at night. The white community in the South found slave funerals a bit strange because they were joyful and celebratory. The enslaved African Americans viewed death as a relief from the misery and humiliation of slavery; while going to Jesus, symbolized going home. There were drums playing, shouting, expressive dancing, and singing, which was nothing like the somber funerals in the white community.

A particular favorite song for slaves in Louisiana was the hymn "There are all my Father's children," which was apropos when the paternal father died. It's possible that all of Granvill's children assembled in the room where the coffin laid. Next, traditionally, they arranged themselves in age and relationship order. Lucy and Jack were the oldest, next Marywether, then Samuel, William, and Handy, if they were there, with most likely Jane as the youngest of his children or maybe there were more children. There could have been eight or more grandchildren. Singing the hymn, they marched round and round the coffin with the lyrics, "Dese all my fader's children" several times, followed by "My fader's done widde trouble o' de world, Outshine de sun." Granvill was done with the trouble of this world. The youngest child was passed over and under the coffin, and then two men took the coffin on their shoulders and carried it quickly to the grave. Once buried, the grave might have been decorated with objects from his life.

Although Granvill died over 150 years ago, researching his life has somehow for me, bought him and the other unnamed slaves who never saw freedom back to life. I have so few records for Granvill. There is no birth record, no marriage license, and nothing written in a Bible. Heeding my Balanta heritage to resist, I sought to fight the politics of his times, which made every law and regulation to exploit him and then cast him aside when he was no longer of any use. Maybe, I could create a death record to make him more real, but I realized I knew so few details, an obituary would have to do. Now he and his descendants have a written history. My old textbook from when I was a child, which jumps from "During the two hundred, some million such captives were sold to the United States…" to the next paragraph about white people of the North in the Abolition Movement. Granvill's life adds a lot a detail in-between those paragraphs. My gift to his legacy is a modern-day obituary, which acknowledges his loss, expresses the pain of his loss, and the joy his remembrance has brought to me and, hopefully, others.

Noticing my gloomy mood, Weilin tried to console me by explaining the Chinese saying, "Only after his death, can a man be judged." He explained that one's sons could give a testament of their father's life. I took that to mean that perhaps his children's lives could tell me more about their father. This brought me hope that even though one's ancestors left little for us to get to know them, their children offer a window which might reveal something more.

The institution of slavery robbed me of my past. It was the backdrop of Granvill's entire life and was firmly entrenched into the fabric of the United States. He and all the other enslaved African Americans continually had to adapt and resist its harmful effects. Slavery was the foundation on which the social, economic, religious, and political structures of the country were built. From social status gained from having slaves, from slaveholders and northern capitalists who gained substantial profits, from religious leaders who gained new converts and from politicians who gained power and used it to prop up the slave economy with laws and codes; slavery could not be easily diminished until it was ripped out by means of war.

Utilizing the lens of political issues to analyze Granvill's life lead to many new insights. One realization was that politics can affect a person's life in many unforeseen ways. So, take the time to examine what was happening at the national and local level for your ancestor. Determine what laws, immigration and military rules, regulations, and codes impacted your ancestor's life. Also check the taxes, working conditions, healthcare, retirement, and safety laws. I now know that these issues affected Granvill's life in unexpected ways. It's incredible that in all likelihood, I know his name, because of taxes. One could also research local marriage laws, education laws, or housing regulations to figure out someone's life. Reflecting on the usually dull topic of politics opened a cornucopia of revelations about my ancestor's life. I am sure if you delve into some of the politics, laws, rules, and regulations that were part of your ancestor's life, you will figure out how your ancestor was influenced by them.

Obituary

Granvill entered the world in 1770 in Georgia and was taken to his Heavenly Mansion in the early 1860s. He was born of West African parents, with his father being from the Balanta tribe.

He completed his upbringing with his family in Georgia. He worked on plantations in Georgia, Alabama, and Louisiana. Granvill accepted Christ and attended church. He spent his free time taking care of his family. He will be missed by his community.

Granvill leaves to cherish his memory his devoted wife Eliza, his daughter Lucy, and her husband Abram, his son Jack, and his wife Barbary, his son, Austin and his wife Caroline, his son Marywether, and his wife Ann, his son Samuel, and his wife Caroline, his son, William and his wife Laura, his son, Handy and his wife and Mary, and his daughter Jane, his grandchildren and a host of family and friends.

Moments

What makes us who we are? That's what I pondered after the death of the 41st president, George Herbert Walker Bush, which ushered in a brief reflective pause in our country. There were multiple articles, pictures, video clips, and stories told about him that embodied the defining moments in this life. They all could be boiled down to his favorite quote, "Be bold in your caring, be bold in your dreaming and above all else, always do your best." Those moments included his love for his wife and family, how he handled the end of the Cold War, and his public service.

This retrospective thinking led me to wonder which moments in life tell you about a person. Using a technique I often utilized with my students, I drew a large circle on a blank sheet of white paper. In the center, I circumscribed the words Memorable Moments in a small circle (see Appendix H). Next, I listed notable moments, big and small, from my life. Then I categorized what I had written into similar clusters. I was amazed by how they embodied me. For example, when I was 6 or 7 years old, I dug a nice, neat little hole and pooped into it to see what would happen. And also, the unceasing questioning of my mother about why the fire (eternal flame) at JFK's grave would never go out, illustrated my unabated curiosity.

Critical times taught me marvelous insights, such as how sometimes, you have to fight. I learned this by my father's insistence that I stand up to the neighborhood bully. Or the absolute best way to study for a test. In junior high school, I was the alternate for our team in a science bowl contest, because I had dug in and tried to write the most challenging questions possible for the contestants, I knew all the answers and won for our team. And my way of dealing with racism, even though it was nothing like the life or death situations my ancestors faced. I had an eighth-grade history teacher whom I perceived had a condescending attitude toward blacks. I took an indirect strategy; I became a thorn in her side by acing all her tests while taking great pride in arguing with her to the point she gave me a U for "Unsatisfactory" in cooperation.

Several very significant moments altered my life. One was the day, not long before completing my degree in mathematics, I ventured to my dad's place of employment at Lockheed Missiles in Space. I observed all those men laboring away in nondescript gray cubicles with little interaction with others. That convinced me that I wanted to work with children as a teacher so I could make a difference in the lives of others. Another life altering moment was how since I couldn't roll my r's, a requirement to be a proficient Spanish speaker, I decided to learn Chinese instead. Lastly, there was the awful moment when I realized that my first husband shared many of my same interests, but not my values.

If these moments in my life revealed me to be ever curious, rationale seeking, and feisty underneath my friendly face, could the study of the moments in Granvill's descendant's lives help to divulge things about them? I wanted to find out about Granvill's values, personality, accomplishment, and physical features by studying his descendants. I planned that after I figured out where his children were, then I will scrutinize as many moments - big and small - to discern what the patterns reveal. I also wanted to understand the Civil War from the perspective of their lives. To find all of Granvill's ancestors, I took the time to upgrade the family timeline of the children of each of his children. Instead of just paying attention to my second great-grandfather's lineage, I had to research and build out all of Granvill's children's families.

Unlike their parents, the children of Granvill and Eliza experienced the most-deadly war in American history, the Civil War. Today, historians have not come to a consensus on the most important cause and consequence of the war. Yet, there is a general view that slavery, religious zeal, a bestselling book, states' rights, violent fights over land, a Supreme Court decision, and the election of Abraham Lincoln, all contributed to the Civil War.

In Louisiana, the lives of the descendants of Granvill and Eliza: sons Jack, Austin, Marywether, Samuel, William, Handy, their daughter Jane, and Granvill's other daughter, Lucy, often seemed far removed from those pressing issues the nation was facing. But the slowly brewing fight over the hot button issue of slavery would eventually creep into their unassuming lives and have life-altering consequences.

About the same time, the twins, Samuel and William, were born, the most famous abolitionist, William Lloyd Garrison, began his uncompromising crusade to persuade the nation that slavery was immoral in 1831. He started with speeches and pamphlets in New England. Garrison published the anti-slavery newspaper The Liberator, mostly supported by free African Americans representing seventy-percent of his paid subscriptions. One such reader was Frederic Douglass, the famed African American orator, and author. He collaborated with Garrison to advance an anti-slavery agenda. I wonder, did this anti-slavery rhetoric ever reach Samuel, William, or their siblings' ears?

The underground railroad of the abolitionists never reached the Red River country in Louisiana; on the other hand, the patrol system, a volunteer police force, did. It was always actively maintaining order by inflicting penalties for breaking the clearly defined rules. Groups of three to six white men canvassed the area looking for runaways and blacks without a pass. For instance, Spyker, Gilmer's son-in-law, wrote in his diary, that his overseer caught a "runaway negro" and promptly marched him back to the neighbor's plantation in Morehouse, Louisiana. The patrol enforced the curfew and broke up any large gathering of enslaved African Americans. There were frequent searches of their homes for guns, stolen property, and books, thus generally keeping enslaved African Americans in line through constant terror. Nowadays, the Fourth Amendment of the Constitution gives us some protection, so it's really tough to imagine random search and seizures with no cause. I am confident that this continual harassment was one of many moments of distress. Not knowing what my ancestors thought about this situation, perhaps they agreed with Frederick Douglass who stated,

I have observed this in my experience of slavery, that whenever my condition was improved, instead of it increasing my contentment, it only increased my desire to be free, and set me to thinking of plans to gain my freedom.

By the middle of the 1850s, Granvill and Eliza's children were probably less content because they had been forced to live on separate plantations. The young twenty-something Sam, William, and their little brother Handy moved from the Plain Dealing Plantation further south to the Bee Bend plantation. Located in an area that benefited from the fertile alluvial soil deposited by the Red River over eons, over 60% of George E. Gilmer's slaves worked at this site. The slave quarters had 16 dwellings, hopefully with vegetable patches, that provided homes for over 70 slaves. The brothers, Sam and William, willingly or maybe not, were married to Fannie and Laura, both who had grown up at Bee Bend.

	Jack	Austin	Marywether	William	Samuel	Handy	Jane
1840 – 1849	*Bossier, LA* 44 Mary Ann 47 Charity	*Bossier, LA* 44 Emmerline 49 Granville					
1850 – 1859	51 Isaac 53 Matilda 54 Tom (John) 56 Eliz. Eliza 58 George W.	*Morehouse, LA* 53 Meriweather 54 Austin 57 Leander 59 Pauline	*Bossier, LA* 57 Laura 58 Louann	*Bossier, LA* 58 Granville	*Bossier, LA* 55 Mariah 57 Jeff		*Bossier, LA* *58* Francis
1860 **Civil War** **1865**	60 Franklin 65? DEATH	60 Martha J. 64 Milly 65 Eliza 66? DEATH	62 Willis 64 Anna Eliza	61 Nancy 65 Isaac 65 Eliza ??			62 Eliza

Plain Dealing Plantation   Morehouse Plantation   Bee Bend Plantation

Wives generally prepared a family dinner in the evening and morning meals at daybreak. Depending on the season of the year, the brothers toiled more than twelve hours a day on the plantation, as most enslaved blacks did. Planting time in the spring, hoeing in the summer, and picking cotton in winter were the more grueling times. As they toiled in the 1850s, the mood of the country was changing. My ancestors may or may not have known about a book banned in the South that had begun to sway opinions about slavery in the rest of the United States. Another dedicated abolitionist, Harriet Beecher Stowe, penned the novel Uncle Tom's Cabins. It depicted the horrors of slavery in such graphic detail that thousands converted to a more sympathetic view of slaves. With compelling Christian values and enduring characters, such as the long-suffering Uncle Tom, Eliza, Sambo, and the arch-villain, Simon Legree, the novel was very influential. The book increased anti-slavery inclinations across the nation. As the second bestselling book in the nineteenth century, after the Bible, it impacted public opinion. President Lincoln declared, "So you're the little woman who wrote the book that started this great war" when he finally met her.

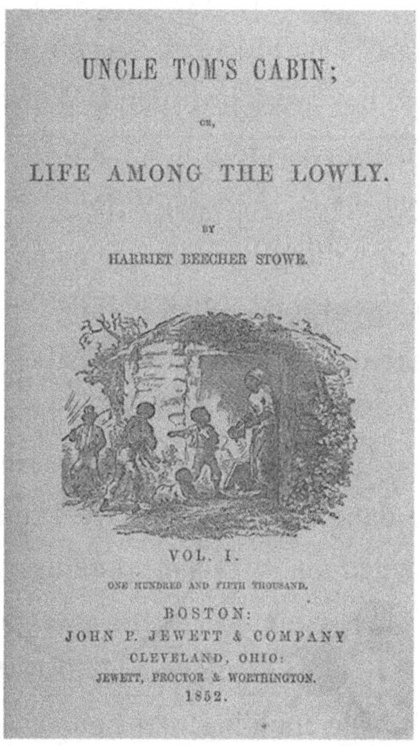

Title Illustration Page from the original 1852 book

Definitely, with no leisure time to read books, Austin and his family were on the Hard Times Plantation. It was located on the north eastern side of the Plain Dealing Plantation. Leonidas Spyker, the husband of Sarah Gilmer, was the slaveholder of Austin, his wife, Caroline, and their daughter, Emmerline and son, Granville. George O. Gilmer had given them to his daughter as a deed of gift just before he died.

The *Diary of Leonidas Pendleton Spyker*, which I unearthed during my trip back to grandfather's birthplace, provided some insight into daily life in Bossier Parish in the late 1850s. He recorded the weather, who visited, how the crops were fairing, and anything of importance on each date. On July 1, a Tuesday, he wrote, "Hands finished hoeing new ground today the second time. Very hot today, 1 p.m., M88: 3 ½ p.m., M90." No doubt, many members of my ancestors were out in the sweltering heat, placing their hoes in the correct spot to whack the weeds and not harm the cotton plants. It was very grueling work, hoeing row after row of cotton under the unforgiving sun. Once they developed the stamina and mental discipline to get it done, would their other activities seem less hard? If my hypothesis is correct, then their stamina reveals that they were tough. Did they harbor a sense of pride, like I do, when I say I had to work several jobs to put myself through college? Maybe they did, or perhaps they were just numb. Whatever the case, I am sure that they detested it. Multiple slave narratives from the 2,300 first-person accounts of slavery from the *Born in Slavery: Slavery from the Federal Writers' Project, 1936-1938*, attest to the fact that they would never want or willingly go back to being a slave.

On July 5, the day after the official July 4 holiday, the "hands were provided a holiday barbecue." Typically, slaveholders held large and festive barbecues for the enslaved blacks. Before the Civil War, pork was associated with feelings of Southern pride and patriotism. Southerners and slaveholders, in particular, considered themselves the true believers in the Constitution, which enshrined the states' rights in the Tenth Amendment. A newspaper, "The American Patriot," commented on a mayor proudly announcing "his devotion to the Constitution and the laws of his country!" as their worthy ideal. They felt that the federal government did not have the right to regulate or abolish slavery within the southern states.

This debate between the slaveholding and non-slaveholding states intensified as the boundaries of the United States reached the Pacific Ocean, when more territories applied for admission as states. As the controversy over slavery slowly built up miles away, nothing changed in Bossier. Besides gathering corn and cotton, Spyker also said the "hands" sheared the sheep and salted up the meat. Working in gangs, the "hands" also went to work at other plantations. For instance, he noted that there was a request for help with raising a gin house.

The notations in Spyker's diary opened a window into the precariousness of running a cotton plantation. At the end of the year, when it was time to pick the cotton, the rainy weather caused him lots of apprehension. Spyker sometimes had the enslaved African Americans picking cotton way into the night. At other times, Spyker sometimes sent Austin to the town of Bellevue to run errands, likely indicating that he was reliable and dependable.

On a cold January morning, Austin, Caroline, and their children, Emmerline and their son Granville along with one hundred others, set off for Morehouse Parish in 1857. The Sunday before they left, Spyker commented about Martha Gilmer negroes telling them good bye. Most likely, they included Granvill, Eliza, his children, Jack, Marywether, Jane, and their children. Although it was not ripping children from their parent's arms, this moment of separation from the family was no less painful and traumatic. An enduring mystery that had something to do with the oldest son in the Gilmer family was the reason for Spyker leaving. On Jan. 14, 1857, Spyker lamented that he was going and wrote, "Injustice had been the cause of driving us from home—and J. B. Gilmer has been at the bottom of it."

Because Jack and his family, Marywether, and Jane were on the Plain Dealing Plantation, they probably knew the inside scoop on the Gilmer empire. The house slaves who worked for the widowed Mrs. Gilmer, were often the eyes and ears of the enslaved African American community. There was unquestionably plenty of gossip about James Blair (J.B.) Gilmer, the eldest son of George O. Gilmer. J. B. Gilmer endured what we would say today was a public, rich, and famous separation. James and his wife, Pauline De Graffenreid, went through a dissolution of marriage after being married 13 years. Splitting two wealthy estates proved so hopeless, the Louisiana government had to get involved in the partition of the property, which included 560 slaves and a multitude of plantations. J.B. next went off to Cuba.

Many of the elite slaveholders thought that Cuba would become part of the South. The Mexican-American War, between 1846-1848, had annexed new territory from the Southwest to the nation, but none of the new territory allowed slavery. Southerners, who desired an expansion of slave territory, pressed the President to send the Secretary of State to try to acquire Cuba in secret meetings. When other countries in Europe and the northern abolitionist got the drift of this arrangement, it caused a firestorm, further distancing the North from the South. J.B. was prospecting for future holdings when yellow fever struck him. The more severe form of yellow fever produces a viral infection that kills 50% of those bitten by an infected mosquito. The popular name for the disease, yellow fever, comes from a high fever accompanied by the yellowish coloring or jaundice of the skin produced by the destruction of the liver.

He died on Aug 8, 1856, in Holguin, Cuba. G. E. Gilmer retrieved the body of his older brother and took it to Alabama to be buried next to his first wife. George R. Gilmer, the former governor of Georgia who was his cousin, called James "enterprising to recklessness and very determined in his purposes." I wonder if they sang the song "Amazing Grace" at his funeral. A former slave trader who later renounced his past wrote the beloved hymn in 1772. Dying young like his grandfather, did he ever reflect on whether his thirst for land and slaves would be the death of him?

Death and illness seemed to be a frequent topic among the pages of Spyker's diary. Spyker seemed to be called on by people, both black and white, when they were ill. Perhaps he was some kind of healer because he had potions listed on the back page of his diary. He also pulled the teeth of several of enslaved children. On Nov. 2, 1859, part of his daily notes included, "George Chisholm died this evening." George, only 34 years old at the time, was at the least an acquaintance and perhaps a friend of Austin who was the same age. A few days later, all "hands" had orders to clean out the negro quarters after three men came in sick in the morning. On that what he called a "clear Indian summer" day, "there was no cotton picked due to everyone was cleaning." Apparently, that stemmed the problem, because no other deaths occurred during that season except for news from Bossier Parish that the twenty-four-year-old daughter of James Blair Gilmer, Sarah Vance, had died. For women, childbirth was a dangerous time for both the mother and her child. No doubt, during each of these tragic moments, everyone felt with the same pain and agony that we experience today.

Meanwhile, down south on the Bee Bend Plantation, Sam and Fanny had two little children, a girl Mariah and her younger brother, Jeff. Not only were they a tiny part of the nation's increase in the African American population from 400,000 in 1808 to just under 4 million slaves in 1860, but they would become a mystery in my family tree.

The average enslaved mother gave birth to about nine children. As the parents of small children, did Sam and Fanny ever have time to discuss the latest issues surrounding slavery? Booker T. Washington, in his book, *Up From Slavery*, stated that throughout the South, the slaves kept "themselves so accurately and completely informed about the great National questions that were agitating the country." If they did, it must have been a disappointment when miles away in Washington, DC, the Supreme Court handed down the Dred Scott Decision. Dred Scott was a slave who tried to fight for his freedom through the American legal system. The Supreme Court ruled that no Negro or anyone with African blood could ever be a citizen. The northern abolitionists were outraged. This decision led to the undoing of some restrictions on slavery in the western territories, probably delighting the slaveholding states. The Dred Scott Decision became the rallying cry in the 1860 elections.

On June 15, 1860, the local newspaper, the *Bossier Banner*, which I found in Chronicling America at the Library of Congress, announced that Joseph Vance, the overseer, was building a road with G E Gilmer or George Edwin Gilmer's hands. That most likely included Sam, William, and Handy. G E Gilmer was now the twenty-five-year-old head of the Gilmer plantations. He was one of only 3,000 slaveholders in all of the South with over 100 slaves. His twenty-three-year-old niece, Miss Mattie Gilmer, was the slaveholder of her late father, James Blair Gilmer's holdings.

Their world was changing rapidly. The Industrial Revolution was catching up to their neck of the woods. Steamboats designed by Henry Shreve, who had previously unblocked the Red River, were chugging up and down the river. About 20 miles to the south, the Vicksburg, Shreveport & Texas Railroad was shuttling passengers and freight. Information from hundreds of miles away was transmitted on telegraph lines. We know from records associated with G.E. Gilmer that he was owed money for work, no doubt, done by Granvill's descendants, on telegraph lines. Factories in the North were busily manufacturing cloth from the cotton grown in the South. The Southern members of the "confederacy" felt they needed to, as the local newspaper wrote, band together against the "flagrant violations of the Constitution perpetrated by the Northern states." They began to build up their infrastructure, their papers, their books, and culture to repel the increasingly meddlesome rest of the United States.

In the fall of 1860, Abraham Lincoln, a Republican, was elected president of the United States with less than 40% of the popular vote, but with a majority of the electoral votes, which included all the northern states. In his diary, Leonidas Spyker recorded how everyone in town was espousing for Democratic positions. Lincoln's most pressing goal was to save the Union. At first, even though he hated slavery, he was not going to interfere with slavery where it currently existed, as long as the South abstained from trying to expand slavery into new territories. With Lincoln's election, the Southern states were afraid that they would lose their "superior" Southern way of life with slavery as its defining feature. A book, *Historical and Geographical Description of Morehouse Parish Louisiana in 1885,* by C.T. Dunn, articulates the reasoning of that time.

This African was admirably fitted to the office he was destined to fill, in his natural adaptation to a southern climate, in his strong physical powers, and in his patient, obedient nature, which rendered him susceptible of being organized and domesticated; under the restless activity and quickening spirit of the white master, his dormant powers were brought into active exercise, and the negro slave proved a most efficient co-laborer with the superior, enterprising white man.

The South almost immediately began to vote for succeeding from the Union. Slaveholders and non-slaveholders felt that they had the "God-given" right to secede from the United States and were willing to fight for it. Bossier Parish sent two representatives to the convention to ratify the ordinance on the Secession of the State of Louisiana in January of 1861. The northern states refused to recognize the legality of secession. By spring, the Civil War began in Charleston, South Carolina. Each side felt that they were uncompromisingly right, and God was on their side.

Meanwhile, my friend Dale Jennings ran across the name Sam on the list of enslaved church members from the 1860s, which meant he was a member in good standing. Spyker's diary also frequently mentioned the enslaved African Americans in the area attending church on Sundays. As the kin of Granvill and Eliza spent time engaged in their Christian faith, they were able to build the amazing resilience to overcome the oppression brought on by slavery.

Soon G.E. Gilmer, and his cousin, ardent secessionists, signed up to join the Confederate side as a member of the 1st Regiment of Louisiana Volunteers. Lincoln had hoped the war would be quick with as little bloodshed as possible. His wish was not to be the case, as the brutal, bloody war lasted for four long years. The single most bloody day in American military history was the Battle of Antietam fought in Sharpsburg, Maryland.

Photographs of this battle horrified Americans. For the first time, with the advent of the new medium of photography, they were able to see the actual carnage of dead soldiers strewn all over battlefields up close and personal. It is equally surprising that through the wonders of the internet, I can take a virtual stroll through the wide-open spaces of the cornfield to the long fence where the Louisiana regiment was surrounded and shot at from both sides. This clash was not the Civil War's battle with the most casualties, that was Gettysburg with over 50,000. Nevertheless, one of the 22,717 fatalities was a Confederate private in the infantry named G.E. Gilmer. His body was never identified nor brought back.

In Louisiana, it took over a year to complete the inventory for G.E. Gilmer's property and to divide it among James Blair Gilmer's daughters. On paper, the family was split up, with Jack and Barbary with their eight children, plus William and Laura, with their two children, along with Handy, going to Mattie Gilmer O'Neill. While Sam and Fanny with their two children, plus Jane, with her two children, going to Eliza Gilmer Graves. A careful examination of the records for G.E. Gilmer's Succession revealed these details.

Even more consequential to our family was the day after the Battle of Antietam, when Abraham Lincoln issued the executive order freeing the slaves, the Emancipation Proclamation. The emancipation appeased the abolitionists who insisted the war should be for liberating the slaves. He made it clear to other foreign countries that the North's noble aim was to abolish slavery, preempting them from entering the war on the Confederate side. The newly freed slaves were now allowed to join the Union cause. Despite being discriminated against, over 200,000 African Americans fought in armed forces in the fight for their freedom, which eventually helped to tip the scales toward a Union victory.

Sam and his family, as did most of the slaves during the Civil War, most likely remained on the plantation. The everyday struggle to survive for enslaved African Americans now mirrored the lives of almost everyone in the Confederacy. The naval blockade of the ports caused shortages of everything that came from the North and Europe. Super inflation sent the prices of the essentials, like bread, skyrocketing to $50 Confederate notes. With 3 out of 4 men serving in the Confederate army, there was a shortage of men. Enslaved blacks sometimes took advantage of the situation. There were work slowdowns and defiance, especially toward the planter's wives. Many southern plantation women struggled as they were left to run the plantations, raise their children, and even work to provide for their families.

In Bossier Parish, similarly, the daughters of the Gilmer's, who were my family's new slaveholders, most likely struggled. There were no battles near the plantation, but it was likely that Sam and others of G.E. Gilmer's hands traveled to work on telegraph lines near Shreveport. As the capital of Confederate Louisiana, Shreveport, a small military-industrial complex for both the army and the navy, was targeted in the Red River Campaign in the spring of 1864. After a decisive victory over the Union forces, several Confederate generals marched their soldiers through the Bee Bend Plantation very near the slave quarters and later near the Plain Dealing Plantation moving toward north toward Arkansas. It must have been quite a memorable moment for the enslaved blacks as thousands of infantry soldiers marched by in a column dressed in their ragtag gray hat, jackets, and trousers, as the mounted cavalry strutted by on their horses and the enormous guns of the artillery lumbered along.

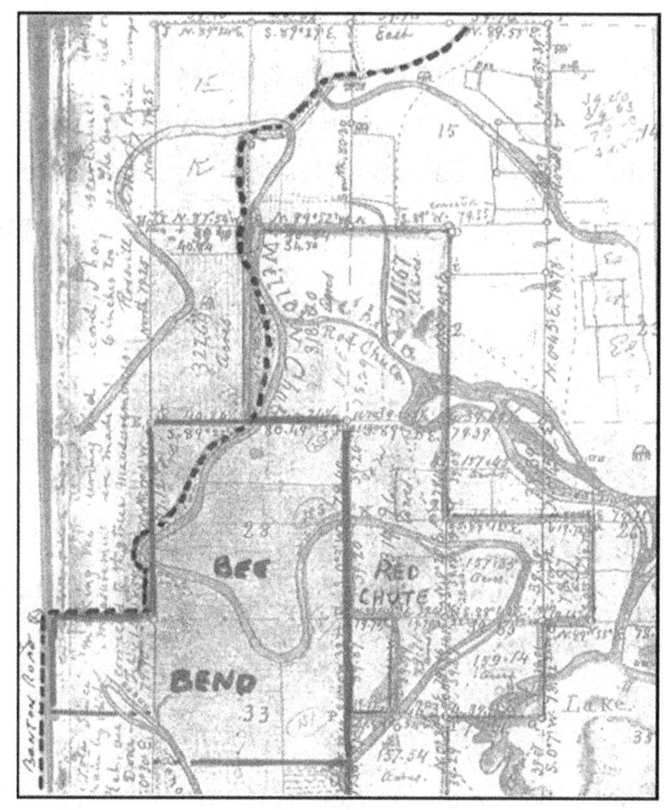

Rough Map by Dale Jennings of the probable route of General Parsons to Arkansas April 1864

In the spring of 1865, after years of bloodshed and over 600,000+ casualties, General Lee surrendered to General Grant. The celebration ending the Civil War paused a few days later as the nation mourned the death of the president. Furthermore, the local paper reported the details of the president's death before it finally announced "capitulation of Gen. R. E. Lee" almost a month later. In the end, Abraham Lincoln had kept the country together and liberated millions of African Americans from the institution of slavery. The war did not begin with the motive of freeing the slaves when it started in 1861, but the magnitude of the sacrifice of soldiers on both sides demanded an equally worthy purpose. At the end of the war, more than 300,000 slaves became free in Louisiana.

Times were tough with the cotton and sugar trade disrupted and runaway inflation. An occupying army sometimes seized and destroyed food crops leaving both the black and white people of Louisiana in dire straits. The thirteenth amendment was ratified on December 18,

1865, which unequivocally freed all the enslaved African Americans throughout the United States. The descendants of Granvill and Eliza were now free. Their freedom was probably the most significant moment in their entire lives. How did they feel? Whatever their thoughts, they had to face the same tribulations that the northern free blacks face, a hostile environment, where they were not welcome. A former slave said it this way, "For we colored people did not know how to be free, and the white people did not know how to have a free colored person about them."

With the chosen last name of Smith, a fresh start for the newly recognized Smith family was just beginning. Since the family was in four different locations after the Civil War, but they all chose the same last name of Smith, this probably reinforces the fact that enslaved people had surnames. Samuel Smith, his siblings, and the rest of the family could finally leave the status of slaves behind them, but the legacy of the institution of slavery would live on for years to come.

The emancipation of the slaves brought an end to the bitter 250 years of slavery in America. The institution of slavery included the brutal treatment of African Americans as property with no rights in the South, as well as the racist belief, shared by most Americans, that blacks were inferior and unequal to whites. David Hume, considered one of the most influential philosophers in Western thought, in 1748, wrote, "I am apt to suspect the negroes to be naturally inferior to the whites."

This racism did not change with the end of the Civil War. I think a fitting Chinese proverb that describes the depth of animosity toward blacks is, "three feet of ice is not the result of one cold day." This analogy summed up the racist norm of American society in the 1800s. The nation was not prepared to accept the full citizenship of the newly freed former slaves. The North had secured its goal of keeping the Union together and abolishing the immoral institution of slavery. Except for a cadre of dedicated white teachers, government workers, and ministers who worked tirelessly to help the emancipated blacks, the north turned its attention to building a prosperous industrial society, which included new factories, new technologies, and inventions such as typewriters and the telephone, the expansion of the railroads, and the growth of cites.

The defeated South had to deal with the ravages of the war and the task of rebuilding a society not based on slave labor. In this inhospitable environment, Samuel Smith, his siblings and their families began the undertaking of managing their own lives as free people with the solidarity and strength of family. It would take at least one hundred years before they would receive all the rights of an American citizen and shrink the level of racism and the bitter legacy of slavery.

Examining the moments in Samuel's and his siblings' lives only revealed a little bit about them. There were hints of being dependable and trustworthy that they may have mimicked their father. The threat of violence almost certainly limited their ability to do what they wanted and express their feelings and preferences.

How much violence did they endure? In Spyker's diary, he mentions one instance of the overseer, Mr. Elton, whipping Painter Dick "for being impertinent." Another time, he "flailed" a female. Does this mean whipping was not a common occurrence, or did he only note major infractions? DNA evidence shows that some of Granvill's descendants are related to the overseer, J.P. Vance, in Bossier Parish and the Elton family in Morehouse Parish. Those are the kind of moments; reluctantly, blacks just have dealt with because, like me, the average African American is 30% European. As African Americans, the traumatic moments of whippings and rape are a source of deep anger, which researchers have evidence to show that this ancestral trauma influences our mental health today.

By studying the lives of my ancestors during slavery, I have come to understand that they possessed incredible strength. Weilin's idea to surround myself with whatever I feared to train myself to overcome my fear has worked. I no longer fear the ugly monster of slavery. That does not change how horrific enslavement was; however, it was what it was. Examining many moments in their lives, I shudder to think of how they endured, but they did. My new understanding is that my ancestors not only survived, but they were incredibly resilient. Nothing I have accomplished can hold a candle to their fortitude. Now, instead of fear and anger, I have worked through my emotions to feel great pride. Hopefully, we, as a country, also need to deal with all these feelings and resolve them.

I am almost sure that most other families have other traumatic circumstances that someone endured. Wars, The Depression, migrating across the ocean or the country, ethnic strife, and more have engulfed the lives of many. If we focus on how they survived, they can provide us lessons of hope and resilience. Isn't that what we want to teach our children?

Again, this is another reason that our ancestors deserve to be studied, not because they were famous, but because they provided us a light to follow.

After enslavement, my ancestors had more control and could run their own lives. Weilin once asked me, "Why couldn't the formerly enslaved blacks become successful after they were freed?" That would be a logical question if there was an equal playing field, but there wasn't. Instead of slavery, there was now racism, deadly violence, and discrimination. How did my descendants struggle with these new hardships? Your ancestors most likely had to deal with hurdles, too. People, and more specifically, our ancestors, reveal their personalities, values, and talents as they fought against whatever obstacles they faced in their lives. What will the moments about their lives tell you?

Values

I always thought the Civil War was over when General Lee surrendered to General Grant. It never occurred to me that the ending date of the war was not the same for everyone. General Robert E. Lee surrendered to General Ulysses S. Grant on April 9, 1865, but it took months for all the commands to surrender. Eventually, the papers also clearly stated that there were "no longer slaves in the United States." The expectation was that the "Freedmen" be employed under contracts with reasonable wages and to be "treated kindly." The children of Granvill and Eliza were now Freedmen. What did it actually mean for them? How did they feel? What was the first decision that they decided to make on their own? How were they going to run their lives? What did they expect? A poignant quote by an unidentified former slave around 1937 said,

We knowed freedom was on us, but we didn't know what was to come with it. We thought we was going to get rich like the white folks. We thought we was going to be richer than the white folks, 'cause we was stronger and knowed how to work, and the whites didn't, and they didn't have us to work for them anymore. But it didn't turn out that way. We soon found out that freedom could make folks proud, but it didn't make us rich.

If hard work is the key to making it, then his thoughts seemed very reasonable. It turned out that freedom was the only beacon of light down a long treacherous tunnel. Stepping out of the shackles of slavery, my ancestors could run their lives according to their own goals and beliefs. But racism would now be an invisible chain holding them back.

The next best avenue to "resurrect" Granvill, since I don't have any of his records, was to look at his children. His offspring had the power to mold their lives using the values they had learned from their parents. Those values included their sense of right and wrong, and what their priorities should be. Choices, goals, motives, and behaviors are explainable in terms of their values system. By carefully studying their actions in a variety of situations, I believed I could estimate the value system of his kin, thus pointing me toward Granvill.

All their descendants, including me, have a part of Granvill and Eliza's values, but which parts? To find out, I proposed an experiment. First, I took a test to find my values on a measure of Schwartz Values. Schwartz Values represent ten universal human goals, which include benevolence, universalism, self-direction, stimulation, hedonism, achievement, power, security, tradition, and conformity. Then I asked ten people to take the same test. They included my DNA cousins, who descended from Granvill and Eliza's children, as well two others who were not related. Using only the responses of Granvill's ancestors, I graphed their top four values to determine which values appeared the most frequently. As you can see, everyone had self-direction as one of their highest values; in contrast, no one in this experiment had the values of hedonism or power.

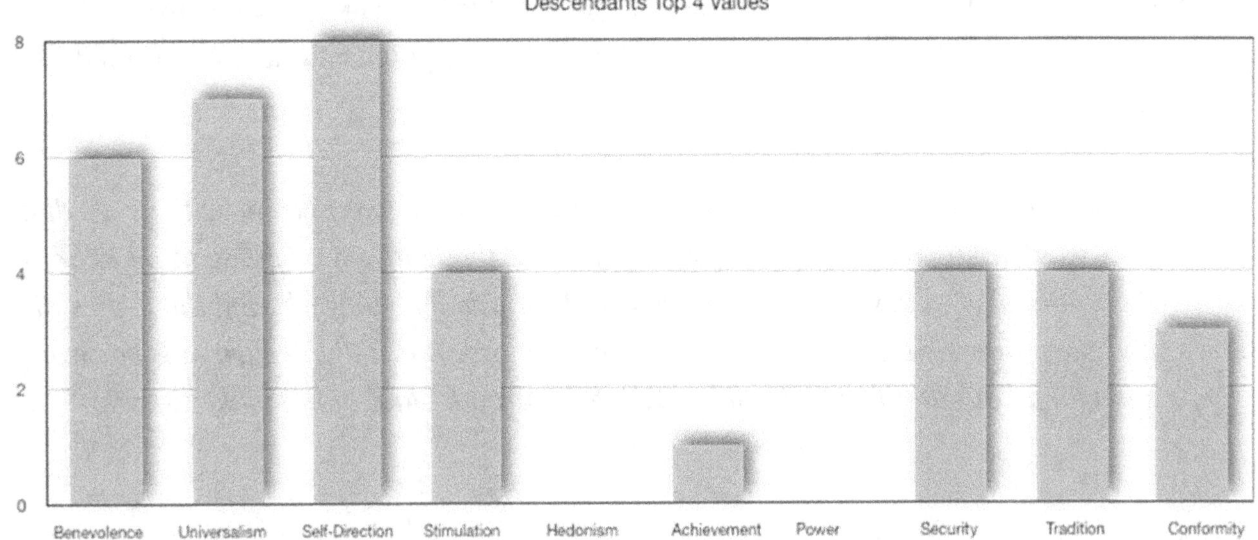

Of course, this was just a rough hint. My next task was to look for evidence of these values of benevolence, self-direction, and universalism, as defined by Schwartz.

SELF-DIRECTION *Defining goal*: independent thought and action; choosing, creating exploring			
curious	freedom	privacy	self-respect
UNIVERSALISM *Defining goal*: understanding, appreciation, tolerance, and protection for the welfare of all people and for nature.			
broadminded	equality	wisdom	social justice
inner harmony	a world at peace	a world of beauty	
BENEVOLENCE *Defining goal*: preserving and enhancing the welfare of those with home one is in frequent personal contact			
honest	helpful	responsible	loyal
mature love	true friendship	a spiritual life	meaning in life

Our family's Schwartz Values with the defining goal and specific values that express that goal

In my ancestral line, was there self-direction, which means independent thought and actions? How about universalism, which is the protection of all people. Finally, was there substantiation for benevolence? Were they preserving and enhancing the welfare of groups such as the family?

Before I started to cross-examine my ancestors, I practiced spotting those values in my life. Considering some of the more specific words that express self-direction, I see in myself as independent, curious, creative, and one who follows my own goals, along with maybe being a bit square. For example, when I learned that "Balanta" means those who resist, it reminded me of my "I don't care attitude" in college, when the male students taunted and picked on me as the only female in some of my engineering classes. The descriptors of universalism pertain to both Weilin and I. Not only have we broadened our horizons by traveling extensively, but our decades-long multicultural marriage demands that we be both tolerant and fair to others. Benevolence is an area where our values routinely conflict in our view of the role of students. Weilin thinks students should always actively be striving to achieve, whereas I put a premium on me, the teacher, being responsible so I can help my students learn. Our family's highest values came out to be the opposite of the top four for the British people. Their top four values included power, achievement, stimulation, and hedonism. Perhaps that explains the British Empire and their quest to colonize the world.

I examined Granvill's and Eliza's children, as well as their grandchildren, to find evidence of these shared values in their lives. In Spyker's diary, Austin displays an aspect of benevolence, being honest and trustworthy. He, among over one hundred enslaved blacks, was chosen to run an errand involving a transaction with nine gold dollars. My daughter reminded me that she knew honesty was important in our family because, as a teenager, when she got caught lying, her task was to write a persuasive essay on why she should always tell the truth and why lying was wrong. Her classmates at college thought this was very amusing.

National Numismatic Collection, National Museum of American History

Dale, my friend who I met while in Bossier Parish, told me that the church records revealed a situation involving another feature of benevolence, having a spiritual life. He found a member of the Red River Baptist Church named Sam. Since it is very near to were my 2nd great-grandfather was, it is very likely Samuel. In 1859, another member of the church of about 40 members faced exclusion for running away. Later, he was allowed to come back. Evidently, besides a spiritual life, the church was a place everyone wanted to belong to, even in slave times. Thus, these actions demonstrate the value of benevolence during slavery.

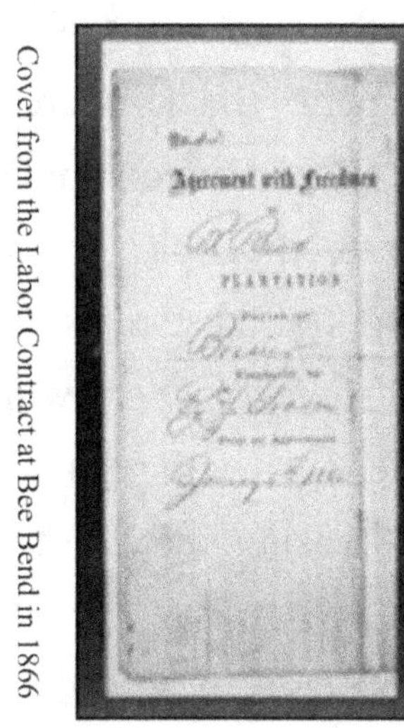

To find more values, I was banking on being able to find more records after the Civil War. I learned another lesson about genealogy records as I researched my family after the Civil War. I was always under the impression that the 1870 Census was the first record that listed my ancestors with surnames. But, from a presenter at a conference, I became aware that I could find Labor Contracts from the Freedmen's Bureau on FamilySearch. First, I entered the state, Louisiana, then Freedmen's Bureau Field Office Records, 1865-1872. Next, I drilled down to the heading (plantation department). Finally, I located the roll for Bossier parish (or county level in other states). I spent an evening flipping through Roll 41, which had Bossier Parish along with three nearby parishes. Eureka, I found Sam Smith, his wife Fannie, and his children, Mariah and Jeff. I had attempted to search the Louisiana, Freedman's Bureau's records before, but now they are organized into categories, I had success. The lesson is to check for updates occasionally. I found my 2nd great-grandfather, Sam Smith, and his family at the Bee Bend Plantation in January of 1868. That left me with a baffling mystery. What happened to Fannie, Mariah, and Jeff?

Over the years, I had had several theories about what happened to Samuel's first family. One hypothesis was Samuel wanted to move back to where his family who were in Plain Dealing, but his wife Fannie wished to stay with her family, so they split. Another theory was the end of the Civil War provided an excellent time for an unhappy couple to go their separate ways. Another idea was his wife and kids died of some disease. After meeting Dale, he provided me with information about a tragic situation that impacted his family

Most white Southerners were both dismayed and angry with the defeat of the South and the ending of the old order based on white supremacy. More specifically, in Bossier Parish, as claimed by the local paper, some found the "liberation of those with questionable character" hard to take. Matters became worse when it became a crime to call colored US troops stationed in the parish the "N" word. Add to this, labor shortages occurred when hundreds of former enslaved African Americans attempted to leave the plantations.

This unease led to the denial of Granvill's descendants' any opportunity to move up the economic ladder outside of agriculture. The Louisiana State legislature quickly enacted punitive laws in 1865 and 1866 meant to keep the blacks working on the plantations. Known as Black Codes, they attempted to restrict the freedmen's movement. Blacks were not allowed to be armed. Orphans, as well as other children, were placed in compulsory apprenticeships. Vagrancy laws permitted local authorities to arrest freed people for minor infractions and put them to work. Having to work within the framework of these racist laws, Congress established the Freedmen's Bureau to help the former black slaves and poor whites. They did their best to look after some of the needs of the African Americans with regulations covering the labor contracts, standard work schedules, provisions for housing, food, clothing, and schools.

That same year, Reconstruction legislation passed by the United States Congress allowed 90% of the black males of voting age to register to vote. Wages and working conditions were improving. Granvill's' male descendants over the age of 21 probably were involved in electing the first African American to a state office, the lieutenant governor of Louisiana, in June of 1868. But circumstances would change later in 1868. The heavy reliance on cotton production in the past in Bossier Parish had skewed the population to 9,170 blacks and 3,505 whites. With almost three out four of the populaces being black, it would mean almost certain defeat for the whites at the polls.

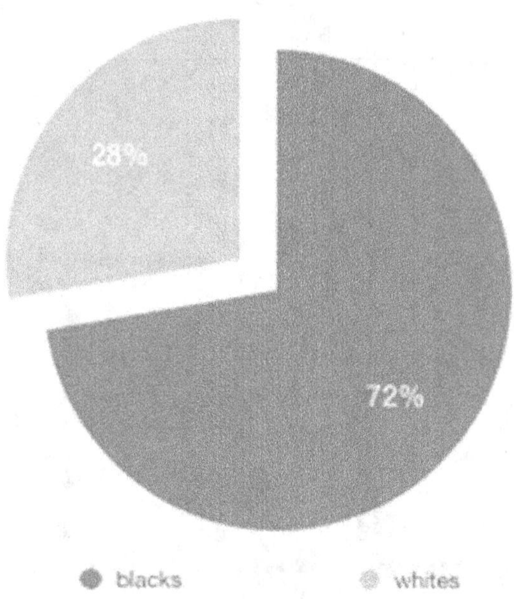

The situation became intolerable for Southern Democrats. Throughout the southern states, but primarily in Louisiana and Georgia, there were large-scale collective violence and massacres. Unfortunately, the influential and respectable men in the community often condoned this behavior.

One such occurrence happened on a hot, humid day in late September on the Shady Grove Plantation. Known as the Bossier Massacre or Shady Grove Riots, it began on one of the former Gilmer plantations located next to Bee Bend. The labor contracts showed that Sam Smith, his family, and friends were nearby at Bee Bend plantation. What actually happened was probably something between widely different versions of the events. The local newspaper said a robbery by several Negro freedmen precipitated the killing. A synopsis from the Freedmen's Bureau claimed "lawless acts of desperadoes" from nearby Arkansas caused the riot. Both accounts agree that two white men were mortally wounded. One of them was related to my friend Dale's wife. In retribution, a large group of over 100 armed white men, supposedly from Arkansas, descended into the area to indiscriminately kill over a hundred, some said 150, freedmen over a wide area. A report for the state legislators concluded that the massacre lasted for 3 or 4 days, during which time 162 people were killed.

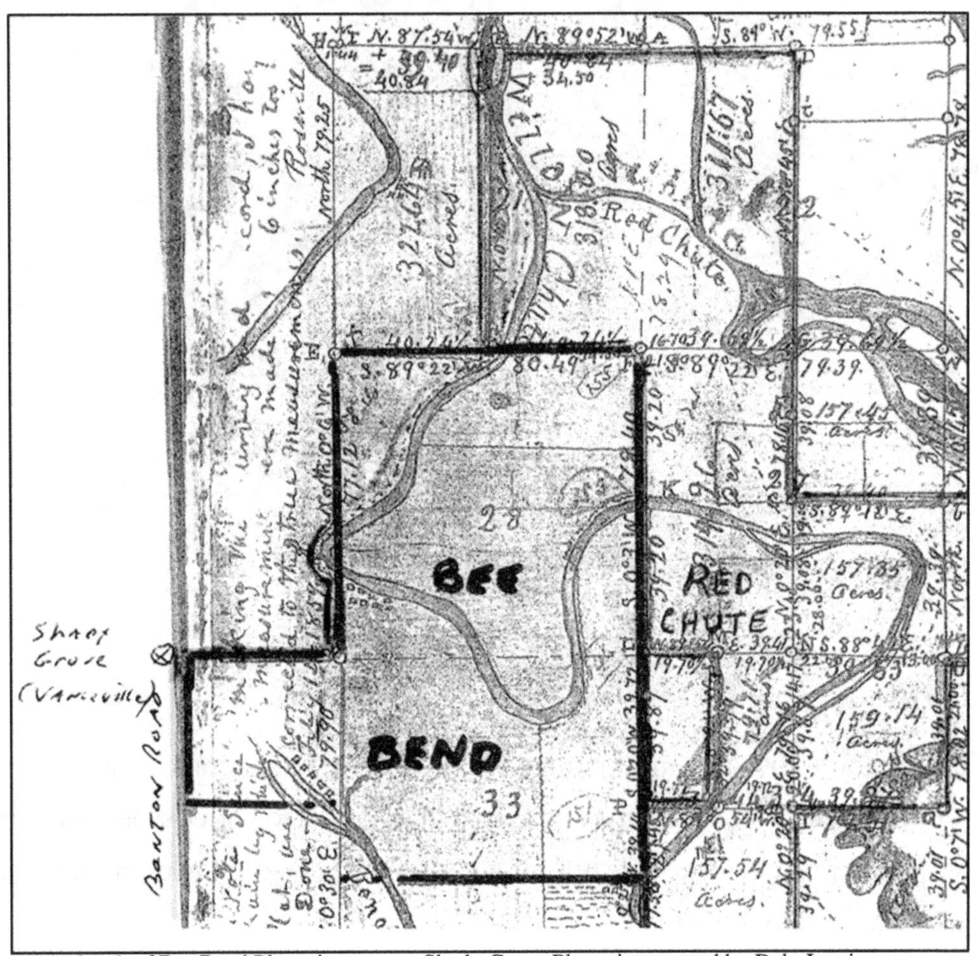

A sketch of Bee Bend Plantation next to Shady Grove Plantation created by Dale Jennings

The reports ended with a comment that only one person in Bossier had voted for the Grant out of about 2,000 registered Republican voters in 1868. The collective violence against the freedmen in Bossier parish intimidated them into not voting for the party of Lincoln and achieved the goal of having blacks "put back into their place." There were killings all over both Bossier and Caddo parishes. Was anyone in the Smith family slaughtered during these days fraught with danger? There is no evidence except that between 1867 and 1870, Samuel's first family, including his wife Fanny and his children Mariah and Jeff, disappeared from the records. Whatever happened, it must have been heart-wrenching to lose your entire family. Samuel's older brother Jack had family, as well some of the children Marywether's children also left no trace. Maybe they died from disease, but my gut feeling is they met a tragic end in the riots, whatever happened, this was a very perilous time. Freedom definitely had not brought forth the values of tolerance, equality, or social justice.

Samuel moved on with his life. On Saturday, April 23, in 1870, Sam Smith and Caroline Johnson signed their mark to certify that they had been married by Rev. A. R. Banks. I researched all the names on the marriage certificate. As an itinerant minister from Arkansas, he was one of the first Presbyterian ministers who took up the difficult task of traveling between churches on horseback in the northern Louisiana area.

J.P. Vance, the former overseer for G.E. Gilmer, bought land, which was part of the old Plain Dealing plantation. As was customary with the regulations set by the Louisiana Freedmen's Bureau, J.P. Vance persuaded Samuel and his friend John Garner to work for him. My DNA cousin, Cheryl, obtained a copy of the 1870 Agricultural schedule for Bossier while she was in Salt Lake City. Samuel Smith was the "manager" of a 50-acre farm and Samuel's longtime friend, John Garner, worked on 35 acres in 1870.

The document listed acres of land, property cash values, livestock, produce, and Total Value. With a range from $480 - $1000, Sam Smith's total for his farm products was estimated to be $1000. His total was the highest for blacks on that particular page. Is this an example of the value of being very responsible or being goal-centered? Whichever, it seems he was very hard-working.

Viewing the rest of Granvill and Eliza's kin after emancipation required that I make sure I completed all the family lines of our tree beyond my lineage. Many people only fill out their immediate family, but looking for examples of values became another compelling reason to finish all the information for Granvill and Eliza's children. In genealogy research, female ancestors frequently present problems, especially when finding their maiden names. Further complicating this problem was the fact that 1870 was the first time the last names of African Americans were recorded. Sometimes, I found that married female family members lived near their parents but this wasn't always the case. Nowadays, the Social Security Applications records on Ancestry is my most effective way of finding maiden names. Researching "finding female ancestors" will give you more techniques for different states and other countries. A side benefit I gained from completing all the information on the other lines of descent was that my genealogical research skills improved.

Examining the values of the rest of Granvill's ancestors has the limitation of only having census records. So, I had to try to squeeze as much data out of those records as I could. First, I decided to find out the exact location of each member of the family. I utilized the actual images of the 1870 US Federal Census to locate the family. I glanced at the page before and the page after the person I was researching. The families of Samuel, his older brothers Jack and Marywether, and Jane were fortunate to be together in the northern part of Bossier Parish. To illustrate what I did, here is a table for the 1870 US Federal Census:

Names of Descendants	County	Ward	Page
Sam/ Marywether Smith	Bossier	3	69
Jack's children/ Jane Smith	Bossier	3	70
Lucy Ann Smith and family	Bossier	3	43
Almeda Smith Bowler	Bossier	3	44
William/ Handy Smith	Bossier	3	95
Caroline Smith and family	Morehouse	1	8
Emmaline Smith Gray and family	Morehouse	1	4

Samuel and his siblings were on page 69, while Jack's family and Jane were on page 70 Likewise, Lucy Ann and her family were in another area of Bossier Parish in the same ward, on page 43. I know that his twin brother William, as well as his younger brother Handy were also in Bossier Parish but in a different section because they were still in Ward 3, but both on page 95. Austin's family was also in two places Morehouse Parish. One group was with Caroline on page 8, and her eldest daughter, Emmaline, who married into the Gray family, was on page 4, which might not have been far away.

Next, I extended the family timeline, which produced a clear picture of the members of the family and their location. Under each child of Granvill and Eliza is a list of their children, when and where they were born, and where they were in the 1870-1880 Federal US Censuses. Finally, I placed them into groups:

Granvill's Family Timeline to 1880

	Lucy Ann	Jack	Austin	Marywether	Samuel	William	Handy	Jane
1840 - 1849	40 Robert *Bossier, LA* 42 Almeda 44 Rebecca	*Bossier, LA* 44 Mary Ann 47 Charity	*Bossier, LA* 44 Emmerline 49 Granville					
1850 - 1859	52 Isaac 54 Jenny 56 Gravnille	51 Isaac 53 Matilda 54 Tom (John) 56 Eliz. Eliza 58 George W.	*Morehouse, LA* 53 Meriweather 54 Austin 57 Leander 59 Pauline	*Bossier, LA* 57 Laura 58 Louann	*Bossier, LA* 55 Mariah 57 Jeff	*Bossier, LA* 58 Granville		*Bossier, LA* *58* Francis
1860 – Civil War 1869		60 Franklin	60 Martha J. 64 Milly 65 Eliza	60 Susan 62 Willis 64 Anna Eliza 68 Fannie Lu		61 Nancy 65 Isaac 65 Eliza		62 Eliza
1870 - 1879				71 Louis T 73 Hannah 76 Pattie 78 Fleming	71 Granville 74 William 75 Frank 76 Joseph 79 Jane		*Bossier, LA* 70 Betsey 72 Benson	

Lucy Group   Austin group   Plain Dealing Group   William & Handy Group

Examining the children of Granvill and Eliza, I would presume that all of them behaved similarly to the newly freed blacks in 1865. According to the History of Morehouse Parish, right after the war, there was a concerted effort to produce a big cotton crop in 1866. Doubtless, Austin's family was part of the undertaking, which included planters, merchants, lawyers, blacks, and whites. People borrowed money. Merchants made hefty advances. But the cotton crop of 1866 was a near-total failure due to storms and insects. Sadly, we don't know what happened to Austin.

The 1870 Federal Census was the first census that had data about all of Granvill and Eliza's descendants. Column 7, which provided the profession, occupation, or trade of each person, male or female, had information that pointed toward another value. By 1870, Austin's widow, Caroline, was keeping the house with her four daughters, while her four sons worked as farm laborers. African Americans everywhere desired a chance to escape anything that smacked of slavery. Not only did they reject slave gangs, but they also insisted on no mandatory work for black women. They wanted their wives to be equal to white women, who were able to stay at home to take care of the family. Most, or about 70%, of the female kin of Eliza, reached this level of equality, as their occupation was "Keeping House" in the 1870 US Federal Census. Equality is an aspect of universalism or the idea that some ideas should apply to everyone.

It is not surprising that my DNA cousins, along with my family, share the value of benevolence. Being benevolent is hard-wired into African American culture. Supporting each other in the family was the bedrock of African American culture through slavery, Reconstruction, and segregation. As enslaved African Americans, Granvill and Eliza's family survived because they supported each other as well as took care of other's kids. Jack's two eldest children were taking care of their younger brothers and sisters. While their uncles, Samuel and Marywether, could also be counted on to help them. In the Lucy group, all her married children lived next to her eldest son, Robert, who took care of her. In the Austin Group, his widowed wife relied on her four oldest sons to work as farm laborers. And the families of William and Handy no doubt supported each other as their two families were right next to each other. My ancestors' penchant for being helpful, loyal, and responsible shone through in the records. Granvill and Eliza's descendants were benevolent.

Life changed in 1877 as Reconstruction ended due to one of the most contentious elections in American history. To become the president, Republican candidate Rutherford Hayes made a compromise deal with several southern states. Louisiana figured prominently in this deal, which included removing the dreaded federal troops from the South. Hence, effectively returning the South to a political climate similar to the pre-war status, including the disenfranchisement of African American voters, a harsher form of sharecropping, lynching, and the emergence of Jim Crow laws. In northern Louisiana, after being "forced out of public offices, burned out of schools, cheated out of a decent living and hunted down," thousands of blacks voted with their feet and fled to Kansas.

The descendants of Granvill and Eliza persisted and, one by one, experienced an opportunity which was formerly forbidden - getting an education. Working and learning together, the family made incremental strides forward. Using the 1880 US census, I collected data for how many of their grandchildren, aged 10 through 30, were able to read compared to the average for all blacks (who were called "coloreds").

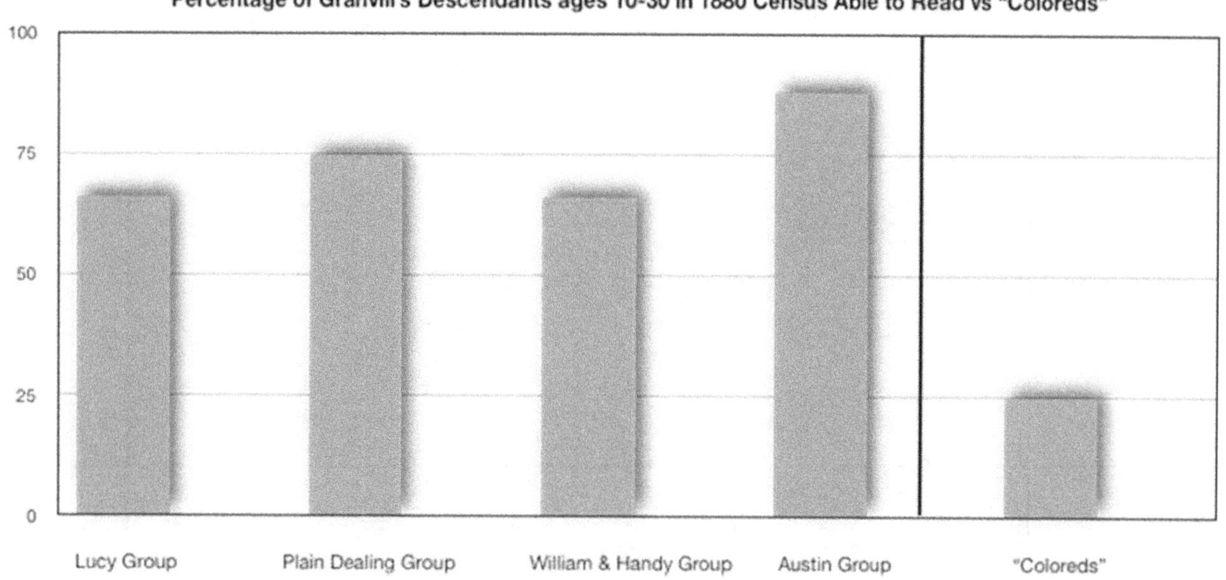

That was definitive evidence that all the groups of Granvill's grandchildren were striving for the goal of being able to read. To me, that illustrates that Granvill passed on the value of self-direction, including being creative enough to find a way to get an education. After the war, universally, black freedmen desired education for their children, but Granvill's children managed to reach that goal.

That was evident when Samuel and two others, Oscar Caldwell and Elijah Stephens, pooled their meager resources. In 1881, they bought two acres of land from the old Plain Dealing plantation from the Gilmer descendants to build the Mount Zion Church. By 1885, Mount Zion, Paysinger, and Cottage Grove were the facilities that housed the colored schools, according to the local newspaper. As was typical at the time, many of the newly organized schools opened in the churches. According to the numbers I found on my trip to the Bossier

Parish Library Historical center, there were dozens of children that began the term in September with an intense desire to learn. Maybe there was a night school to accommodate the wish at that time of many older blacks who wanted to learn to read the Bible before they died. These schools were not just for the Smith family, but all students in the area.

Bossier Parish Deed book,   P. 140 Deed to purchase land for the church in 1881

As an educator, it pains me that these eager students with a thirst for learning had teachers who received one-third less than the white teachers and taught class sizes that were 50% larger. Segregation meant what little money there was for education was stretched thin to the detriment of both black and white students. Despite this, the Smith family pressed on.

The Plain Dealing Group, which included the children of Jack, Samuel, Mayweather, Jane, and their families, demonstrated the value of universalism by making sure all around equally received an excellent education. The husband of their niece, S.Turner James, or S.T. James, also seems to have been very influential. S.T. James was married to Eliza, the daughter of Samuel's sister, Jane Smith, and J.P. Vance, the former overseer. In the 1880s, S.T. James' name was often in the local newspaper as being qualified to be a juror. In the 1890s, his name returns several times in the paper as a Trustee for the Mount Zion Colored School. Sometimes the mandatory white trustee was J.P. Vance. John Garner, who married Jack's daughter, was also sometimes the trustee. With S.T. James, J.P. Vance, and John Garner controlling the school, it may explain why while about 31% of the school-age population of blacks enrolled in school in the United States, in comparison, Bossier Parish had over 60%. And while most blacks at the time received only an elementary school education of first through fifth grade, the one-room school with N.L. Paul listed as the teacher, provided the Smith children a primary school education all the way from first grade through eighth grade. This value of universalism was also evident in the Lucy Group; most completed 5th grade, with one in her group, Jacob Smith, also a Trustee for a colored school in Bossier Parish.

Jane Smith(1836-1892)

Granvill and Eliza's kin in Morehouse Parish seemed to take a different path than the other groups. In a book written in the 1880s about the parish, the writer claims there were public schools supported by taxation for the "colored children, but they are poorly attended." Austin's descendants had the wisdom to exploit this situation. They went to school, with almost 90% of them being able to read, according to the 1880 census.

By the end of the 19th century, most of Granvill and Eliza's children were gone. In 1887, Lucy Ann passed away. Then, Jane Smith died in 1892. Samuel, along with Caroline, met some kind of tragic end around 1894. We are not sure when, how, and why, but according to Cheryl, my DNA cousin, her grandmother, Addie Lee Smith, became an orphan when she was about eight years old. Since Joseph P. was a teenager at the time, it's probably when he first went to live with his older brother, Granville, on his farm. Did Rev. S. T. James become a father figure who shepherded Joseph P. toward a religious inclination? Joseph P.'s bible, which the family still has, shows it was given to him by Rev. S. T. James. Hopefully, Rev. S. T. James was able to comfort the entire Smith family after the death of Samuel at 62 and Caroline's untimely death at only 40 years old, which continued to reinforce the value of benevolence.

Studying the historical context of their lives, and also reflecting on their values, helped me to understand my 2nd great-grandparents better. I had no firsthand knowledge of them, so they were the first ancestors I learned about only using records. Each of those records I uncovered about Samuel and Caroline evoked a range of strong emotions. Not only was there the dread and bitterness of seeing them as slaves on bills of sale, but there was also the perplexing question: what does that color of copper mean for a human being? Then there was the marriage license when they were legally wed. Their mark for their signatures distressed and saddened me as I was painfully reminded me that they were forbidden to read or write. There was the thrill of seeing their full names listed as freed people in the United States Federal Census. And finally, their son, Joseph P. Smith, remembered them in his obituary, providing the giddy moment of finding Caroline's maiden name was Johnson. There is the exasperation of knowing I will not get my wish to find a death certificate to tidy up all the loose ends of their lives.

At first, with aid from the policies of Reconstruction, the Granvill and Eliza kin had made some fledgling progress. But soon, collective violence, such as the Bossier Massacre, led to the scare tactics meant to keep the black majority from ascertaining its rights as voters and limit their economic opportunities. In this segregated environment, their children found a way to provide for the growing educational and religious needs of their families. With a passion for learning, most of their grandchildren obtained an American education.

Looking at their children, it seems that Granvill and Eliza did their duty. One of Weilin's sayings about the importance of family is, "It is the responsibility of your family to teach you because you didn't spring out of a rock." He is referring to one of the very famous characters in Chinese literature, the Monkey King. Unlike everyone else, he had no family to teach him what' was right and wrong because he sprang out from a rock. Some of the values the children of Granvill and Eliza developed and reinforced, have withstood the test of time. I conclude that most likely, Granvill had the same values of self-direction, benevolence, and universalism that his descendants have today. These family values, including faith with a spiritual life, reaching for your goals such as education for all children, and supporting each other, guided them through many adversities that struck throughout the nineteenth century.

Every family has a unique set of values. A way to uncover your family's values is to quiz members of your ancestor's extended family. After understanding those values fully, you need to find examples of those values in your life. Finally, search for examples of those values possibly in your ancestor's life or in the children of your ancestor. Squeezing every bit of information that you can squeeze out of the census data can require some creative thinking. For example, for the value of power, you could investigate professions and, for the value of tradition, determine if they stayed in the same place over multiple census years. Learning how your family used these values in the past provides a unique opportunity for you to emphasize those values to your ancestor's descendants. Appreciating your family's values is a vital link to "resurrecting" your ancestor and honoring them today.

Patterns

The year 1900 was somewhat unusual. It did not officially begin the 20th century, nor did it follow the usual pattern of being a leap year. Ordinarily, if the last two digits of a year can be divided by 4, it's a leap year. But the rule also says if the year is divisible by 100 like 1900, it must also be divisible by 400, to be a leap year. So, if any of Granvill and Eliza's dozen or more descendants who were born in 1896 happened to be born on Feb. 29th, they would have to wait eight years until they had another birthday in 1904.

Nevertheless, changing from the year 1899 to 1900 evoked some kind of closure and reflection in the minds of many, especially since the first day of that year fell on a Sunday. Society reflected on its accomplishments in the 1800s. There were revolutionary inventions from American inventors such as Alexander Graham Bell with his telephone and Thomas Alva Edison with his light bulb and the phonograph. They wondered what the 1900s would bring. Perhaps a better society?

Of course, Granvill, who had been born in the 1700s, didn't make it to the 1900s to experience these new technologies, but the legacy of his name did. Continuing naming patterns that the African American culture utilized to honor family members over the centuries, the name Granville was all over northern Louisiana. In the Lucy group, there was one son of his daughter named Granville, in the Plain Dealing group, there was one grandson named Granville along with a great-grandson. Further, Granville Stephens was the son of a friend and the minister of the local church. Far away in Morehouse in the Austin group, there was another grandson name Granville. And finally, the William and Handy group had one grandson and two great-grandsons, all named Granville Smith. Many followed the naming pattern in the 19th century for sons, which included naming the first son after the paternal grandfather, the second son after the maternal grandfather, and the third son after the father. Correspondingly, there were many girls named Eliza or had Eliza in their name, such as Eliza Jane and Anna Eliza.

Not only did Granvill's descendant name their children after him, but they also utilized a pattern of giving them the names of people in the family's history. African American genealogist Nicka Smith proclaimed, "Your history is in your names." On the 1900 Census, the record for a grandson, Isaac "Ike" Smith revealed many interesting names for his sixteen children. He had named several of his sons, George E. Smith, Spyker Smith, and John Milton Smith, after the former family slaveholders George E. Gilmer, Leonidas Spyker, and John Milton Sandidge. He also named another son, Garner Smith, after his brother-in-law, John Garner. This naming pattern also happened in the Austin Group. And not only were there the family names of Granville, a Meriweather, and Samuel, but there was a Leonidas George Gray. Besides the legacy of patterns in names, I wondered if I could decipher other patterns in the lives of Granvill's descendants that may help resurrect him.

Figuring out patterns was one of my favorite topics in my middle school mathematics curriculum. Students were pleasantly surprised that the multiples of 5 (5, 10, 15, 20, 25, 30…) end in a repeating pattern of five then zero. Of course, as a teacher, I lived for those days to see the sparkle in their eyes when they realize adding the digits in the multiples of nine equal nine and adding the digits in the multiples of three will also be a multiple of three. (For example, the sum of the digits in 18, 27, 36 is 9 and the sum of 30, 33, 36 is 3, 6, 9). Now they were ready for other problems included extending a pattern, like what comes next 28, 31, 34… the answer is 37. Or if these first three figures have 4, 6, 8 blocks, can you predict how many blocks will be in the 10th figure?

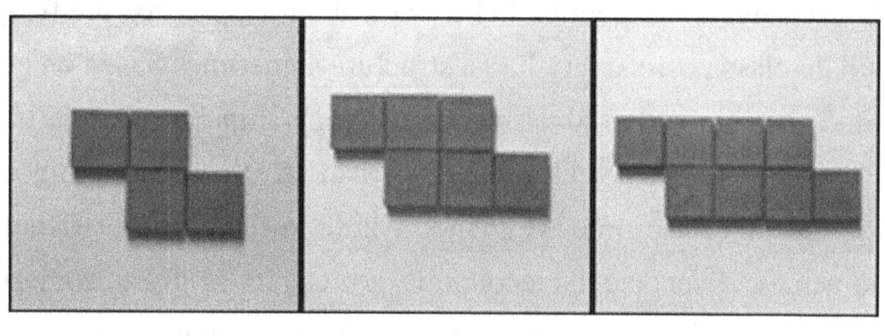

Figure 1   Figure 2   Figure 3

With guidance, they found the rule for this pattern is to multiply by 2 and add 2, which in algebra is $2n + 2$. The answer is 22 blocks. My students started hunting for patterns everywhere in their lives. They discovered them in the hundreds chart, the multiplication tables, and even in the designs on their clothes. You can find them in reoccurring cycles like the 24-hour day, the seasons, in crystals, in the stock market, and even the trek of lives beginning at birth. Patterns also occur in families influencing your diet, your beliefs, your social traditions, your career, your personality quirks, and even your hobbies. I hoped I could find exciting patterns in the lives of Granvill's descendants and then trace the rule or origin back to Granvill.

One pattern that continued from the 1800s was that Granvill's descendant's economic life depended on the life cycle of cotton, but some things had changed. Now they decided when to plant the cotton seeds, when to hoe, and when to pick the cotton. Additionally, there was an inescapable difference between who now owned the land. A detailed analysis of the 1900 Census revealed that slightly over the majority of Granvill's adult ancestors owned their homes. That was significantly more than most blacks at the time and about the same as whites.

Interestingly, this correlated with those of Granvill's kin who could read in the 1880 Census. Also, even though each group of Granvill's descendants did not live near each other, each group of families had about the same number of home-owners versus renters. That pointed toward a pattern worth noting.

145

Henry Louis Gates, Jr. explained in his book about Oprah that the fledgling beginning of the black middle-class post-slavery had a structure sometimes based on color, sometimes on education, and sometimes based on property ownership but always based on literacy. I wondered what the improvement in literacy had to do with buying land. My husband reminded me that since the time we visited China in the early 1980s until we revisited in 2004, China achieved spectacular economic growth in its gross domestic product (GDP) because they made a significant investment in raising their literacy rates and education. Recent research demonstrated that increased education correlated with increased GDP. So, improving literacy and education played a significant role in boosting economic development in China, just like it did for Granvill's descendants.

Of course, my curious mind pondered why or how this happened. Sweeping the cobwebs back to discussions of literacy in my education classes, the name Paulo Freire popped up who proclaimed that once you learn to read, you also learn to think; breaking the bonds of ignorance. Once you learn to think, you can use your brain in many ways. Indeed, researchers using brain scans found that teaching illiterate people to read produced enormous brain changes. That makes sense; we know your brain grows new brain cells called neurons when you learn. With more neurons, your brain functions at a higher level. It crushes my soul to think about all those enslaved African Americans who missed the opportunities that literacy brings.

Granvill possibly learned rudimentary reading when he was a boy in Georgia. Christian women taught some enslaved children how to read the Bible as part of their religious training, but this stopped after the United States became a country. Since Granvill had such a long life, he may have passed on some knowledge of the benefits of reading to his children and grandchildren. Maybe he did, or perhaps this pattern was due to an inherited go-getter mentality.

In October of 1900, two more of Granvill and Eliza's grandchildren became property owners. Granville, Joseph P.'s older brother, and he signed the papers to buy 80 acres of former timberland. (This was the same land that I would see over a century later when I visited northern Louisiana that I found was now part of a legal fight, one which is not over yet.) The growth of cities had spurred the need for more lumber, particularly as Americans settled in the timber deprived Great Plains. By the 1900s, the seat of the lumber industry had slowly moved from the depleted forest of New England to the South. Due to this soaring demand, lumber-rich northern Louisiana enjoyed a lumber boom in the early 20th century. Seizing on this opportunity, Jeff Smith, their younger brother, and Garner Smith, their cousin, worked for sawmills just outside of Plain Dealing.

Some small sawmill operations profited as they grabbed new cheap land sold off by the railroads. First, they quickly cut down the timber and then made even more money by selling the stump-filled lots of land. Joseph P. and Granville, as well as some of their other siblings, bought this type of land plot. It was very inexpensive, and was purchased for a little less than two dollars an acre. Their 80 acres were more substantial than most farms in Louisiana, which averaged under 50 acres according to the Census of Agriculture for the year 1900. Their new land required a punishing amount of hard work to get it ready to produce results. But at least they owned it. That was a step up from most African Americans, who at the time were sharecroppers or tenants.

They were just one example of many of Granvill's and Eliza's descendants who were determined to control their destinies. Granvill's last surviving son, Marywether, still worked his land with his children. Others in the Plain Dealing group, included another brother and sister, and Rev. S.T. James and his wife, Eliza, who slowly continued to buy pieces of land. Jack's son, Isaac "Ike" owned a farm on which fourteen of his children worked with him. In the Lucy group, the Ford siblings inherited property from their father. In the Austin group, there were three family namesakes Austin, Granville, and Merriweather, who also acquired property.

Finally, there was another Granville Smith who bought some land. At first, I thought it was William's son, but after carefully examining all the documents for William, I no longer think so. But possibly there was a connection to an older brother of Lucy. I will need DNA evidence to show this is indeed the fact. Nevertheless, many of Granvill's kin found a way to buy land, or how to get good jobs working in the lumber industry. They did whatever it took to achieve their goal. I don't know precisely what they had to do each day to reach the desired result, but I know they didn't give up. It would seem that the origin of this high character of determination very likely came from Granvill.

4—772.

The United States of America,

TO ALL TO WHOM THESE PRESENTS SHALL COME. GREETING:

Homestead Certificate No. 4618

Application 7305

Whereas, There has been deposited in the GENERAL LAND OFFICE of the United States a CERTIFICATE of the Register of the Land Office at *Natchitoches Louisiana* whereby it appears that, pursuant to the Act of Congress approved 20th May, 1862, "to secure Homesteads to Actual Settlers on the Public Domain," and the acts supplemental thereto, the claim of *Granville Smith* has been established and duly consummated in conformity to law, for the *South West quarter of the South West quarter of Section six in Township twenty one North of Range twelve West of Louisiana Meridian in Louisiana Containing thirty nine acres and ninety two hundredths of an acre*

The deed for Granville Smith, a possible Granvill ancestor

Not all of the family's patterns were desirable. The Smith family had long ago hoped to leave behind everything having to deal with their life under slavery. Yet beginning in 1902, regrettably, they stumbled back as they came face to face with the American legal system. It was in a clash over the contested will of J.P. Vance, their former overseer on the Gilmer's plantation. The Smith family had many dealings with Joseph Patilow Vance. Right after the Civil War and during Reconstruction, Jane Smith, Granvill's youngest daughter was listed as the cook for J.P. in the 1880 United States Census. Jane and J.P. Vance had a daughter named Eliza.

In time, her husband S. Turner James became Rev. S.T. James, who was a prominent member of the Plain Dealing community. Vance also had served as the white Trustee for the local Mount Zion School along with S. T. James. Eliza, as well as her husband, Rev. S. T. James, cared for the frail Vance during the last seven years of his life. They took care of him as well as did the household chores and managed his several farms.

Wanting to repay those who helped him in his "old and helpless days," Joseph P. Vance's will clearly stately that he wanted most of his real estate to go to Eliza James. South Carolinian relatives of J. P contested the will and alleged that Eliza James was "a full woman of color." They claimed she was a bastard because she was an unacknowledged daughter of Vance and "a colored woman" named Jane. Even though everyone knew that Eliza was J. P.'s daughter, as stated by John Garner, a long-time family friend in the court documents, Jim Crow laws maintained that only the testimony of Whites was admissible. Only one white person, who was a friend, recalled that Mr. Vance lamented the fact that he didn't have a family, which he blamed on doctors who cautioned him not to have children due to an earlier disease he had contracted. But J.P. offered "Turner's wife as healthy as anybody," to contend the doctors were wrong.

With a backdrop of Jim Crow mentality, the case went against S.T. James, who appealed it to the Supreme Court of Louisiana. The court upheld the lower court's ruling. Undeterred, James sued the estate of J.P. Vance to recoup payment for assisting Mr. Vance in his later years. Again, the court ruled against him, and one more time, James appealed to the appellate court, which reversed the lower court ruling and awarded Rev. S.T. James $300 and court cost.

That would not be the only court case involving members of Granvill's descendants, land, and issues of interactions with blacks and whites. One of Lucy's daughters, Rebecca, had seven children with a white man, James A. Ford. In court testimony, he and his brothers were vilified because of "this strange and shameful departure from the paths of social rectitude and racial integrity" because all three Ford brothers "took up with negro women" and "reared families." The children of the eldest brother were trying to paint the youngest brother as insane in a property dispute.

Do these cases illustrate something about Granvill? Granvill's daughter, Lucy Ann, was listed as "yellow" in the bill of sale, which very likely means she was light-skinned. Austin, Marywether, and Samuel all married mulatto spouses. I wonder did they take a cue from Granvill to pursue mulatto spouses. Perhaps they wanted for their children the preferential treatment of mulattoes, who were more likely to be house and skilled slaves. Maybe it was something more sinister such that they had internalized feelings about blackness. Martin Luther King recognized that in the English language, the color black is used to connote evil, low, and dirty in words like blackmail, black sheep, and blacken. I am not sure what this pattern reveals. But on the other hand, these court cases, along with 489 recorded lynchings across the United States from 1900 to 1905, show legal protection from the law was not something African Americans could bank on. The unfairness of the treatment of African Americans in the legal system was very evident to our family.

I noticed another family pattern that also turned up in my life. My great-grandfather, Joseph P. Smith, found the circumstances of his life markedly changed in January of 1906. Rev. S.T. James signed the wedding license indicating that he had joined together in holy wedlock, Mr. Joe Smith, and Miss Pauline Lindsey. Pauline was the fifth child of Moses and Melvina Lindsey.

Around 1898, Moses and Melvina had moved to Bossier Parish across the Red River from nearby Caddo Parish with their eleven children due to several possible reasons. Extreme violence could have motivated them, since Caddo Parish was rife with the Klu Klux Klan. Caddo Parish leads the list for lynchings in Louisiana while coming in second for the whole country. Or it could have been an uptick in the yellow fever cases that occurred near the end of the century. This may have prompted them to seek the "fresh country air," hoping to avoid the disastrous 1873 outbreak of yellow fever that killed hundreds in Caddo Parish. Or maybe it could have been the lure of new land. The 1900 US Federal Census recorded that Moses Lindsey owned the property free and clear. Conveyance records showed that in 1898, Pauline's father had purchased 80 acres of valuable land not too far from the Red River.

Joe's marriage to Pauline followed a pattern seen in marriage all the way back to Granvill and Eliza. Joe was 29 years old while Pauline was 18. This age difference was wider than the median age of 25 for males and 22 for females in 1900, according to the US Bureau of the Census. This eleven-year age difference was no way near the 28-year gap for his grandparents, Granvill and Eliza, nor the 22-year difference for his parents, Samuel and Caroline. Those were not first marriages, just like his uncle William was 13 years older than his second wife, Laura. In the same way, Weilin is 16 years older than I am.

With first marriages, his uncle, Marywether and Ann, had a 12-year difference, and unbeknownst to him, there was a difference of 20 years between his uncle, Handy, and Mary, while another uncle, Jack, and his wife, Barbary, were seven years apart. Several Smith females, including Lucy Ann, with a 10-year-age difference, and Hanna Lou with a 16-year gap, also exhibited this pattern. Researchers today have found in cultures and times when the male is the provider, and the female is the homemaker, there is a broader gap in the ages of the two. Seemingly, this pattern points to Granvill and his male descendants feeling a strong drive to "bring home the bacon" and be great providers, while the females wanted wise and mature husbands.

I asked Weilin what he thought of these cross-generational age differences in my family, including us. He stopped for a moment and crossed his arms. He glanced down as he was thinking. Looking up with a sly grin on his face, he replied, "Maybe Granvill and the males on your father's side of the family age well, just like me!"

Whatever my great grandfather's reasoning, the new groom probably saw the qualities in Pauline Lindsey that many black women had in the 1900s in the South. Religion was central to her life, and the church was a refuge from the ugliness and oppressiveness of Jim Crow segregation realities. She sought to uplift the character of the Negro, as had been promoted by Booker T. Washington, by fervently adhering to the teachings of the Bible. When their first son arrived, Joseph P. and Pauline strove to bring him up in the ways of the Lord, always knowing right from wrong by using the words of the Bible to guide them.

They were continuing another pattern that ran both through the generations, actions that pointed to a strong religious faith. To find evidence of their religious practices, I collected as many obituaries of the Granvill's descendants as I could find. First, I started with my family with my grandfather, great-aunt, and uncle. Next, I requested obituaries from my DNA cousins. And finally, I scoured the information on Ancestry and Newspaper.com. I checked every family member with a Find-A-Grave link and found several had obituaries there. I was able to locate obituaries from most of my ancestor groups.

Granvill's descendants		List of activities dealing with religion in the obituaries
Lucy Group (1)		Sunday School teacher, on Mission Board, president of the Deacon Wives, attended church regularly
Austin Group (2)		Called to the ministry later in life Treasurer of the South Louisiana Conference, Stewart and Trustee for the church
Plain Dealing Group	Jack (3)	1 minister Adult Sunday School teacher, Superintendent of Sunday Schools, active and faithful for 90 years A deacon
	Marywether (2)	Sunday school teacher, deacon and elder later in life Sunday school teacher
	Samuel (7)	Chairperson on the Trustee Board of the church, 2 deacons 2 ministers later in life, loved reading the bible 1 elder 2 faithful and loyal members
	Jane (2)	Loyal church member for 50 years Sang in the choir
William & Handy Group (1)		Member

Table Listing a sample of religious activities found on obituaries in each of the groups

Placing them in a table, I saw several unmistakable patterns. First, like most African Americans, the descendants of Granvill found strength and unity through their church, where they were loyal members throughout much of their lives. But what struck me was how many of them had leadership roles. They were respected leaders in their church community, just like Joseph P. Smith, who obtained his minister license a few years after his marriage in 1911. Obviously, this list is only a tiny sample of Granvill's progeny, but since it spans across and through the generations, it very likely means that this pattern shows Granvill was loyal and respected by his community.

Meanwhile, the hostile environment of Bossier Parish became even worse. No doubt, Joseph P. and others in the Plain Dealing group, like other immigrants all over the United States, turned to ethnic newspapers to help them navigate their frightening world. For the first time, blacks over vast areas could know about events pertinent to themselves all over the United States. Besides the spread of African American newspapers, Black porters, such as Cheryl's uncle, while working on the railroad, relayed the news, gossip, and papers, which helped to keep the African American community informed. One of the most famous of these newspapers was the Chicago Defender, founded by Robert S. Abbott, who became very influential and was one of America's first black millionaires. Not only did these newspapers chronicle the plight of African Americans in brazen details, but they also wrote about places to live and job opportunities.

Another form of communication was the circular or what we would call a poster used for promotional purposes. Edward P. McCabe, a land developer and politician, used circulars to promote the All-Black towns in Oklahoma. Appealing to blacks that they could live in a safe haven free of Jim Crow laws, the Ku Klux Klan, and a chance for self-determination along with proving one's self-worth, McCabe was very successful at promoting All-Black towns. The largest settlement, Boley, was visited by Booker T. Washington in 1908 and featured in the same prestigious New York magazine that published his autobiography. Did Joseph P. and the rest of the Smith family read and discuss the news of their day in barbershops, at church, or in town meetings as other African Americans did at the time? We can never know.

Near the end of the first decade of the 1900s, those in the Plain Dealing group faced even more challenging times. The frightening ordeal began with something so small; it was barely the length of the white part of your fingernail. It was a tiny beetle - the boll weevil. Native to Mexico and Central America, the weevil had entered the United States in 1892 through Texas. Traveling an average of about 100 miles per year, it would infest the entire Cotton Belt by 1922.

The adult weevil laid their eggs inside the cotton plant just as it began to form. First eating the leaves and then the young cotton bolls, the weevil's life cycle completed itself with the release of adults ready to wreak their own havoc. One pair of weevils could generate two million descendants in one season. Once the little creature hit, farmers and officials were helpless to prevent a 50% decline in that area's cotton production. At the time, the local newspaper pages in Bossier Parish were filled with remedies such as burning or syrup to try to defeat the pest. With your acreage producing only half of its usual production, the only real way to maintain your income level was to increase your acreage, which most farmers were unable to do.

The economic impact of the boll weevil even caused small cracks in the application of  Jim Crow. In December of 1908, a letter appeared in the Bossier Banner under the heading of "Colored People Grateful." The letter, written in glowing terms to the Bossier Parish Fair Association, expressed their appreciation and praised those running the state fair. Written by S.T. James, it was signed "Your friends, The Colored Citizens." It turned out

Adult Boll Weevil

that the attendance for the Bossier Parish Fair was less than previous years due to the reduction of most everyone's income caused by the boll weevil infestation. An extra day was set aside for the previously excluded blacks to deal with the shortfall, and for them to present "colored people's exhibits." The extra day nearly brought the receipts up to the previous year, and the letter implied that the blacks hoped to for an invitation back the next year. Understanding what was happening right at that moment really gave me insight into what that letter insinuated and how much locale affects the life of an ancestor.

The year 1908 was also the year my grandfather, Lindsey, was born. They named him after his mother's maiden name. His birth increased the number of mouths needing to be fed to four, thus adding more weight to the predicament the boll weevil had caused. With many hurdles facing them in Louisiana, many in the Plain Dealing group finally felt compelled to leave Louisiana. Life was not easy for blacks in the South. Since the start of the century, the violence of over 600 lynchings had shattered their sense of security. Jim Crow segregation laws had thoroughly touched their schools, public housing, restaurants, theaters, trains, and so on. Louisiana was one of the first to place restrictions on voting using the grandfather clause, which gave African Americans no voice to try to improve their lives. Not only were blacks treated like less than second class citizens, but then they were called out for not living up to the highest moral character.

The coming of the boll weevil in Bossier Parish made making a living almost impossible. The last of Granville and Eliza's children, Marywether, had passed away in 1908. Their grandchildren decided to follow a script that had been developed by the Smith family while in bondage to the Gilmer family, and they moved to new lands. In the past, the Smith family had been moved from Georgia to Alabama and then to Louisiana. In their quest for better places to plant their crops, they now decided to move to Wagoner County, Oklahoma. As had been the case for over one hundred years, the exceptionally strong bonds in the Smith family provided support as they uprooted from Louisiana and moved to put down roots in Oklahoma. Twelve members of the Marywether Smith branch, including wives and children of Willis and Lewis as well as twelve members from the Samuel Smith branch, with Granville, William, and Joseph P. along with their wives and children, rode the train to Porter sometime in 1909. Advertisements about Porter claimed it had many lots of fertile land suitable for farming.

The new century had brought many struggles for the Smith family, and the groups took different paths. The younger men in the Plain Dealing didn't follow the pattern of most of Granvill's descendants. The Lucy Group mostly stayed in an area west of Plain Dealing. The members of the Austin group gradually spread out from where they started to other parts of the parish or nearby parishes. This was especially true for the females who married spouses in nearby Arkansas. In the Plain Dealing group, Jack's descendants tended to slowly spread out from Plain Dealing, with many going to Shreveport. The small William and Handy group had a small group in New Orleans and another in Shreveport. In pursuit of stability, almost all except a few chose to continue the pattern of the cotton way of life.

The day the Plain Dealing group of Smith family decided to start that journey to Oklahoma must have been chalk full of emotions. Typically, the train station was a communal event for blacks in the South. Apprehensive crowds included both those patiently waiting to leave and those who wished them farewell. The stylish travelers usually wore their Sunday best. Of course, no adult could step outside without a hat. The females wore long dresses or skirts with dark stockings. The men sported white shirts with some kind of tie, long jackets, and pants suited to the season. The small children in the group, which included my toddler grandfather, were probably as wide-eyed as any kid today, watching the commotion of all those animated people. Those in the family who stayed behind probably silently wondered if would they ever see the others again. Joseph P., Pauline, and the almost three dozen members of the Smith clan more than likely took the train together because a group discount lowered the cost for everyone. Jim Crow was ever-present as they had to buy the tickets in the "colored" ticket booth and traveled in the less than optimal, shabby Jim Crow coach. Did someone say or think of the words to the old hymn, "I am bound for the promised land?" When the shiny black steam locomotive puffing up steam finally pulled into the station, did the migrants associate the steam power with freedom and escape as blacks once did during slave times?

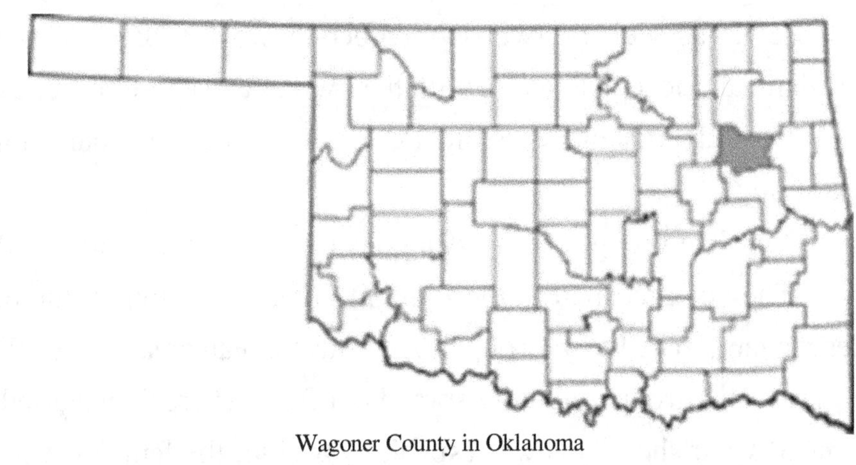

Wagoner County in Oklahoma

The Smith clan finally arrived in Oklahoma, the 47th state, created from former Oklahoma and Indian Territories. Situated in the Great Plains of North America, much of it was flat plains dotted with rolling hills, ridges, and small mountains. Their final destination was an area near the small town of Porter located in Wagoner County close to one of the three significant rivers in Oklahoma, that drain into the Arkansas River. They were part of a massive surge in the state's population from 1907 to 1910, including a 15% increase in the Porter area. Simultaneously, they contributed to a sizable decrease of blacks in Bossier Parish.

After leaving the Missouri, Kansas and Texas Railway depot station, the Smith clan most likely headed north to the Negro district. They needed to find the building where they could lease those farms that were available on formally Indian land. The slaveholding Five Civilized Tribes were required by Post Civil War treaties to free their enslaved African Americans and give them citizenship in the tribe with rights to land. Delayed for many years, many Creek freedmen in this area had only recently received their land. One of Lucy Ann's grandsons, who married a freedman of one of the other tribes, the Chickasaw, received her allotment in 1904. Each of my great-grandparents on my father's mother's side was Creek Freedman, who did not acquire their property until 1903. They then lived on his forty acres and leased out her allotment. These kinds of land allotments were what was available when the Smith clan arrived. The 1910 Federal Census showed the Smith family was spread out, living near a patchwork of farms that were both owned and rented. For the first time in over 75 years, the Smith clan broke the pattern of living together. However, it still must have been a blessing that the extended Smith family of my great-grandfather, Joseph P, including his brothers and cousins, could provide both physical and emotional support as they started their lives in this new land.

I had a little knowledge about the patterns of life on a farm because I was able to interview my 90-year-old great-uncle, who lived during this time. He told me they settled into a well-functioning routine of farm life, typically up early to take care of the animals and then out to the fields excluding Sunday, which was for church. When the older two boys trotted off to the Negro school, Pauline had her hands full with small children running around the house. She did the cooking, milked the cow, tended to the chickens and their eggs, hoed her garden, and cleaned too. And then, how did she get through corn shucking and cotton-picking time? This scene was similar to all of Granvill's and Eliza's grandchildren and great grandchildren's lives in Oklahoma and Louisiana.

The years from 1910 until 1914 turned out to be the golden years for agriculture in the United States. There were high prices for the fruits of their labor due to the increased demand for farm products. The US Department of Agriculture created demonstration farms to advise farmers on the latest techniques that improved productivity with hybrid seeds and fertilizers, developing ways various methods for controlling pests and diseases in plants and animals. New products were only a turn of a page away as the Sears Catalog carried the latest for the farm and the family. Joseph P.'s life was typical of the other members of the Smith family and close to half of the population in the US who lived in rural areas on small diversified farms that produced about five different commodities.

Life changed when the United States declared war on Germany. The Selective Service Act passed by Congress required men like Joseph P., between the ages of eighteen and forty-five, to register for the draft. Historians now know that The Great War, its name back then, had been caused by several notable factors. The Western Powers had become wealthy as they dominated and controlled almost all of the countries on every continent. By the time it began in 1914, Western imperialist countries had no way to grow except by taking territory away through war. The Great War dragged on for many years as neither side was able to advance. The soldiers on each side were trapped in trenches topped with barb wire and machine guns. We are left today with expressions that entered our lexicon, such as "in the trenches, "no man's land," and "over the top" as vivid reminders of that tragic war a century ago. These factors that caused this far away war finally crept to the US shores and even affected Granvill's kin.

When Joseph P. Smith was forty-two years old, he signed his name to the World War I Draft Registration card in 1918; he was the oldest of Granvill's 23 male kin with a Draft registration card. Using the data from these cards, I was able to gather data on whether their height was either short, medium, or tall, and if their build was either stout, medium, or slender. The results showed that the majority had a medium height and a medium build. Here is a chart of the results. Looking at the pattern of the heights and builds of Granvill's descendants, there is a strong probability that Granvill was also medium tall and medium built.

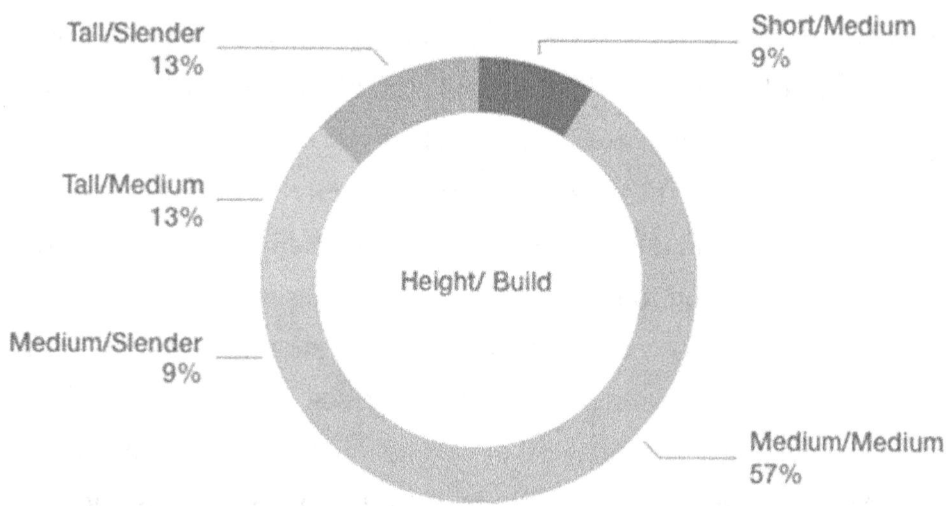

Percentages in each category of the 23 descendants with World War I Draft Registration cards

If Granvill's descendants were like most typical African Americans at the time, they were indifferent to that faraway European war. A weekly published black local newspaper, the Muskogee Cimeter, complained about President Wilson. He had boasted of keeping the US out of that war. But they thought he should worry more about the Americans (many who were the segregated unit the 10th Cavalry, known as the Buffalo soldiers) who had been killed by Mexicans in their mission to capture Pancho Villa in Mexico in 1916. These sentiments eventually changed. Germany's quest to get Mexico to join the Central Powers by sinking the British luxury steamship the Lusitania, with many Americans passenger one board, shifted public opinion. Both blacks and whites in the United States favored joining the war on the side of the Allied Powers fighting with the British, the French, and the Russian imperial powers.

By the time of the draft registration, World War I had been a boon to farmers like the Smith clan for several years. Prices for their agricultural products had been exceptionally high. With millions of the European farmers off to war in the military, the United States had been a critical supplier of not only agricultural products, but Model T cars, trucks, tractors and military equipment. Not only had the war been a boon to African American farmers but to factories in the North, which had ramped up production. The flow of immigrants from Europe had been halted due to the war. This caused labor shortages that were filled by blacks from the South. This change fueled the beginning of what became known as the Great Migration. Between 1914 and 1920, about 500,000 black southerners courageously migrated to the big northern cities, such as Chicago and New York. They were part of the first wave who sought better opportunities and relief from the effects of Jim Crow laws in the South. Most of Granvill's descendants didn't follow this pattern and waited until the later second wave of the Great Migration to move.

About 370,000 blacks joined the war effort. As some black soldiers from Oklahoma left for war, they carried a banner that said, "Do not Lynch Our Relatives while We are Gone." Some like Turner James Jr, who was the grandson of Jane Smith, joined the navy. The grandson of Austin, John Luther Loche, who lived in Louisiana, was one of the over 200,000 African Americans who crossed the Atlantic to serve. These men were most surprised by the warm welcome they received with little overt racism in France. Even though African American soldiers had to endure racial segregation at home, they had shown their patriotism, broadened their world perspectives, and been treated with respect in France. African Americans felt they could assert their rights as citizens as they protested racial injustice. The local newspaper wrote, "…we believe that since we have entered the world politics, Europe will be quick to see our hypocrisy in reference to our so-called democracy." African Americans had done their part, and now they felt they could demand that the nation live up to its ideals of democracy and rights for all of its citizens, no matter their race.

Turner James, grandson of Jane Smith

After World War I ended on what is now Veteran's Day, Nov. 11, 1918, Joseph P. and the rest of the world tried to get back to some semblance of normalcy, but the next year, 1919 turned out to be rather eventful. On March 15, a warm spring day, there was a break in what had been on and off showers. I wonder where Joseph P. and his family were when suddenly a black rotating cloud produced a funnel which zigzagged across the landscape. Did they hear the roar which sounded like an explosion followed by lightning and thunder punctuated by a torrent of heavy rainfall?

A tornado had struck Porter in the "thickly settled Negro district." With twenty-five houses demolished, it was miraculous that there were only two black fatalities, along with scores that were injured. A cotton gin, the Missouri, Kansas & Texas Railway depot, six business, the Negro Baptist Church, and the Negro schoolhouse were all destroyed. The report on this weather event recounted that of four teams of horsed tied near the railroad station, the tornado dipped over the first team, lifted the second and fourth teams while leaving the third team unscathed.

With no school for their three oldest children and no church to go to on Sundays, Joseph P. and Pauline, with their five children, left Porter. Did they stay with either of his siblings in Tullahassee or with her sister Mary in Tulsa? Whatever happened, I only know by the 1920 Census, they had moved to a nearby county.

The twentieth century brought new surprises and challenges for Granvill's progeny. As I examined their lives, I found many patterns, such as spouse age spans, the intensity of their religious activities, as well as their physical appearance.

These are the steps I took to find those patterns. First, I made an extensive timeline, gathering every document I could find for one person. I began with my great-grandfather. Next, I examined each record, looking for something unique. I kept in mind each census had something different, finding that the 1940 census provided the highest grade completed in school and the 1900 census asked mothers, the number of living children and how many children. Then, I researched to see if that aspect also occurred in other family members of my ancestor. If you have more records besides the census, marriage, military and land records, and obituaries, hopefully, you can discover even more patterns among your relative's descendants originating back to your ancestor.

Tendencies

It was a hot, humid day in the small village of Hosston, Louisiana. Jane Boyd, a granddaughter of Granvill and Eliza, was traveling 30 miles south to the city of Shreveport. This moment was the worst time for her to be sick. She desperately needed to take care of her children, who were still reeling from the death of their father. After the lumber jobs dried in Bossier Parish, he had taken the family across the Red River to work as a laborer on a farm in the Caddo Parish. Life was even more complicated since they didn't live near family. She tried not to think about her problems, especially since once she made it to the city, she had to watch out for automobiles.

Inside the hospital, white-clad nurses escorted Jane to the colored section. This newly built Shreveport Charity Hospital was a massive three-story building constructed with red brick. The diagnosis was not encouraging. The doctors told her she needed surgery for her fibroids. Unfortunately, a few weeks later, she died from complications of that surgery, orphaning her hapless children.

This heartbreaking account illustrates many of the dramatic changes in Western society. Granvill's descendants faced a world full of upheaval. This turmoil was due to the profound clash between all things traditional and the advent of the modern world beginning in 1920. Ready or not, economic, political, and social transformations were sweeping the world. Numerous countries granted women the right to vote. For the victorious nations in World

War I, there was an economic boom, especially in the cities. It was known as the Roaring Twenties in the U. S. and the Golden Age Twenties or Crazy Years in Europe. For the first time in history, urbanites made up the majority. In the cities, the beginnings of a mass consumer society motivated people to flock to buy cars, furniture, washing machines, movie tickets, and radio sets. While those in the rural areas, where almost all of Granvill's kin lived, saw their standard of living fall. The farm economy began its long downward trend. All over the world, the spread of nationalism, socialism, and workers' activism accompanied social unrest, unease, and heightened racial tensions. With opposite forces pulling the world forward and backward, how did the progeny of Granvill fare?

To find out what was happening to Granvill's descendants in the 1920s, I decided to create a spreadsheet listing the members of each generation of his kin. I began with Granvill and his daughter Lucy Ann along with his wife Eliza and their seven children. Generation 1 was Lucy Ann Smith and Jack Smith, born in Georgia, then Austin Smith, Marywether Smith, Samuel Smith, his twin William Smith, Handy Smith, and finally Jane Smith, all born in Alabama. For Generation 2, I listed each of their children, adding married names for the females. Thus, one of Lucy Ann's daughter was Amelia Smith BOWLER, and one of Austin's daughter was Emmerline Smith GRAY. Using the 1880 Census, I recorded whether they could read or write. From the 1900 Census, I listed whether they owned land, the number of female and male children. I tried to find the age of that the oldest and youngest child born to female descendants. I also tried to find the age at death, but it was not clear for many in the second generation due to a lack of records. This spreadsheet is a huge undertaking and not for the faint of heart. I labored a long time on this formidable goal. Fortunately, it yielded some insights, but it is also possible I could have just gathered data on specific topics.

By 1920, there were over 200 members of Granvill's heirs. Of these, there were 12 formally enslaved family members. The oldest was Emmerline Smith GRAY, daughter of Austin. Eventually, she would become the first of many descendants of Granvill, who lived to or passed the age of ninety-year-old, just like Granvill. Using the tag system recently introduced on Ancestry, I found 29 of Granvill's descendants under my 90+ custom tag. This longevity was one of many tendencies I noticed as I labored on my spreadsheet. After locating 630 plus of the first four generations of Granvill descendants, many, but of course, not all, were prone to behave in similar ways. Following the story of my family as the base, and adding on examples from the other lineages, I resurrected more of Granvill by identifying his offspring's tendencies. I also wanted to figure out how strongly was their inclination toward each tendency as they dealt with a changing world.

In 1920, Granvill's kin resided in the South Central States, including Louisiana, Arkansas, Oklahoma, and Texas. They probably lived there due to the similarity in climate and geography. Using their residence in the 1920 Federal Census, I established that most of the family still lived in Louisiana. But many had branched out to parishes outside of the former plantation areas of Plain Dealing, Bossier, and Bastrop, Morehouse. Many of Granvill's grandchildren that were born in the mid-1800s proudly owned their land. Others like James E. Gray, one of Austin's grandson, owned his grocery store in the town of Bastrop. Outside of Louisiana, one of Austin's daughters, Pauline Smith HUNTER, raised her family in Arkansas. One of Lucy Ann's granddaughters went to Texas. There were several groups in Oklahoma, in or near All-Black Towns. One large group of Lucy Ann's grandchildren lived in Boley, the largest and the best known of the over 50 All-Black Towns in Oklahoma. That group was in Boley very near its inception in 1904. I located my great-grandfather, Joseph P, near the All-Black Town of Red Bird in Gatesville Township, while his brothers, a sister, and several cousins were close by in another All-Black town named Tullahassee.

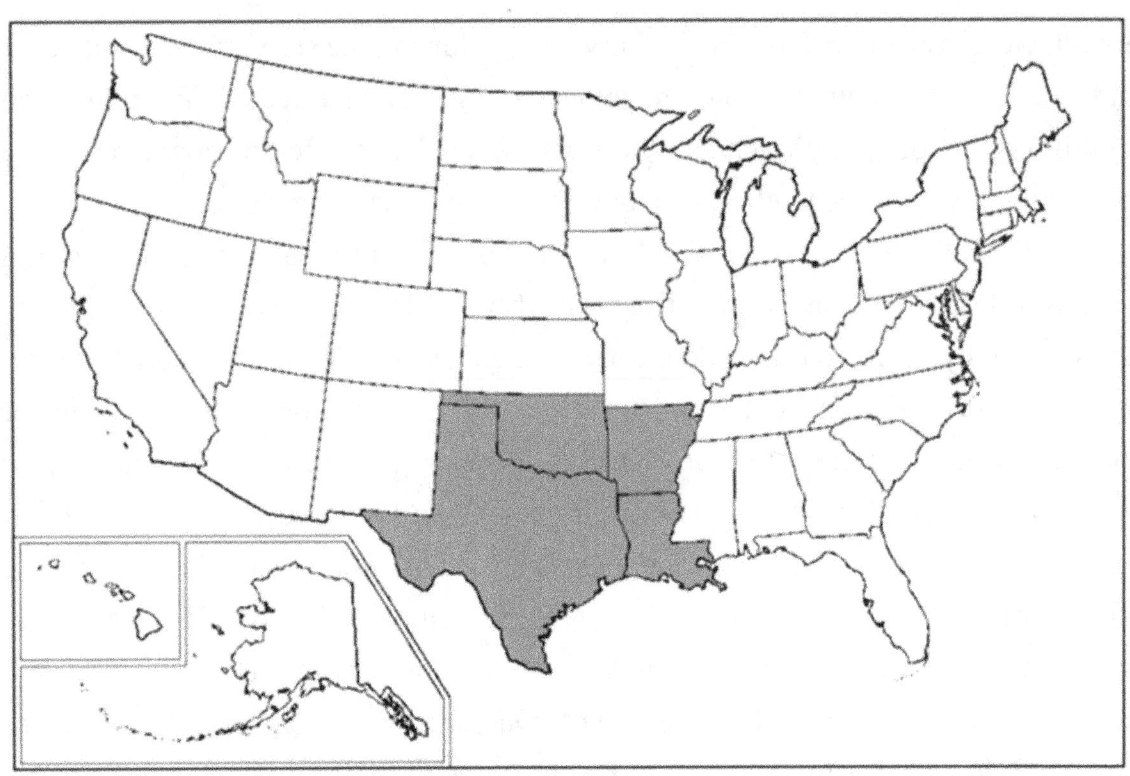

Map of the South Central States of Louisiana, Arkansas, Oklahoma, and Texas

At first, I didn't see any tendencies in looking at where Granvill's kin moved. Then one day, it all became clear after a misunderstanding between Weilin and I. It was a sunny day, so I began to adjust the vent in the car. Weilin nonchalantly chimed in, "You have to push the button if you want to turn the air conditioner on." After a long silence, he glanced over to notice my best "teacher look." That elicited from him both a shrug along with 'What did I do?" I crossed my arms and responded, "Why do you have to tell me what to do?" Since we are pros at understanding that this probably had to do with culture, we defused the situation by discussing his collectivist and my individualist point of view. He thought he was just being helpful, but then he wondered out loud why it bothered me so much.

Reflecting on the situation for a while, I realized that I am fiercely independent. I hate people telling me what to do, especially more than once. I take great pride in taking care of things before you even ask me. Not only that, if you tell me I can't do something (like girls can't learn math) ,I will prove you wrong. Suddenly, I understood the spirit of the Balanta people, those who resist. We tend to "do our own thing" like buying land or a store. After adding a column for occupation from the 1920 Federal Census, I found that over 75% were either farming on their own behalf or had other jobs, such as a teaching or even electrical work. Just under a quarter were laborers working on a farm for an employer like Jane's husband. Given a chance, I believe they wanted to toil on their own farm or live in a place where they could be self-sufficient, like in All-Black Towns. On a scale from extremely independent to not independent at all, I would say the inclination of being very independent was evident in many of Granvill's descendants.

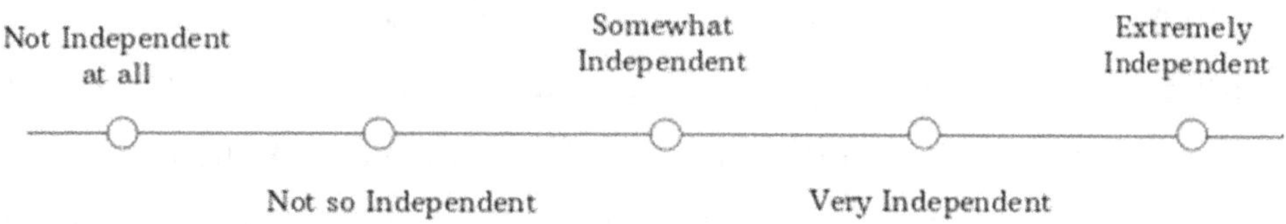

As hard as they worked, being a tenant farmer, or even a farmer in general, meant just scratching out an existence during the 1920s. Whatever they had, no matter what, the family was taken care of, no excuses. For example, near the end of 1920, a little five-year boy, one of Jane Boyd's hapless children, must have felt fearful as he scanned his new home and family. He needed somewhere to go after a personal tragedy had struck his parents. There was no remaining Smith clan in the Plain Dealing area after his father, Allen Boyd, had succumbed to the chronic bright disease, and his mother Jane died. The family decided that this little boy and his brother would go to Oklahoma. He came to live with his Uncle Joseph P., while his brother sent off to Uncle William. With the addition of five-year-old Allen Boyd, the family grew to six children. It must have been traumatic and scary for this little one. He had endured the agony of losing both his parents and being sent to live to a new place with relatives he barely knew. Knowing Joseph P., he turned to the Bible for comfort. Being a firm believer in living by the precepts of his Christian faith, it is plausible that he read the family the verse from the Bible. 1 Timothy 5:8 states, "If anyone does not take care of his own relatives, especially his immediate family, he has denied the faith worse than an unbeliever."

Other members of Granvill's offspring also were just as caring. In 1920 in Louisiana, Matilda Smith Ford, Jack's daughter, and her husband Rev. Leon Ford, as well as Marywether's daughter Fannie Lou Smith AIKENS, were raising their grandchildren. Julius A. Smith, a grandson of Austin, was providing for his mother and youngest sister, which delayed him marrying.

The most interesting case, I discovered, was Carrie Ford JACKSON's case. She was a twenty-three-year-old widow with three toddlers living with her mother, her younger siblings, and other small children of her cousins. As I usually do, I scanned the page just before, and immediately after the page she was on, so I could get a sense of her neighborhood and look for other relatives. It was striking that five women were widows, including her mother, on that page. This result was very likely due to the Spanish Flu.

This Influenza Pandemic of 1918-1919 killed between 20 to 50 million worldwide, with some estimates as high as 100 million victims. For some unexplained reason, it was the most fatal to people in their prime between the ages of 20 and 40. Another surprising fact is that the epidemic was far less devastating to African American communities. Why this was the case is still up for debate. Were blacks less susceptible to the Spanish flu or did segregated neighborhood function as a quarantine that limited exposure to those who had the flu? The light-skinned Ford's lived in a mixed-race neighborhood with other white farmers. Perhaps it was the latter. There is no way of knowing.

Granvill's descendants may have considered themselves to be following good Christian values. They may not have known that that child fosterage or the raising of children by relatives or even non-relatives was a widespread tradition in West Africa. They were following actions with deep roots, which if I put it on a scale of a strong sense of taking care of the family to not a strong sense at all, they - like most blacks - had a strong sense of taking care of the family.

At this same time, Granvill's descendants were not among the most ambitious African Americans in the United States. There was a group of hardy blacks who left the rural South in search of better economic opportunities between 1910 and 1920. Many were employed in industries in major northern cities such as New York, Chicago, Detroit, and Pittsburg in the first wave what was known as the Great Migration. Possibly Rev. S.T. James was among them. He had sold his land in Plain Dealing and headed to Oklahoma. He probably moved from Louisiana because there was a steep drop in the price of cotton after the end of World War I. Without the high demand for cotton, he, like other black tenants and sharecroppers, had abandoned cotton farming. On the other hand, those who tried to stay in agriculture saw their situation deteriorate. In rural areas, they lived on rented land typically in old, dilapidated houses.

The clash between rural and traditional versus city and modern was playing out in the United States and hit very close to my family. In a few places in large cities, blacks were thriving. A "New Negro Movement" sprang up in Harlem that espoused black pride, dignity, and creative expression. African Americans, who had spread to Chicago, Philadelphia, St. Louis, Detroit, and even closer in Tulsa, Oklahoma, wanted to drop the old negro slave image. The New Negroes movement, promoted by Marcus Garvey, was an avid preacher of "Back to Africa" as well as others such as the Oklahoma publisher, Roscoe Dunjee. In his newspaper, Black Dispatch, he promoted separate communities based on black pride.

These social and economic changes caused racial tensions, which erupted into violence. In 1921, the Greenwood District of northern Tulsa, Oklahoma could pride itself as one of the most affluent African American communities in the country. It was known as the "Black Wall Street," in part due to the oil.

On a summery day in June, everything would change for the sister and brother-in-law of my great-grandmother, Pauline, who lived in Tulsa. Sometime during the night, they were confronted by the smell of smoke. People were screaming with cries of anguish and running literally for their lives. An angry mob of white men was ordering everyone out of their homes, setting fires everywhere, and then preventing the arriving firetrucks from putting them out. Maybe they saw the terrifying airplanes dropping firebombs on the town. Was her husband part of the group of men awakened to be whisked away to a detention area?

Tulsa Riots in 1921

When it had ended, thick black smoke billowed toward the sky over a bleak landscape of 35 city blocks, reduced to nothing more than the charred ashes and rubble. Up to 10,000, people lost their homes and businesses, and up to 300 people died. An inflammatory article which accused a young black man, who had ridden the elevator to navigate to the only available colored bathroom, of inappropriate behavior toward the young white female attendant, set in motion the Tulsa Riots of 1921.

Enraged white masses attempted to lynch the young man, but were thwarted by both the police and a group of armed blacks. So, they turned their attention to loot and burn down Black Tulsa. The National Guard, based in the area, rounded up the blacks trying to defend themselves, leaving their property in Greenwood defenseless. Just like the over 3,000 cases of lynching of African Americans, no whites were ever charged in this grievous riot. Unbelievably, some whites sent others postcards of the smoking remains of the destruction to celebrate the violence. The Ku Klux Klan would never be indicted for starting the riot, but their "spirit of lawlessness" paved the way for this brutality to occur.

Where did Pauline's sister and brother-in-law go after these horrific riots? The Red Cross provided tents for the victims. Did they stay with the Smiths as they tried to rebuild their lives? Joseph P. and the other blacks in Oklahoma were probably baffled by conclusions of the grand jury at the time who place the causes of the riot squarely on the African Americans for trying to stop a lynching. Further reasons included "the agitation among negroes of social equality," and the added excuse of the breakdown in law enforcement, who didn't enforce vice laws in Greenwood. This rationale referred to displeasure that W. E. B. Dubois, the head of the NAACP, had visited this area in the last year and that "whites and colored" mingled together to listen to jazz in the dance halls. Probably embarrassed, the residents of Tulsa wanted to brush this incident under the rug as quickly as possible and did not thoroughly investigate it again until 1997. But many in the rest of the United States were appalled. Ministers in pulpits across the land condemned these actions, as did major newspapers.

As one of the worst race riots in U. S. history, the Tulsa Riot could be considered the lowest point in black/white relations. Even during slavery, slaveholders did not indiscriminately kill African Americans because they were valuable property. But I was shocked to find this was one of 26 racial conflicts that raged between 1919 and 1921. There were riots near other branches of Granvill's tree. For those in Northeast Texas, there were the Longview Race Riots of 1919, and even worse, the Elaine Race Riot of 1919, five white men and 200 African American men, women, and children were murdered in Arkansas. I can't imagine how tense and traumatic this period must have been for African Americans. Somehow, they had the mental tenacity to move on. It seems that they were able to manage the stress and the crisis. Maybe with comfort from Bible verses like 2 Corinthians 4:8-9, "We are afflicted in every way, but not crushed: perplexed, but not driven to despair: persecuted, but not forsaken; struck down, but not destroyed."

As life went on, in June of 1922, Joseph P. and his wife Pauline, along with Granville and his wife Carrie watched as the notary public for Wagoner County carefully typed out the information about their property in Bossier Parish, Louisiana. They were dividing the previously undivided property. Granville had 20 acres because he had already sold 20 acres. With his signature, the other 40 acres now belonged to Joseph P. and his heirs forever, as it said. It was very likely that Granville needed the extra money to make ends meet on the farm he owned in Oklahoma. Unfortunately, besides having to deal with upheavals in the political area, farmers were dealing with economic uncertainty. New technology and the modernization of farming techniques led to an expansion in agriculture and overproduction. Prices plummeted, which increased the desire for farmers to grow more to make up for lost revenue, which only made matters worse. Soon the living standards for farmers declined.

Even as many urban Americans prospered in the 1920s, it was a disastrous period for farmers. As prices for seed, fertilizer, and machinery went up, their incomes declined markedly. Over time, farmers had moved from being self-sufficient to the bare minimal subsistence farming and poverty. Tenant farmers, like Joseph P. in Oklahoma, his brother Frank Smith in Texas, relatives George Paysinger in Arkansas, and Lucian Ford in Louisiana and could barely scrape together a living. In cases where the father of the family died early, such as William, Handy, and Jeff Smith, along with the husbands of Amelia, Jane, and Fannie Lou Smith, life for their children was even more tenuous.

Several of Granvill's male descendants found work in the lumber industry. In Morehouse Parish, for some reason, many of Granvill's kin did not show up in the 1920 census, even though they were in the 1930 census. Of those found, most were in the city, just like a few others, who found work in the cities of Shreveport and Benton, Louisiana. One of the highest achieving descendants of Granvill and Eliza was a female. Rosa Lee Smith was the great-granddaughter of Lucy Ann, and a teacher, according to the 1920 census. Granvill and Eliza's descendants did not tend to be the ambitious type. Slowly, in time, more and more of Granvill's kin would follow the more ambitious African Americans, and leave the agricultural way of life.

Under Jim Crow laws, Granvill's offspring attended segregated schools since the early 1900s. For example, Joseph's children sat in one of the 604 black schoolhouses in Oklahoma. Unlike some parents who kept their children home to work on the farm, being a huge proponent of education, Joseph P. made sure his children went to school. Back when Joseph P. had gone to school in the 1890s, the enrollment rate was only 1 out of 3 blacks in school. By 1900, blacks who attended school averaged to get to a 5th-grade level education, while Joseph P. and his siblings had obtained an impressive 8th-grade education. It was so important to him that Joseph P. would later register his disapproval of his children dating anyone who didn't have a good education. In the Austin group, James, my DNA cousin, told me that the Gray and Smith families put pressure on themselves to do well in school. As a group, they always wanted to maintain their reputation for being smart.

Sadly, in 1920, there were only ten accredited black high schools in the entire state of Oklahoma. By 1933, a report on secondary education showed that there were only 16 accredited black high schools between the states of Louisiana, Florida, Mississippi, and South Carolina. Noting gross inequities such as the value for library holding for the black schools was about $5,000. At the same, it was almost $300,000 for the white schools. Perhaps Joseph P. was among the numerous groups of parents who filed lawsuits that tried to improve the situation to little avail. Nonetheless, he also required reading and studying the Bible, a big part of his children's education, and found a way for them to attain the highest levels possible.

The 1940 Census showed there was a wide variation in the level of education Granvill's descendants acquired from first grade through four years of college. It seemed to depend on how close one was to a high school or college. Those in the cities had a better chance of getting more education. Lucy Ann's great-grandchildren in the All-Black town of Boley either finished high school or attended college. My DNA cousin, Cheryl's mother, and her uncles and aunts also went to college in the city of Beaumont, Texas.

The extent of schooling also depended on the individual. In some families, some of the children were able to get more education. For example, in an article about Zelda Ruby Cullen, one of Jack's great-grand-daughters, it noted that she "had a good vocabulary, was good in math, and had excellent reading skills," so she became a teacher. She later received a BA from Grambling University. Zelda was a teacher after my own heart. She received awards for teaching in both first grade and high school math. Yet her siblings had from a 5th to 7th-grade education. Being committed to education was an aspiration of many of Granvill's progeny. This tendency was not as strong as being extremely committed to education.

Before I met my husband, I wondered, probably like others, why the Chinese had a reputation for doing well in school. I found the Chinese are extremely committed to education on a scale of extremely committed to no commit at all to education. I was better able to understand this characteristic with an explanation from Weilin and watching how his family operated. He explained the Chinese have a well-known saying that goes something like this, "Even if you are not smart, diligence and hard work can make up for it." A poor villager from China, who eventually went on to be the first to attend college in the village, illustrates this quote. He said:

"As a student you must be good. You have to be the top student. But I'm a slow student. I'm not clever or smart compared with many of my fellow students. I had to spend more time studying than the others because I'm not a quick learner. In high school, I spent most every Sunday studying, but in those days, we could not stay up very late because at 10 p.m. the whole school turned off its lights. So, I always got up at least one hour earlier than the other students and did my morning reading and memorizing and reading aloud before they got up. That's how I became a good student."

Not only is effort stressed over ability, but everyone in your family from your parents, grandparents, aunt, and uncles set high and consistent expectations for you to do well in school. So, the first utterance from family members or even one of his friends was, "how is (your child's name) doing in school?" All this helped me to observe how being extremely committed to education looks like. It's interesting that the former First Lady, Michelle Obama, came from a family that was also extremely committed to education.

With separate and unequal schools, what other ways did Granvill's kin press on? Joseph P. Smith, his brother Granville C. Smith and some of their children forged a way to fight against segregation. They became members of the oldest and most active fraternal groups in their state, the Prince Hall Masons. The fraternity was also in Bastrop, where Julius Smith, a grandson of Austin, was a member. The Grand Lodge in Boley, the largest All-Black town at that time, served as the headquarters for Oklahoma's Prince Hall Masons. Lucy Ann had several ancestors who possibly were members, especially since Prince Hall freemasonry was an integral segment of the black community.

Many of the founding fathers such as George Washington, Ben Franklin, and Paul Revere were Freemasons. Prince Hall, an African American, started a branch for blacks by establishing a Lodge near the end of the 1700s. They became an indispensable part of the community. There were hundreds of Lodges in Oklahoma, as well as other states by the 1920s. The primary purpose of the Freemasons was to cultivate character and self-improvement through study while promoting social equality, individual liberty, religious freedom, democracy, education through philanthropy, and volunteerism. While Jim Crow attitudes sought to keep the "colored in their place," the Prince Hall lodges provided both social opportunities and a training ground for leadership development.

This cultivation was yet another way to fight against entrenched stereotypes of inferiority. Besides affording companionship, these men tried to meet the needs of society by sponsoring recreation projects and dances. Their charitable activities included providing funds for the needy as well as burial insurance. Joseph P. was a contemporary to many very famous Prince Hall Freemasons such as Garrett A. Morgan, the inventor of the traffic light and gas mask, Robert Abbot, the founder of the Chicago Defender newspaper, Booker T. Washington, W. E. B. Dubois as well jazz artists Duke Ellington, Louis Armstrong, and Count Bassie. Being connected to the community through Prince Hall Freemasons was evidence of Granvill's kin being at least somewhat committed to the community, which researchers give as another one of the characteristics of strong families.

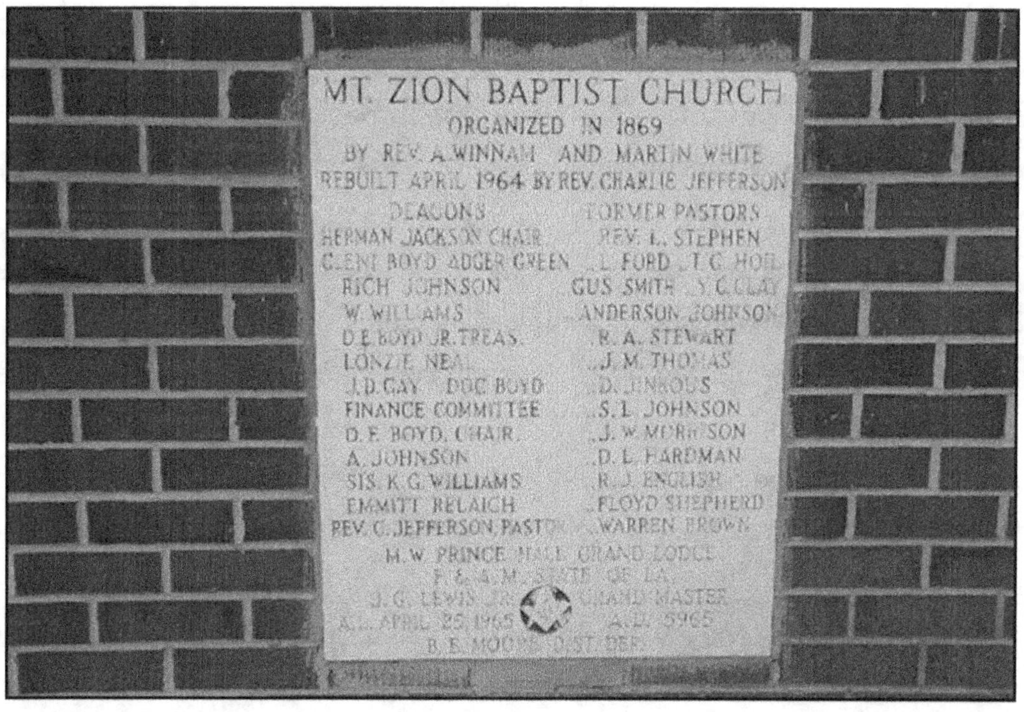

Plaque on the Mt. Zion Baptist Church with Freemasonry Inscription

As I was finishing up the last edit on this chapter, I decided to find out if I could find more family members of Granvill's progeny who were Prince Hall Masons. I posted this photo of a plaque that is on the side of the Mt. Zion Baptist Church on a private group on the Facebook page dedicated to Plain Dealing Genealogy. The Administrator, Karen Berney, recalled that a fellow genealogist wrote a book about the Prince Hall Masons. She had a list of the members for Plain Dealing Lodge # 52, which she had on a flash drive. Eventually, she provided the list of members from 1907 with my great-grandfather and two of his older brothers as officers. Other members included cousins, in-laws, and other relatives. I couldn't believe my eyes. Over one hundred years ago, Granvill's kin were systematically helping their community in an organized fashion, and there are records to prove it. That just goes to show you that genealogists rock; you never know what documents you might find, so never stop trying.

Being in Prince Hall Freemasonry was a place to retreat from facing the growing pains of the 1920s. With growing urbanization, many lashed out against what they saw an affront to their traditional values. Many of the whites had strong an affinity with Southern ideals, especially church-going Christianity, political conservatism, and segregation. Noting the "Roaring Twenties" seemed to bring vices such as bootlegging, prostitution, gambling, as well as a fear of the growing communist ideology and black nationalism, the Ku Klux Klan (KKK) found a fertile place to grow its membership. The adherents mushroomed in Oklahoma and other Southern states, as the civil leaders, local law enforcement officers, Protestant ministers, businessmen, and even members of the white Masonic lodges began their reign of violence and terrorism. Not only did they target blacks, but the Klan also targeted European immigrants, American Indians, Jews, Catholics, other religious groups, and anyone else that did not uphold their moral standards. Midnight whipping parties were a notorious form of punishment used to flog any offender and sometimes even white criminals.

As if the KKK was not enough to be worried about, the 1930s brought more misery. Granvill's offspring probably didn't pay attention to what was happening far away on Black Friday on Wall Street. During that week in October of 1929, the market lost an astonishing $30 billion, which would be more than a third of a trillion dollars in today's economy. Most farmers had already struggled through the agricultural depression in the 1920s, but by 1931 prices for produce and other farm products had tumbled down to disastrous levels.

Joseph P.'s income fell, just like the gross income of all Oklahoma farm crops and livestock, dropping from $314 million in 1929 to $115 million in 1932. That was in line with an average 60% drop for income across the country. Then once more, in their early fifties, Joseph P. and Pauline or Big Papa and Big Mama, as they were called, took in another little boy. His young mother had just died, and she was the daughter of his sister who had passed away. Fortunately, for this boy named John L., Big Papa, and Big Mama, lived into their 80s. Not only was longevity, as stated before, was a tendency in Granvill's descendants but Granvill, his son Samuel, and several others had children in their fifties and sixties. Come what may, life at this time was trying.

The Great Depression affected both black and white farmers with an equal vengeance as they were steadily ground down to the poverty level. The famous black sociologist William Julius Wilson stated, "The Great Depression had a leveling effect, and all groups really experienced hard times: poor whites, poor blacks." Sometimes the weather also seemed to turn against them with drought, record heat, and pestilence that destroyed their crops. Farmers had little money to buy anything. Everyone was poor.

Fortunately for Granvill's kin who were still on farms, they could feed themselves with produce from the farm. Perhaps they had a garden which was meticulously tended to by others just like Big Mama. The boys got up each morning before school to milk the cows, which bought in a little money. Big Papa and probably others lived by the motto used during the Great Depression "Repair, reuse, make do, and don't throw anything away." He was often trying to tinker and fix things. Did Big Mama or any of other mothers in Granvill's progeny use the big sacks of flour or livestock feed to sew dresses, boy's shirts, and even underpants? As part of the emergence of consumerism, which encourages buying "stuff," flour and chicken feed sacks often had patterns and flowers as an incentive to get people to buy their products.

For African Americans living in the cities, life was even worse. By 1932, almost half of black Americans were out of work. Whites called for blacks to be fired as long as whites didn't have jobs. African Americans received little help from the government, including both the small tenant farmers in the rural areas and the workers in the urban areas. Nevertheless,

African Americans were impressed with the ideas and energy of President Franklin Roosevelt. Leaving the Republican Party of Lincoln, voting patterns changed as blacks swung to the Democratic Party. Many blacks felt "a sense of belonging they had never experience before" from Roosevelt's fireside chats. Roosevelt did bring blacks into his administration as advisors, but discrimination continued in New Deal housing and employment projects. Without a doubt, with continuous support from prayer, Granvill's clan was not driven to despair.

Rated on a scale of religious conviction, having a very strong conviction was probably Granvill's descendant's highest-rated tendency. There was evidence in almost every obituary that I could find. Members on every line of Granvill's tree have references to being loyal and faithful members of their respective churches, along with many being active as Sunday school teachers, deacons, and ushers. This iron-clad conviction began when they were young. For example, my father joked about putting on his Sunday best and not being able to go out and play in his clothes when he was a boy, which conveyed the message that church always came first. My DNA cousin, Cheryl, had fond memories from her childhood of her grandmother. Addie was kind and deeply religious. She became an elder who ministered in Louisiana and Texas, similar to Ray Hester, a descendant of Marywether, who served in Oklahoma. Just before her beloved grandmother's death, she recalls, "she told me someday that she would see me in heaven. She said it with authority and conviction, and I believe her."

This strong religious conviction meant that not only did they talk the talk, but they walked the walk. A granddaughter of Samuel was typical in that she was the choir director, school teacher, and clerk at her church. There were several Reverends including Rev. Emmett C. Smith from Austin's side and my great-grandfather, Rev. Joseph P. Smith, who began his career on the pastoral team at Blue Creek Baptist Church.

As a matter of fact, my grandparents, Lindsey and Luticia, met and were married at the church in 1931. John L., the little one whose grand uncle and aunt took on the roles of Big Papa and Big Mama, recalled watching the festivities of the reception at the house and him getting his first taste of liquor. No doubt it was homemade because this was during the waning years of Prohibition.

How did they survive personal tragedies in the family, deal with the worst race riots in American history, and an unwelcoming racist society teeming with the KKK, plus live in poverty because of horrific financial conditions due to the collapse of farm products prices and the worst weather in years? What kept Joseph P., along with most African Americans, from being crushed under all these burdens? In 1972, Dr. Robert B. Hill, a black social psychologist, set out to identify the family strengths that allowed blacks to not only survive but advance in a hostile world. By going beyond the usual US Census statistics, which reinforce negative stereotypes of African Americans, Hill focused on what contributed to the resilience of the black family. He found five strengths — strong kinship bonds, a strong religious orientation, adaptability of family roles, a high achievement orientation, and a strong work orientation.

Granvill and Eliza's descendants demonstrated all of these strengths. For example, Joseph P.'s siblings kept a strong bond with the other siblings through letters, especially the youngest sisters Addie Lee and Bessie. Then there was the previously demonstrated unselfish generosity, Joseph P. and his wife, Pauline, took in a small little boy who was their grandnephew after his mother died. Dr. Hill found that black families were more likely than white families to absorb a younger related family member, which strengthened kinship bonds. And, like many of Granvill's kin, the family lived very closed to each other right after the Civil War, where a group of Hodge siblings, Lucy Ann's kin, supported each other in Michigan. All these examples were evidence of strong kinship bonds that seemed to continue through the generations.

John L., who grew up in Big Papa house, told me that he and the two younger sons understood that they had to work hard on their chores and equally achieve at school. Remarkably, doing this time of deep financial distress, somehow enough money was finally saved to buy their land in 1935. As was typical for most African Americans, they were told that they had to work twice as hard as whites just to survive. The grandfather of my DNA cousin, James E. Gray II, was teaching at the Morehouse Parish Training School, where he was more than likely instilling this work ethic in his students. The enduring memory of the grandchildren of Eva Alford, one of Austin's descendants that lived for over 90 years, was she instilled "a strong work ethic." Hence, Granvill's descendants had the tendencies of taking care of the family, a strong religious conviction, a commitment to education, and a strong work ethic, which helped them to be resilient. Many African American families had these characteristics, but by using a scale for each characteristic, this reveals the unique emphasis each family put on each area. Some may have been more committed to education, while others, like our family, were more committed to religion. Dr. Hill noted back then as well as now that blacks have the lowest suicide rate of all races. Again, pointing to how these factors helped create supportive environments that shielded against the suffering and adversity of the times.

For Granvill's descendants, the 1920s ushered in a time of economic uncertainty and political upheaval in a modern world with electricity, shiny automobiles, talking motion pictures, radios and airplanes. Many of the tendencies of our family enabled them to endure. The tendency of many of Granvill's kin to live long ensured their families had a long, stable environment. Being committed to their families, churches, and community was instrumental in building resilience needed to combat racism. And the tendency to taking care of the vulnerable family members provided a safeguard against tragedies.

Others found different ways to handle these hardships. The creative genius, Walt Disney, released the hugely popular animated film, The Three Little Pigs, in 1933 during the Depression. Its memorable song "Who's Afraid of the Big Bad Wolf?" became a rallying call. It symbolized that if everyone worked together, they could defeat the Big Bad Wolf, which was symbolic of the Depression. Ushering a new era of consumerism and movies, this was the first film to have a higher gross-receipts from merchandising than from the movie, which included storybook, watches, sand bucker, and soap figurines dedicated to the Pigs.

Most families endured these trying times but were not unscarred by anxiety that it could happen again. Sometimes they demonstrated their resilience, their dedication to time-honored principles such as taking care of the family's children, and others even used creativity. Each of us needs to find how our ancestors used their strengths to endure whatever life threw at them to get a better understanding of their unique inclinations and tendencies.

In Your Genes

With every intriguing story or perspective, I have found about Granvill and his life, Weilin never fails to ask me, "Is that enough to show him as a distinct individual?" He's right; if I am going to resurrect my 3rd great-grandfather, Granvill, I will need to find his uniqueness. When he was alive, his body, like all humans, would have had been made of trillions of cells. Each cell had a nucleus with 23 pairs of chromosomes. The chromosomes have short segments of DNA known as genes. He would have had almost the same genes arranged in the same order as all other humans. In the year 2000, scientists discovered that humans are 99.9% alike, when they mapped the human genome. That 0.1% difference in the total genetic code for our species is what makes each of us unique.

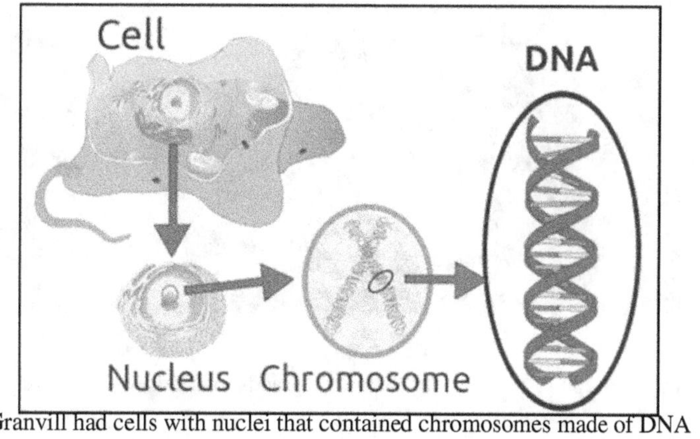

Granvill had cells with nuclei that contained chromosomes made of DNA

The key to our uniqueness is literally in our genes. Genes are strands of DNA that have the instructions like a recipe of how the body should function and what genetic traits should be expressed. For example, almost certainly, Granvill had very curly hair because the genes he inherited from his parents instructed each of his hair follicles to grow very curly hair. Humans have over 20,000 genes. Less than 1% of them contribute to the small differences between people. Since each gene has two copies, one part is inherited from each parent. Siblings each get half of the genetic information from each parent but don't inherit the same combinations. So that's what makes each of them different from each other. Each of Granvill's children inherited about 50% of his genetic information, while his grandchildren inherited about 25% of his genes. Since each succeeding generation receives half as much as the previous generation, I might have inherited about 3% of Granvill's genes. Which of my physical features, traits, abilities, personality traits, health disorders, diseases, and other characteristics could I have inherited? And what have his other descendants have inherited?

One of the hints I found was a startling discovery I made why developing a poster on DNA in my family. First, I edited each photo of my great-grandfather, Joseph P. Smith, his son, Lindsey Smith, and my uncle, Charles Smith, into a square so I could fit it on the poster. Suddenly some similar features of their faces popped-out. Curiously, I began hunting through the Gallery on the Ancestry website of as many of Granvill's kin as I could find. My DNA cousin, Rashawn, had a photo of Eliza Jane Garner. She was born one year after Joseph P., and even though they were 1st cousins once removed, they looked so much alike.

Samuel Smith's son, Joseph P.   Samuel's grandson, Lindsey   Jack Smith's granddaughter, Eliza Jane

Next, I continued checking every photo I could find of Granville's descendants, especially those not on my lineage on Ancestry. Within the images I found on the families of Lucy Ann, Jack, Austin, Marywether, and Samuel, I encountered a mix of similar features. There were slightly wider set eyes. The triangular-shaped nose was more prevalent in the lineages of Jack, Marywether, and Samuel. I also found the smaller ears in the males on the Austin and Samuel lines. I will never know for sure, but since I know Granvill was dark, I believe the tone was deep brown, but not ebony. He very likely had brown eyes and black tightly curled hair in his youth. I hypothesize that Granvill had an oval face with wide-set eyes, sparse eyebrows, a not to large triangular pointed nose, slightly thin lips, and small ears that were attached. It seems that working in the realm of genetics might be a way to learn more about Granvill. What other traits, characteristics, and attributes could I find?

Let's look at an example that involves personality. In 1935, the hardy band of Joseph P. Smith's household trampled over the loose dirt as they scaled the small slope leading toward the one-story house with to a wide porch. Once inside the door, my dad told me there was a living room suitable for hosting guests. It had enough room for a towering player piano and the usual sofa and tables. In the kitchen, which was small by today's standard, Big Mama was delighted to find just the place for all her special cookware and fancy blue and white dinnerware. It didn't have indoor plumbing, which meant that if the well out back went dry, one of the strapping teenage boys had to get water from the creek about a mile away. But it did have electricity. Big Papa could read day or night by the light of a lamp. Now at any time, if any of the boys misbehaved, not only would there be stern looks, but there was enough light for fetching the Bible to read the required scriptures. But the most monumental fact of all was that it was their own house. For almost two hundred years, since the removal of their first ancestor from their home in West Africa, this Smith family had lived in tiny, decrepit dwellings provided by the slaveholder or landowner. Joseph P. now had stepped beyond just freedom to what "Blacks held firm to perceived economic truth: land ownership held the key to success." At the time, Joseph P. could be counted as the one in eight blacks that owned the land on which he worked. He was probably the last of the 60% of Granvill's kin that owned land at the time. Like the aging couple in the Bible, Abraham and Sarah, Big Papa and Big Mama, now in their late fifties, must have felt similarly blessed finally to have their very own home.

One remarkable thing about this home is that Big Papa built it. It took a long time because he had to plan and tediously construct it after the completion of the daily chores. Unquestionably, all the boys helped, just like his contribution to building the church and school in Plain Dealing. He was not the only Granvill descendant that constructed his own home. I heard and read about several others. Another one of the descendants of Lucy Ann Smith named Porter Lee Ford was described as a jack of all trades being skilled in auto maintenance, carpentry, plumbing, and any type of electrical work. James Austin Gray told me his family developed a family crest that had a hammer to symbolize their connection to construction. From the Jack side, Kerry Williams, a DNA cousin, formed a construction/engineering firm. In my spreadsheet, I have three carpenters listed under occupation. Was this just a coincidence? Ever since I found out that my DNA cousin James Austin Gray and I both had careers that involved studying mathematics, I wondered if there was any connection to Granvill.

With a little digging, I found that an American psychologist, John L. Holland, had developed a theory of six types of careers and vocational choices based on personality types.

Job Personality and Work Environment Types (and what they do)	
Realistic	(Doer)
Investigative	(Thinker)
Artistic	(Creator)
Social	(Helper)
Enterprising	(Persuader)
Conventional	(Organizer)

Table listing the Job Personality and Work environment types with a descriptive word about what they do

Each category has a range of jobs depending on how much education is needed. Under the Investigative listing, I found loggers, brick masons, carpenters, ironworkers, construction, contractors, aerospace engineers, civil engineers, mathematicians, psychiatrists to lawyers. Many of those occupations are in my spreadsheet from census data on Granvill's progeny in the past. It also includes the careers of many of my DNA cousins.

The personality traits for Investigative Personality Types include being analytical, curious, independent, and preferring to work with ideas. That sounds a lot like me. Since I found evidence of the Investigative Personality Type on multiple lines, working backward, we could have inherited this job personality type from Granvill. I wondered if maybe all blacks come out with this personality type. I used this process on my mother's side of my family. It disclosed a long line of teachers and ministers from the Social Personality (Helper) type. Next, Weilin's side had chefs, merchants, clergy, Training managers, and financial department heads all under the Enterprising Personality (Persuader) type. As a math teacher, I am a bit of both of my parents. This split makes perfect sense because researchers have found that musical ability is 50% inherited. Thus, others of Granvill's descendants could have inherited another personality type from the non-Granvill side's parent. Inheritance and finding career personality types are tricky, but I do believe it points us in the right direction.

I am sure my great-grandparents felt blessed and proud to have their own home, but I often wondered what kind of personality trait helped them to survive under Jim Crow segregation. An American politician, Sen. Jim Webb, once said, "The injustices endured by black Americans at the hands of their own government have no parallel in our history, not only during the period of slavery but also in the Jim Crow era that followed." How did they handle the racism and constant humiliation of being treated like second-class citizens?

No one really talks about how it felt. I must confess, I have not had to deal with that kind of racism. To me, racism in the twenty-first century is akin to the tree nut allergy my daughter has. It is always in the back of your mind, and at mealtimes, you have to be especially careful to avoid eating tree nuts. Hence, racism is always in the back of your mind. And, you are always careful with your behavior, especially while dealing with law enforcement. Racism back in the early twentieth century seems more like having my dreadful spring allergies all year long. You are always miserable, and relief is only relative.

How much did these little victories, such as finally getting a home, help those like Joseph P. to cope? I utilized the Big Five Personality traits to examine the behavior the Granvill's kin. Perhaps one reason they survived is due to the Big Five personality trait of neuroticism.

If you score high on neuroticism, you are vulnerable to unpleasant emotions such as anger, anxiety, and depression. Research found at the National Institute of Health confirms the fact the most African Americans tend to score low on neuroticism. It is almost certain Granvill's descendants inherited low scores on neuroticism. That result means their emotional stability helped them to weather racism.

Their new home was near Taft, a small town just west of the city of Muskogee, in Muskogee County. Located south of their former residence in Wagoner County, Taft was on land allotted to Creek freedmen. Joseph P.'s grandnephew, who he raised, commented he only saw blacks throughout the town and neighborhood. This town was one of more than fifty All-Black towns. He didn't know at the time, but there was no other place that boasted more All-Black towns than Oklahoma. Spanning from right after the Civil War in 1865 up until 1920, African Americans found some relief from discrimination and the indignity of segregation in All-Black towns.

What in this place could aid him and his family lighten the bitter effects of racism, segregation, and discrimination? In these towns, everyone depended upon each other for help and financial assistance. These communities supported businesses, schools, and churches as well as being small agricultural centers run by blacks for blacks. Most of the others of Granvill and Eliza's kin did not live in All-Black towns, but they did live on farms or worked at businesses that they owned. They all tried to control their world as much as much as possible, be independent, and supportive. Being loyal, helpful, and kind are components of the Big Five personality trait of agreeableness. That's another way they could have lessened the impact of racism.

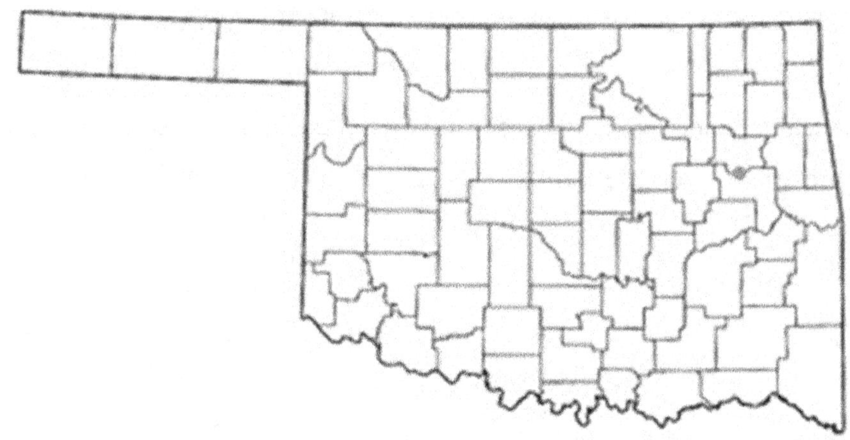

Taft, Muskogee, Oklahoma

The summer after they moved in 1936, the weather became their oppressor. Day after day, it was so scorching hot, it was reminiscent of that biblical "you know where" place. The usually talkative Big Mama had nothing to say, and Big Papa could do nothing to fix it. The typically moderate climate gave way to one of the nation's worst heat waves with one of the hottest summers in history. Located just south of the river in the Arkansas River Valley, Taft usually had favorable conditions for agriculture. But a heat dome had produced extreme heat from the "Dust Bowl" phenomena. Poor farming methods had left little of the natural vegetation, which made the region's prolonged drought even more pronounced. The sweltering temperatures had begun in the Rocky Mountains, slowly shifted over the Plains, Upper Midwest and Great Lakes regions.

In Muskogee County, the average July high temperature of 93 degrees shot up to a record-shattering 118 degrees on July 18. Known as the Great Heat Wave of 1936, over 5,000 people died from the scorching heat across the nation. The high levels of heat gave new energy to the smothering dust storms that blackened the skies further west in Western Oklahoma. Not only did the extreme weather hit Oklahoma, but all-time highs of 120° hit in Arkansas and Texas, and Louisiana hit 116°F, and those high record temperatures still stand today.

For many Midwestern farmers, the recording-breaking heat was the final straw. They had fought economic hard times as well as the calamities of dust storms and drought. As was described by the great American author John Steinbeck, in *The Grapes of Wrath*, thousands of "Okies" left Oklahoma for California. This fictional account follows the woes of a poor White tenant farmer forced out by drought, money problems, and hopelessness. Nevertheless, Rev. Joseph P. Smith and most of the other Granvill's progeny stayed. Maybe they were stubborn, or conceivably I am naïve to think that blacks had any choice under pervasive segregationist policies.

Nevertheless, the weather finally broke. With patience, prayer, and resilience, they worked hard to make something of their land. The characteristics of being down-to-earth, consistent, and cautious coincides with those who score in the lower range on another one the Big Five Personality traits of openness to experience. Granvill was probably like his kin, who seem to have gotten fulfillment through perseverance, as those who score low on openness to experience tend to do.

Joseph P. had bought his land just as a massive collapse in agricultural employment was excluding poor tenants and sharecroppers, both black and white, in the Southern states. As part of the New Deal to combat the Depression, Franklin Delano Roosevelt's (FDR) administration began paying farm owners to take land out of production to reduce surpluses. This solution, along with mechanization, slashed the need for workers. Still, with these efforts, market prices only went up minimally, so Joseph P. took on a part-time job. He became one of the evening guards for the State Hospital for the Negro Insane located at Taft. Maybe he got the job because of his famously calm demeanor or because he lived just a stone's throw away. Each day, Joseph P. walked from his home to the ward where he worked. He had a double set of keys to let himself in where he would watch the patients during the late shift. On Sundays, sometimes his teenage grandnephew would sit in for him while Joseph P. conducted his evening church services.

The stately, three-story brick building, which housed the State Hospital for the Negro Insane, was another by-product of Jim Crow segregation. All of the African American mental patients in the state of Oklahoma came to Taft in the mid-1930s. Built for 700 patients but soon housing 800, Dr. E.P. Henry, the superintendent, tried not to be defeated by this tough situation. With only he, his assistant, and his non-medical staff to care for all those patients, they did their best to provide a clean and humane environment. Dr. Henry wrote to the great African American botanist George Washington Carver requesting information on ways to make money. Getting inspiration from Carver, food, dairy products, brooms, and of course, peanuts were produced on the hundreds of acres of land. (Dr. Carver had published an article explaining 105 ways of preparing peanuts.) Dr. E.P. Henry was proudly in the Who's Who in Colored America for heading "the largest hospital of its kind in the world."

At the time, patients living in hospitals where professionals treated them was considered the most effective way to care for the mentally ill. This remedy was a step above the stigmatization and jail confinement of the mentally ill in the past. In time, the State Hospital of Negro Insane consolidated with the Institute for the Deaf, Blind, and Orphans of the Colored Race along with the Training School for Negro Girls. This employment base ensured that Taft was the most successful of the All-Black towns in Oklahoma. It provided Joseph P. With a stable job working as a guard for fourteen years. I don't know if any of Granvill's other descendants also had a part-time job, but many of them had the box for other sources of income checked "yes" on the 1940 Census.

With a secure income, the family was occasionally able to purchase some modern conveniences of 20th-century life. Corporate America was one place where everyone was treated as equal. It didn't really care who spent the dollars as long as they flowed into their pockets. Perhaps Big Mama influenced by the black news media to bring about social change through collective economic actions, exercised her power as a consumer. She bought some elegant blue tableware. No doubt, the group of Jack's and Lucy Ann's kin that went to Michigan also flexed their economic muscles once they left the agricultural way of life after the 1940s.

One of the pieces we inherited from my great-grandmother's set

There was an action campaign spearheaded by the newspapers in the northern states during the Depression. It espoused, "Don't Buy Where We Can't Work." First, it pushed for companies to hire blacks, later it spread throughout the country. This successful direct action by ordinary African Americans revealed the power of African Americans when they collectively flexed their economic muscles. These tactics would be utilized with even more profound results during the Civil Rights Era.

Another must-have item Big Papa and Big Mama bought was the large polished radio sitting in the living room. Taking up a prominent place just as the television does today, the radio console was a tall rectangular box with a rounded top shaped like a cathedral. Obsessed with listening to exploits of their favorite sports heroes, African Americans often gathered around a radio. One hero triumphed at the 1936 Olympics in Nazi Germany. Hitler planned to use the Olympic Games to support his belief that the German "Aryan" people were the superior race. The son of a sharecropper shattered his plans. A young twenty-two-year-old black athlete named Jesse Owens impressively won four gold medals. Even though FDR, who by neither sent a telegram of congratulations nor invited him to the White House, snubbed him and his achievement, Jesse not only destroyed false negative stereotypes about blacks but bought a sense of hope and pride to African Americans.

Another hero, who also was a son of a sharecropper, was the fighter, Joe Louis. My father vividly remembers traveling in the wagon to Big Papa and Big Mama's house to listen to Joe Louis' fights on the radio. As was strictly enforced, the kids stayed out of the adults' hair on the porch, patiently churning the homemade ice cream. Big Mama, as usual, was directing the lively adults inside in the living room. The uproar of talking and laughing would suddenly drop to the level that a pin drop could be heard just before the announcer started introducing the fighters.

The most famous of Louis' fights was the rematch against the German boxer Max Schmeling in 1938. After Schmeling had defeated Louis in 1936, the talk in the press instilled this fight with the fervor of an epic battle between Nazi ideology and American democracy. When Louis convincingly knocked Schmeling out in the first round, he became an instant American hero. He became one of the most popular blacks in this deeply segregated country. African Americans beamed like proud parents as one of their own was finally afforded respect and admiration. These magnificent athletes, along with Jackie Robinson in the following decade, moved the perception of blacks forward. President Carter, who later made a statement about Jessie Owens but was true of Joe Louis and Jackie Robinson, "Perhaps no athlete better symbolized the human struggle against tyranny, poverty, and racial bigotry."

There is research evidence that there are heritable genetic factors such as height and muscle strength that are critical for success in sports. Obviously, I don't know about all of Granvill's descendants, but as far as I know, none had elite athletic abilities, although there were some athletes. Cheryl, my DNA cousin, told me about the athletic ability of her uncle. Theodous Norris, a great-grandson of Granvill, was known as "Battling Norris from Beaumont" on the boxing circuit in the 1930s. He was a Junior Welterweight. Cheryl told me he boxed in the army and always loved to watch sports. All the same, I assume Granvill did not have elite athletic abilities.

Lots of changed occurred near the end of the 1930s. Sometime in February of 1939, Big Mama received word that life of her dear mother, Melvina Jordan Lindsey, had come to an end. She and her younger sister, who lived in Tulsa, arranged to go to the funeral in Shreveport, Louisiana. Attendance to a loved one's funeral was nearly mandatory in the black community, which was a fact that was known by one of Austin's grandsons, who founded the Smith Mortuary in Bastrop, Louisiana. The high amount for the Value of Home column in the 1940 Census illustrated he was doing quite well. In a world filled with negative stereotypes for African Americans, black funeral directors took exceptional pride in delivering a positive, respectable, and sometimes lavish home-going funeral. It was both a somber and celebratory occasion for eight of Melvina's children as they gathered with their father, Moses.

In death and as in life, the hand of Jim Crow dictated segregated facilities, and obituaries were not permitted in the mainstream newspaper. So many times, the funeral directors created the funeral programs. Hers may have read, "Melvina Louis Jordan, a former slave, was born in Mississippi. After moving to Louisiana, she met Moses Lindsey, and they married in 1879. Their marriage lasted over six decades and were blessed with eleven children. Good luck followed the family's move across the Red River to Bossier Parish. (The twenty-nine-year-old Joseph P. was impressed and eventually married Moses and Melvina's eighteen-year-old daughter Pauline Lindsey in 1906 in Bossier Parish.) Moses purchased land in Bossier Parish and sold it for a premium just at the right time. He and his wife used the money to open a store in Shreveport. Moses also became the pastor for Ebenezer Baptist Church, located twenty miles north of Shreveport. Melvina had been a good Christian wife, mother, and member of the church."

Pauline Lindsey SMITH in 1939

Not only had Pauline lost her mother, but one by one, the "Smith boys" joined the exodus of blacks from the South Central states, such as Oklahoma, emigrating to California. More than a third of a million African Americans moved to the western half of the country during the 1940s. Several reasons may have spurred her grown sons to move. First, there were rumors that some of her "preachers' kids," now grown, started acting out when they were no longer under the strict authority of their mother and father. Perhaps the long switches, sharp pinches, and pressure to be perfect caused the opposite effect, at least temporarily. Second, opportunities for jobs on the farm were being squeezed out by better machinery as well as the government's push to pay farm owners not to grow. The Great Depression and FDR's administration's agricultural subsidies together had ended widespread sharecropping in the South.

For many of Granvill's progeny, another impetus was the enlistment into the military. More than two dozen of Granvill's great-great-grandsons had to report to duty at cities such as Shreveport, Tulsa, Little Rock, and Los Angeles. Another reason for moving was the lure of better educational opportunities for their children. My grandmother fervently wanted her children, including my father, to get a good education.

Coming to California from Oklahoma was one of my father's most impressionable moments of his early life. On his mind was this burning question of "What exactly was the mysterious fog in California?" First, he and his siblings, who could hardly contain their excitement, spent a restless night at his grand-aunt's home in Tulsa, Oklahoma. The four boys, who were nine, eight, six, and four years old, barely were able to stay out of trouble, while his mother kept his two-year-old and eight-month-old sister near her. Somehow, she managed to make some fried chicken before getting a few hours of sleep. Once they finally boarded the train, the kids begged to try the food on the train. Of course, all eight of them squeezed into a small area in the colored section of the train. There was one either side of the dining cards. My grandfather relented and allowed the treat of the train food, very likely served by kindly, black railroad workers. He stayed back in the seat and ate the chicken.

A while later, my father noticed my grandfather was looking sick. He started vomiting, sweating, and looked listless. My grandmother told my father, who was the oldest, to take his brothers for a walk. Soon a walk turned into turning running up and down the aisles of the train. An older gentleman, who suspected the boys needed some supervision, asked the rambunctious boys to come to join him. They ended up sleeping in his section, along with their little sister at night, which gave my grandfather enough space to rest and eventually recover from an awful case of food poisoning.

Once in California, the weary family was greeted by uncles, aunts, and cousins. My dad was anxious to find out how long he would have to wait to see the fog. His cousins assured him that he would see it soon enough, but they asked: "How is Uncle Lindsey?" When he quizzed them on how they knew his dad was sick, they explained that their pastor had told their father that his brother was very ill, but he would be okay. Amazed by this minister, after that incident, my father always made to point never miss going to church!

As their children went to California, they followed the Smith family tradition. Similar to what happened after the end of slavery, 75 years later, they moved next door to each other in a tight-knit group in Los Angeles. The family supported each other financially and emotionally. My father remembers sometimes having almost a dozen people occupying their small two-bedroom house. Whoever needed help, family was always welcome. I found the same thing happened in Flint, Michigan with the Hodge siblings a decade later. Using the City Directory, I found these descendants of Lucy Ann lived very close to each other, presumably to provide support as they moved from Louisiana to Michigan. Granvill must have modeled this when he was alive.

Meanwhile, everyone was trying to deal with what had happened almost a year prior on one cold crispy December day in Taft. Everyone in the Smith household was putting their final touches on their outfits while they were getting ready for church. When the radio was turned on, on that fateful day of December 7, 1941, it reported the devastating news of a surprise military attack by the Japanese on a minuscule place in the vast Pacific Ocean. The US naval base at Pearl Harbor had been attacked with over 2,400 Americans killed and over 1,000 wounded on "a date which will live in infamy." The next day the United States declared war on Japan. Within a week, Adolf Hitler had declared war on the United States, and the United States responded with a declaration of war on Nazi Germany.

One son and a son-in-law of Joseph P. and Pauline, as well as over two dozen of Granvill's great-great-grandsons were soon enlisted to become part of the "Negro Problem" in the army. The military brass was just as susceptible as anyone to the prevailing stereotypical thinking that negroes were dirty and carriers of disease. Of course, this warped thinking justified Jim Crow. "The army of the 1940s was a microcosm of American society—it was segregated and thoroughly racist." The famous prizefighter, Joe Louis, probably exemplified the thoughts of many African Americans when he stated, "Lots of things wrong with America, but Hitler ain't going to fix them." Not all blacks wanted to fight in the "White Man's war," but Joseph P.'s son was part of the over one million African Americans that entered the armed forces. Certainly, Rev. J. P. Smith led his congregation in many a prayer to protect our troops and especially "our boys" during the war. Pauline did what almost every other mother did. She became part of the home front in buying bonds, growing victory gardens and making do because of rationed commodities such as sugar, butter, lard, cheese, and even nylon stockings.

My uncle, who was a young boy in Los Angeles during the war, told me a tale that made me laugh out loud. It involved rationing sugar, which was difficult to get during the war. He was over at a friend's house when he was offered a round, flat food item for a snack. My uncle wondered what this circular shaped piece of food could be. Since he had never seen a cookie, he asked if it was a cookie. His friend roared with laughter and told him it was a tortilla. My uncle's lack of knowledge of cookies was due to the rationing of sugar because it couldn't be shipped from the Philippines nor Hawaii. Whatever sugar was available was utilized in making everything from antiseptics to explosives, but not cookies.

Even though the black service members, like Joseph P.'s son, lived in substandard housing, were poorly trained, received the worse equipment, and lacked the chance for advancement, they still were patriotic and hoped their country would reward their loyal service. Change would come in small victories laying the groundwork for more substantial successes in the decades after World War II. Even before the war began, the threat of mass protest in Washington by African American activist groups such as the NAACP and the Urban League had forced FDR to issue an executive order banning discriminatory employment practices in war-related work.

Hoping for more change, one of the major black newspapers launched a "Double V" campaign, which stood for "Democracy: Victory at home, Victory Abroad." The goals of the campaign was to encourage African Americans to both support the war effort and fighting for civil rights. The hardest challenge was to fight the perception of many white Americans that blacks were inferior in intelligence, character, and ability. By the end of the war, more than 1.2 million African Americans had proudly served their country on the Home Front, in Europe, and the Pacific.

Just recently, an African American hero was recognized with a ship named after him. He usually was only allowed to work in the mess hall, but courageously grabbed an anti-aircraft machine gun and continuously fired until he was out of ammunition as the battleship U.S.S. Arizona was sinking at Pearl Harbor. Black newspapers kept the story alive for months until the Navy finally identified and awarded a medal to Doris Miller.

Famous segregated units, such as the Tuskegee Airmen and the 761st Tank Battalion, showed that blacks could master complex tasks and fight with valor. One of the lesser-known but equally distinguished groups included the 452nd Anti-Aircraft Artillery Battalion, which proved the value of the black soldier. By 1945, for want of men due to troop losses, the military was forced to place African Americans into many positions, even as officers, where they served with honor, distinction and courage equal to any other American.

As it happens, one of Granvill's descendants, James Austin Gray, received a military honor. He was the Staff Sergeant for the 1313th Engineer General Service Regiment, which was manned by African American soldiers in Germany under the command of General Joseph Collins near the end of the war. As part of the US First Army, the 1313th fought in the Battle of the Bulge. In the winter of 1945, the Germans tried unsuccessfully to push the Allies back from German home territory. James Austin Gray was awarded the Bronze Star for Bravery for his actions in Germany. This medal is the fourth-highest award for military combat in bravery. My DNA cousin James Austin Gray II explained that his father crept behind enemy lines to analyze each shot and relay information back to the artillery gunners. Being drafted just before he finished college, he was able to utilize his exceptional mathematical ability to improve the precision of each shot.

James Austin Gray II

Both James and I also show an aptitude for mathematics, since we both majored in it in college. If we inherited genes that made us strong in math, there's a good chance they came from Granvill or possibly Eliza, since they are our common ancestor. To find out, I submitted my raw DNA data to the website <Genomelink>, where I received a genetic trait report stating, "You have a stronger tendency for having acute math ability." Although many genes are involved in the ability to do mathematics, researchers found a possible gene underlying mathematical ability. According to a one-to-one comparison of James and my DNA on <GEDmatch>, we have two segments that match on Chromosome 6 and one section on Chromosome 8 for a total of 56.5 centimorgans (cM). That's not much, because I shared 3,427 cM across 78 segments with my father. James also submitted his data and got the exact same result. There is a real chance that James and I share that math gene we inherited from Granvill. I love the fact that the math smarts of my family contributed to winning World War II.

An ironic result of the segregated armed forces was that of over 400,000 killed in combat during World War II, only 708 were African Americans. Not only were Joseph and Pauline's prayers were answered with the safe return of their son and son-in-law but all the other great-great-grandsons of Granvill. After the war had ended, Joseph P.'s grandnephew served in the army. Not long after that, President Harry Truman issued an executive order to desegregate all of the U.S. Armed Forces in 1948. One institution of American society had moved on as one pillar of government-sponsored racism was finally destroyed.

With the weight of segregation, discrimination, and government-sponsored racism always pulling many African Americans down, the church was their lifesaver. A Baptist minister, Rev. Adam Clayton Powell Jr, became a prominent spokesperson for racial equality for blacks. The congressman from New York was first elected in 1944. Powell was both an outspoken leader and a skilled politician. Adam Clayton Powell, Jr's feisty, independent style curried favor with most African Americans because they felt that there was at least one person who championed their cause. Powell irritated the foremost segregationist, who want to keep blacks and white separate, by continually finding a seat next to him.

Whereas Powell, who was assertive, outgoing and friendly, and would score high on the Big Five Personality trait of extraversion, Rev. J.P. Smith would score lower. Multiple family members have reported he tended to be reserved, quiet, and serious. My DNA cousin, William Smith, also asserted that his father, Granville C. Smith, was also that type. My other DNA cousin, James Austin Gray II, maintained some of the relatives on the Austin line were also dignified, reserved but always ready to remind you of the proper way of doing things. Sometimes those who on the other end of their pronouncements might call it self-righteousness. I believe that Granvill was on the reserved side and commanded respect as an elder full of wisdom from years of navigating the multitude of people and places in his long life.

Nonetheless, because his grandson, Rev. J.P. Smith, was the pastor, he was considered one of the most honest, most devoted, and an outstanding person in the small town of Taft. The church was the anchor of life for Taft as it was for most African Americans. On Sunday mornings, the simple, nondescript church sprang to life as its "Negro brethren" left the isolation of farm life to partake in a shared community experience. The Sunday church clad females, who were mostly past their prime, chattered incessantly about the latest gossip. The gray and balding spruced up males talked about the weather, how things were going, and politics. When their pastor signaled it was to start, they found their seats in uncushioned pews.

Each Sunday, many, no matter how weary, came to this safe place where church members could feel a sense of self-worth. African Americans used their religion to battle the effects of racism in their lives. The words of the Bible and the power of prayer helped them to forget their oppression on this Earth. If they were patient now, they could look forward to a brighter day in the afterlife. It was that old-time religion delivered with calls and responses, shouting and music. It was a deeply spiritual experience, lifting your voice to God with glorious music and intense emotions.

His church was very typical of the state of rural African American churches near the end of the 1940s. It also had the same problems. Almost half of the rural churches had decreased in size with many members who were middle-aged or old folks being cared for by aged pastors like Rev. Smith, who had reached his seventies. His children, nephews, and many of the church members' children had moved on as part of the Second Great Migration. Most of them went to California. He and Pauline were steadfast in their task of taking care of the spiritual and physical needs of their waning flock.

They may have helped out their parishioners in a unique way. County Treasurer's Resale Deeds, show they bought up lots of properties in blocks. Perhaps they bought the land so that their church members could remain on their land as neighbors and friends did in penny auctions. These actions are in line with what researchers have found. Religiousness correlates most reliably with the last of the Big Five personality traits of conscientiousness. They, as well as the majority of Granvill's descendants, were both religious as well as careful, reliable, hard-working, and disciplined people. There's an excellent probability that Granvill was, too.

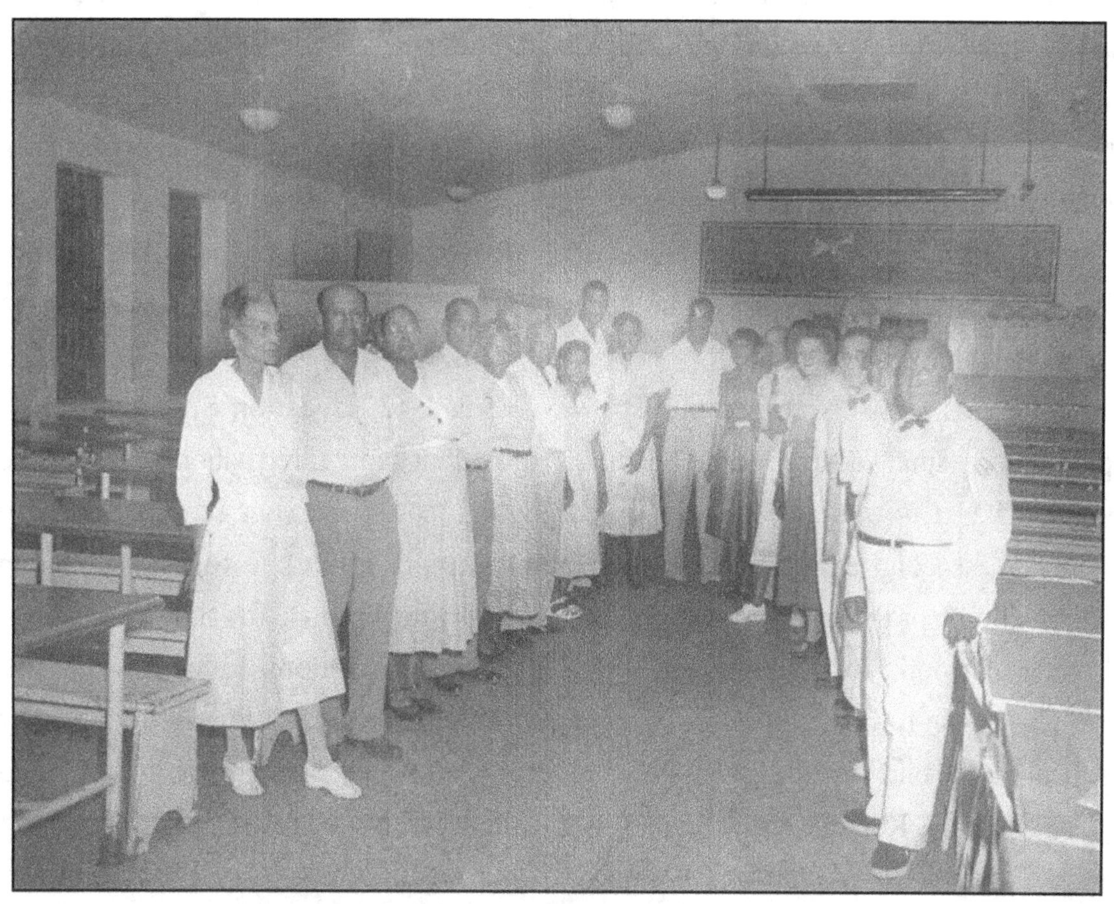

Blue Creek Baptist Church members with Rev. J. P. Smith in the 1940s

As 1950 rolled around, Joseph P. had lived over seven decades. Much had changed over his lifetime. When he was a carefree young boy in Louisiana, could he possibly have imagined that the changes in technology like electric lights, automobiles, movies, airplanes, or television would forever alter his existence? His experiences of racism in American society do not offer such stark transformations, but in sharp contrast, they slowly improved over time. Even though he lived in the South, Joseph's father, Samuel, along with his mentor, Rev. S.T. James, had embraced the opportunity given them after slavery to provide both a religious upbringing and a solid education. With that education and upbringing, Joseph P. had been able to rise up a little on the economic ladder. What had changed was the violence toward African Americans such as lynchings, riots, the KKK, and ruthless intimidation had greatly diminished. In fact, in 1952, there were no lynchings reported for the first time in 70 years. Negative stereotypes had moved from subhuman, inferior, and servant-like to not as smart nor equal but perhaps musical or athletic. Throughout Joseph P.'s life, Jim Crow laws that enshrined segregation were slowly eroding. Continuing political pressure persuaded both President Roosevelt and Truman to issue executive orders that had desegregated the defense industry before and the armed forces after War World II. The NAACP, for whom ministers were typically members, launched several major court cases, particularly several in Oklahoma that continued to chip away those laws.

Finally, in 1954, the momentous Brown v. Board of Education Supreme Court ruling toppled the idea that separate could be equal, ruling that segregated schools were "inherently unequal." The *Chicago Defender*, the leading African American newspaper, called the decision "the second emancipation proclamation…more important to our democracy than the atomic bomb or the hydrogen bomb." Although some places in the South had to be forced with federal troops to integrate and other locales took actions to thwart it, Oklahoma peacefully began to dismantle the foundations of its segregated public-school system. In a twist of fate, the end of segregation may have been the catalyst for Joseph P. having to leave his job as a guard. Records show that the segregated Taft State Hospital for the Negro Insane became integrated after 1954.

In 1955, Joseph and his wife Pauline left Oklahoma, the place they called home for over 45 years. They were moving on from the place they had raised their children and tended to their church. They followed their children to California to live in their waning years. Perhaps Joseph P. or Big Papa or Rev. Smith now felt spiritually stronger. He had relentlessly studied the Bible given to him so many years ago by Rev. S. T. James. But that old body full of aches and pains couldn't run a farm and a church as his eighth decade was just over the horizon. Like most senior citizens of his day, he had worked past the age of 65, passing the average life expectancy for American males in 1955 of about sixty-six years old. He more than likely didn't receive Social Security. Due to racist tactics used by Southern politicians, agricultural and domestic workers, where 4 out of 5 African Americans worked, were initially ineligible for benefits. But even if he did, in the 1950s, the average Social Security benefit was about $30 a month. There were definitely no "golden years" of retirement in those days. Playing golf, eating at a restaurant, or even long-distance telephone calls were luxuries that most retirees could not afford.

Joseph P. didn't sell his land, just as he hadn't sold his property in Louisiana. He and his wife headed west to the city with the largest African American population at the time, Los Angeles. They found a place to stay near their family in Watts. It was one of only two neighborhoods available for blacks in Los Angeles, with the other being South Central LA. They left the world of government-sponsored segregation and racism. They didn't have to suffer more unfair voter requirements because they could vote in California. There would be no more legal discrimination in public places. No more government-sponsored segregated school. No more legally segregated workplaces. No more being governed by openly racist government officials. Even though they had lived in an All-Black town, maybe they had less day to day confrontations with racism than blacks in the cities, but Jim Crow was always creeping into their lives. It would seem that going to California would mean moving on from racism, but I wonder, would it? The majority of the next generation of Granvill's progeny, who left Louisiana, ended up in California. Some in Oakland, but most were in the Los Angeles area. Others went to the Detroit area while others moved to Texas. They were part of the second wave of the Great Migration of African Americans. Beginning in the 1940s, millions of African Americans moved from the southern states to urban areas in the West, the Midwest, and the North.

Our family's story is not unique. It captures not only African American history but the story of America itself, as it grapples with moving toward the self-evident truth that all men are created equal. I began my quest to learn about my 3rd great-grandfather. Starting with the smallest sliver of genealogical evidence, I studied him through his cultural roots and his place and times. Next, I scrutinized similarities in his children and grandchildren. I shifted through the data of his descendants. I analyzed photographs and data from the draft card possible to resurrect some of his physical features. Then, to get a pulse on Granvill's personality, I examined the inheritable genetic characteristics of Granvill's descendants. I was amazed at the end to feel that I had accomplished my goal. And in the end, our land is fine. Of course, we will never know which of my conjectures are correct, but we do know that each of Granvill's kin carries a little bit of him in their genes. And James and I have discovered we both have genes that make us have a tendency for having a strong math ability and memory performance. Hopefully, some of these characteristics had helped his ancestors not only survive but thrive in a world that did not always welcome them.

I began the process of "resurrecting" my 3rd great-grandfather determined to find a way. Through studying the cultural, regional, historical, and other life experiences, I slowly revealed many aspects of his life in the context of African American history. As I created a chronology of his descendants' lives, I wrestled with the dark specter of racism. Time and time again, the strength, conviction, and persistence of Granvill's kin overcame the obstacles put before them. I can almost call these attributes the superpowers of my family. Once more, one of the Chinese sayings Weilin told me, describes what I have gained. It says, "One cannot know sweet without tasting bitter." Granvill, my enslaved ancestor, has left me the legacy of knowing that the bitter sting of racism can be conquered. Plus, I now have the sweet knowledge that I most likely inherited the math gene from him, as well as other attributes such as perseverance, diligence, and an independent streak.

In today's world, not having a lot of records will not stop you from resurrecting your ancestor. Hopefully, you can utilize some of the methods, which I've simplified after my long and arduous search. My goal was to clear the way, making it much easier for you. Using the graphic organizers will lead to unlocking hidden information and data about your ancestor. The narrative in the book presents just one of many possible ways to find insights into your relative. I now realize that studying the obstacles your ancestor had to face such as war, immigration, economic downturns, disease, etc., can help you understand your relative's life and personality. You can find the superpower in your family history, which is a legacy that will strengthen your family for all times. From my family to yours, I wish you a fruitful pursuit!

Selected Bibliography

Chapter 1: Challenges
Ancestry. http://www.ancestry.com/.

Burroughs, Tony. Black Roots: A Beginner's Guide to Tracing the African American Family Tree
New York: Simon & Schuster, 2001.

Cardin, Clifton D. Bossier Parish Headstones. Princeton: Clifton D. Cardin, 1997.

Smith, Edith & Lehman, Vivian. "No Land…Only Slave!" Abstracts from the Deed Book of
Bossier Parish Louisiana. Vol. 1 Balch Springs, Texas, 2004.

Chapter 2: Culture

Carteret, Marcia. "Culturally-based Differences in Child Rearing Practices." 2013.
http://www.dimensionsofculture.com/2013/09/how-individualism-and collectivism
manifest-in-child-rearing-practices/.

Martha H, Gilmore. Louisiana. Bossier Parish. U.S. census (Slave Schedule). 1850. Microfilm
publication M432 citing line 36, Washington D.C., National Archives.

Hawthorne, Walter. Planting Rice and Harvesting Slaves: Transformations along the Guinea-Bissau Coast,
1400-1900. Portmouth: Heinemann, 2003.

"Table of the Flags under which Slave Ships Operated." Slave Voyage, Trans-Atlantic Slave
Trade- Database. Assessed December 5, 2019. https://www.slavevoyages.org/voyage/
database#tables

The Center for Culturally Proficient Education. https://ccpep.org/home/what-is-cultural-proficiency/the-
continuum/.

World Culture Encyclopedia. https://www.everyculture.com

Chapter 3: The Locale

Bell, Karen. B. "Rice, Resistance, and Forced Transatlantic Communities: (Re)envisioning the
African Diaspora in Low Country Georgia, 1750-1800." Journal of African American
History 157-182, 2010.

Berlin, Ira. Many Thousands Gone: the First Two Centuries of Slavery in North America. Cambridge: Harvard University Press, 2009.

Lawrence, Paul et al. Negro American Heritage. Sacramento: State Department of Education, 1966.

Morgan, Philip D. Slave counterpoint: Black culture in the eighteenth-century Chesapeake and Lowcountry. Williamsburg: 1998.

Piercy, William. n.d. "William Piercy letter book, 1773-1783." South Carolina Historical Society.

Smith, Gordon Burns. "Siege of Savannah." New Georgia Encyclopedia. September 2013. Accessed October 1, 2015. https://www.georgiaencyclopedia.org/articles/history-archaeology/siege-savannah.

Weir, Robert M. Colonial South Carolina: A History. Columbia: University of South Carolina, 1997.

Chapter 4: History

Georgia, Headright and Bounty Land Records, 1782 – 1909, Gilmer, John-Gobert, Joseph, image 2 of 464: Georgia State Archive, Morrow.

Georgia. Oglethorpe County. Oglethorpe County Courthouse, Oglethorpe. Will Book "A", 1794 to 1806 Oglethorpe County Wills, Deeds and Estates.

Gilmer, George R. 1926. Sketches of Some of the First Settlers of Upper Georgia, of the Cherokees, and the Author. Baltimore: Clearfield Company.
HistoryLines. https://historylines.com/

Chapter 5: Economics

Bureau of Land Management. https://glorecords.blm.gov/default.aspx.

Dupre, Daniel S. Transforming the Cotton Frontier, Alabama 1800-1840. Baton Rouge: Louisiana State University Press, 1997.

"Georgia Archives County Tax Digest from Microfilm, Oglethorpe County Tax Digest, 1795. Georgia Archives Virtual Vault, University System of Georgia. Assessed September 19, 2019. https://vault.georgiaarchives.org/digital/collection/tax/id/484/rec/18.

Sawyer, Ralph D. Sun-tzu the Art of War. New York: Basic Books.

Smith, David Livingstone. Less than human: Why We Demean, Enslave, and Exterminate Others. New York: St. Martin's Press, 2011.

Williamson, Samuel H. & Cain, Louis. "Measuring Slavery in 2016 Dollars." Measuring Worth, 2020. Assessed January 14, 2019. https://www.measuringworth.com/slavery.php

Chapter 6: Politics

"Geographical and Historical Memoirs of Northwest Louisiana" LA AHGP. Nashville: 1890.
    Assessed May 10, 2016. https://laahgp.genealogyvillage.com/Bigraphicalmemoirs13
    /bossierparishbh1.html

"Gilmer Family and Bossier Parish." Bossier Parish Library Historical Center. Archive Record (1997.122)

Jennings, Dale. "Cash Point Plantation." Bossier Parish Library Historical Center. Archive Record (2000.002)

Jennings, Dale. "Hard Times." Bossier Parish Library Historical Center. Archive Record (2000.052)

Jennings, Dale. "Slave Surnames." Bossier Parish Library Historical Center. Archive Record (1998.067)

Louisiana; Morgan, Thomas Gibbes. Civil code of the state of Louisiana: with the statutory amendments, from 1825 to 1853, inclusive; and references to the decisions of the Supreme Court of Louisiana to the sixth volume of Annual reports. 1861. Duke University Libraries. Assessed February 1, 2019. https://archive.org/details/civilcodeofstate00loui /page/28/mode/2up.

Spyker, Leonidas Pendleton. "Diary of Leonidas Pendleton Spyker, July 1, 1856 to October 31, 1860." Bossier Historical Library Center, Northeast Louisiana State College, Monroe Louisiana.

Chapter 7: Moments

Antietam Virtual Tour. American Battlefield Trust. https://www.battlefields.org/visit/virtual-tours/antietam-360-virtual-tour.

The Bossier banner. [volume] (Bellevue, Bossier Parish, La.), 15 June 1860. Chronicling America: Historic American Newspapers. Library of Congress.   https://chroniclingamerica.loc.gov/lccn/sn85034235/1860-06-15/ed-1/seq-1/

Douglass, Frederick. Narrative of the life of Frederick Douglass, an American slave. Boston: Anti-Slavery Office, 1849. Library of Congress. http://hdl.loc.gov/loc.gdc/lhbcb.25385.

Dunn, Capt. C.T. Historical and geographical description of Morehouse Parish Louisiana in 1885. State Library of Louisiana. Assessed August 18, 2018. https://louisianadigitallibrary.org/ islandora/object/state-lwp%3A4377

Chapter 8: Values

"Global Values: Where Do You Fit?" BBC Taster. https://www.bbc.co.uk/taster/pilots/global-   values-where-do-you-fit. (Note: this website is the most user friendly on values, but it may be discontinued at any time).

Jennings, Dale. "Trouble on Red River." Bossier Parish Library Historical Center. Archive Record (1997.124)

"Revisiting the Bossier massacre of 1868 according to the Freedman's Bureau," The Freedmen's Bureau Online. Assessed March 27, 2016. http://www.freedmensbureau.com/louisiana /outrages/bossierandcaddo.htm.

Sam Smith, "United States, Freedmen's Bureau Labor Contracts, Indenture and Apprenticeship Records, 1865-1872. FamilySearch. https://familysearch.org/ark:/61903/1:1:Q2W3-FV3F.

"The Success Quiz." VisualDNA. https://www.visualdna.com/quizzes/. (Note: this website is directed toward one's career and the names of some the categories are slightly different).

"Two Short Measures of Values (TIVI and TWIVI). Department of Psychology, University of Texas. https://gosling.psy.utexas.edu/two-short-measures-of-values-tivi-and-twivi/. (Note: this is a pencil and paper of the questionnaire, which is not as engaging, but probably it will not disappear).

US Census Bureau. "Agricultural Schedule 1870," State of Louisiana, Bossier Parish, P.29.

Williams, Heather Andrea. Self-Taught African American Education in Slavery and Freedom. Chapel Hill: The University of North Carolina Press, 2005.

Chapter 9: Patterns

Brown, Nikki. "Jim Crow." In KnowLA Encyclopedia of Louisiana, edited by David Johnson. Louisiana Endowment for the Humanities, 2010–. Article published January 21, 2015. http://www.knowla.org/entry/735/.

Fitts, Leroy. A History of Black Baptists. Nashville: Broadman Press, 1985.

Franklin, Jimmie Lewis. Journey Toward Hope. Norman: University of Oklahoma Press, 1982.

Jennings, Dale. "J.P Vance and His Succession." Bossier Parish Library Historical Center. Archive Record (2000.052)

Johnson, Hannibal B. Acres of Aspiration: The All-Black Towns in Oklahoma. Eakin Press, 2002.

Chapter 10: Tendencies

Brophy, Alfred L. Reconstructing the Dreamland: The Tulsa Riot of 1921: Race, Reparations, and Reconciliation. Oxford, 2002.

Larry O'Dell, "Ku Klux Klan," The Encyclopedia of Oklahoma History and Culture, https://www.okhistory.org/publications/enc/entry.php?entry=KU001.

Louisiana. Louisiana State Board of Health, Caddo. Death Certificate, Jane Boyd.

Raymond, Ken. "Black Freemasons have Long History in Oklahoma," The Oklahoman, February 24, 2013. https://oklahoman.com/article/3757711/black-freemasons-have-long-history-in-oklahoma.

Waites, Cheryl. "Building on Strengths: Intergenerational practice with African American Families." Social Work, 54, no.3 (2009): 278-87.

Chapter 11: In Your Genes

Assari, Shervin. "Neuroticism Predicts Subsequent Risk of Major Depression for Whites but Not Blacks." National Center for Biotechnology Information, U.S. National Library of Medicine.Assessed May 11, 2019. https://www.ncbi.nlm.nih.gov/pmc/articles /PMC5746673/#

Cowan, Tom., and Jack Maguire. Timelines of African-American History: 500 years of Black Achievement. New York: A Roundtable Press/Perigee Book, 1994.

Genolink. Assessed October 14, 2019.https://genomelink.io.

Khoynezhad, Gholamreza et al. "Basic Religious Beliefs and Personality Traits," Iranian Journal of Psychiatry, Spring 7, no.2 (2012):82-86, US National Library of Medicine. Assessed March 8, 2019. https://www.ncbi.nlm.nih.gov/pmc/articles/PMC3428642/.

Meier, J.D. "6 Job Personality and Work Environment Types." Sources of Insight. Assessed September 19, 2018. http://sourcesofinsight.com/6-personality-and-work-environment-types/.

Morehouse, Maggi M. Fighting in the Jim Crow Army: Black Men and Women Remember World War II. Lanham: Rowman & Littlefield Publishers, Inc., 2000.

U.S. City Directories, 1822-1995. Michigan, Flint, 1958, Johnnie L Hodge and others.

APPENDIX

Appendix A

Who is in Your Single Line Family Tree?

After you have chosen an ancestor to "resurrect," an easy way to get started is to gather the information on the direct line between you and your chosen ancestor. Begin at the bottom with you, and as you move up, check the box for either the maternal (mother) or paternal (father) side. Continue filling in as much as you can for each generation until you reach your chosen ancestor. The information you gather, answers the "who" and "what" were my relatives in the Five W questions.

☐ Paternal ☐ Maternal 3rd great-grandparent

Name	
Birth	
Death	

☐ Paternal ☐ Maternal 2nd great-grandparent

Name	
Birth	
Death	

☐ Paternal ☐ Maternal great-grandparent

Name	
Birth	
Death	

☐ Paternal ☐ Maternal grandparent

Name	
Birth	
Death	

☐ Paternal ☐ Maternal Parent

Name	
Birth	
Death	

↑

Self

Name	
Birth	

After you have chosen an ancestor to "resurrect," an easy way to get started is to gather the information on the direct line between you and your chosen ancestor. Begin at the bottom with you, and as you move up, check the box for either the maternal (mother) or paternal (father) side. Continue filling in as much as you can for each generation until you reach your chosen ancestor. This answers the "who" and "what" were my relatives in the Five W questions. (Here is a sample.)

☒ Paternal ☐ Maternal 3rd great-grandparent

Name	Granvill
Birth	1770
Death	Abt 1861

↑

☒ Paternal ☐ Maternal 2nd great-grandparent

Name	Samuel (Sam) Smith
Birth	1832
Death	Abt 1894

☒ Paternal ☐ Maternal great-grandparent

↑

Name	Joseph P. Smith
Birth	24 Dec 1876
Death	8 Aug 1960

☒ Paternal ☐ Maternal grandparent

Name	Lindsey Curtis Smith
Birth	24 Jun 1908
Death	12 Aug 1984

☒ Paternal ☐ Maternal Parent

Name	Cornell Rubin Smith
Birth	18 Jun 193x
Death	

Self

Name	Donise Lorene Smith
Birth	13 Apr 195x

Appendix B
Making a Timeline for your Ancestor

Taking the time to construct a timeline for your ancestor allows you to examine his or her life in a systematically, carefully reexamine your records, and spot overlooked information as well as gaps. You will need to gather primary source documents such as birth, marriage, military and death records, photographs, and oral stories. Next, consider online records such as census information and newspapers that pertain to your ancestor. Online sites such as <FamilySearch> and <Ancestry.com> will make a timeline for you, but creating one yourself will provide better insight into your ancestor.

Next, consider the time frame for your timeline. Many timelines are just lists, but if you set up increments of every 10 or 5 years, it will allow you to see gaps in the records, documents, and information.

When? Where?	Who and What information? (*Source*)	I wonder why or if
1760		
1770	Granvill was born in 1770 in Georgia (*1854 Bill of Sale, 1850 U.S. Federal Census - Slave Schedule, 1880 Census*)	I wonder why he was named Granvill.
1780		
1790		
1800		
1810		
1820		
1830		
1840		
1850 Bossier Parish	Granvill (84), his wife Eliza (56), his daughter Lucy (50), his son Jack (37), his son Merriweather (26), the twins William and Samuel (22), his daughter Jane (17), and son Handy (14) (*1854 Bill of Sale*)	I wonder why Jane and Handy's ages are very inconsistent with later documents
1860	G E Gilmer has an 85 year-old black male (*1860 U.S. Federal Census -Slave Schedule*)	I wonder if they didn't believe Granvill was 90 years old

Timeline for

When? Where?	Who and What information is in the record? (*Source*)	I wonder why or if

Sample Timeline for __Samuel Smith_________

When? Where?	Who and What information? (*Source*)	I wonder why or if
1830 Madison or Montgomery, Alabama	Samuel and twin brother were born in 1832 in Alabama (*1854 Bill of Sale, 1880 Census*)	I wonder if George O. Gilmer moved before the land he purchased in Montgomery in 1833 was recorded.
1840 Montgomery, Alabama	Samuel is most likely one of the 14 listed as Slave-Males-Under 10 (*1840 U.S. Federal Census for George O. Gilmer for Montgomery, Alabama*)	I wonder why only 31 out of 68 total slaves were employed in Agriculture, while 10 out 10 were in Louisiana
1850 Bossier, Louisiana	Samuel is most likely one of the two male blacks listed as 20 years-old (*1850 U.S. Federal Census of Martha H Gilmore*) Samuel is listed as 22 (*1854 Bill of Sale*)	I wonder when the ages needed to be more accurate
1860 Bossier, Louisiana	Samuel is most likely the 29 black male listed with a wife and 2 children. Another 29 year-old black male also has 2 children (*G E Gilmer Slave Schedule*) Sam (28), Fanny (25), Riah (9) and Jeff (7) (*Secession of G E Gilmer in 1864*)	I wonder why Sam and his twin William were both 28 years old but William was appraised at $1,450, and Sam $1,300
1870 Bossier, Louisiana	Samuel married Caroline Johnson (*Bossier Parish, Louisiana Marriages, 1851-1900*) Sam Smith (40) and his wife Amanda (18) (*1870 Census*) Sam worked 50 acres of land (*1870 Agricultural Schedule*)	I wonder why Caroline's name was Amanda
1880 Bossier, Louisiana	Sam Smith (48), his wife Caroline (26), sons Granville (8), William (6), Frank (5), Joe (3), and daughter Jane (11/12 months) (*1880 Census*) Samuel Smith with 2 others buy land for $20 to build a church and a school (*1881 Deed for Land for Church and school*)	I wonder what the 1890 Census said

Appendix C
Cultural Life Experiences

Understanding the cultural life experiences of a person reveals a great deal about how a person's life was lived. The early life of a person is influenced by whether a person grew up in an individualistic or collectivist culture. It is easier to grasp how culture impacted your ancestor's life after you first consider how culture influenced your own life.

First, decide whether you were born into a very strong individualistic, a somewhat individualistic, a somewhat collectivist, or a strong collectivist culture. If you were born into a Western culture, any prior culture from your family was pulled toward being more individualistic. (A rough average for certain regions)

Strong individualistic	Somewhat individualistic	Somewhat collectivist	Strong collectivist
English speaking countries	Mediterranean countries	Brazil	East Asian
Northern European	Spanish speaking	India	Central American
German Speaking	Southern European	Northern Asia	African

-Geert Hofstede

Next, using the chart of Individualistic Cultures and Collectivist Cultures, select examples in your life that illustrate tendencies from either side for each stage of your life. Note, that schooling in individualistic countries exert a push toward individualism even if your home culture was more collectivist. Try to find examples for each stage of your life.

Then, use the information from <everyculture.com> to a find out aspects of your ancestor's culture. You may want to research childbirth practices or traditions of a particular ethnic group, country, or region. For example, I researched West African childbirth traditions. Reflect on how your life was similar or different from your ancestor's.

Connect the information you found to your ancestor. Of course, you will never know for sure how your ancestor lived his or her life, but this gives you a clearer understanding of how culture influenced the life of your ancestor.

Finally, research more about the culture and values of your specific ethnic heritage.

Individualistic Culture	Collectivist Culture
Taken care of by immediate family	Born into an extended family or clan which protects them in exchange for loyalty
The value of independence is nurtured	The value of interdependence is nurtured
Education is for learning how to learn	Education is for learning how to do
Is encouraged to be assertive	Is encouraged to be obedient
Sees others as individuals	Sees others as either in-group or the out-group
Always mindful of "I"	Always mindful of "we"
On personality test, people score more extravert	On personality test, people score more introvert
One strives toward personal goals and achievements	Works with others in a cooperative way that always maintains harmony
Individual rights most important	Groups rights overrule the individual
Competes with others	Duty to cooperate with group
Prefers to work alone	Prefers to work in groups
Media is primary source of information	Social network if primary source of information
Respect accomplishments, innovation and expertise	Respect tradition, status and the experience of age and wisdom

Time	Your life	Your Ancestor's Life
Birth		
0 - 4		
5 -13		
14 - 18		
19 - 22		
23<		

*Which cultural experiences assist in "resurrecting" your ancestor's life? What other information can you find on the culture and values of your ancestor's culture?

Time	My life	My Ancestor's Life
Birth	I was born into a somewhat **individualistic culture** in a hospital. I slept in a crib next to my mother.	My ancestor was born into a **collectivist culture** where his mother was surrounded by female family members. He slept with his mother.
0 - 4	I lived with **my immediate family,** which included my mother and father. I was put on a schedule. I learned to be **independent** by feeding myself and became potty trained.	Typically, in West Africa, my ancestor would live in a **large extended family**. He was allowed to fall asleep naturally. His mother fed him longer into the toddler years. Because she carried him on her back, she tried to read his body clues for bowel movements building a bond of i**nterdependence.**
5 -13	I went to school at 5 years-old, where I learned the basics of **how to learn**. After elementary school, I went to junior high, where I interacted with the **friends I chose**, both girls and boys.	My ancestor was put in the youngest age-grade, where he **learned how to do** things like taking care of the livestock. As my ancestor grew up, he learned his **duty to cooperate** and maintain harmony with boys in his group and to be **obedient.**
14 - 18	In high school, I took typical classes, including government, where I learned about my **individual rights. I consciously** decided on my educational goals after I graduated.	As a teenager, my ancestor was allowed to carry weapons and have contact with girls. The **rights of his group** dictated that he was **we conscious** as he worked for the survival of his village. If he reached the end of his teens, it was celebrated by the adults.
19 - 22	I **independently** chose my university, my major, and my career path in line with **my goals**. Later I chose my mate and a place to live **separate from my parents**	My ancestor had to follow the **traditional** transition from youth through an elaborate initiation ceremony. Afterward, he would be eligible to marry but was **dependent on his father** to provide cattle and land.
23<	I continued to strive toward my **unique** dreams. As I age, respect will be bestowed upon me for my **accomplishments** and **expertise.**	My ancestor strove to keep his **family** happy. As my ancestor ages, respect will be bestowed on him for his **experience** and **wisdom.**

Appendix D
Possible Factors from the Locale

Research the following factors to determine how they may have affected your ancestor.

Environmental	Economic
• How did **Geography** influence why people first settled where your ancestor lived? • What significant **Natural Disasters** occurred in __________? • How did the **Climate** affect your ancestor's daily life? • List **Health hazards** in ____________. (e.g. mosquitoes, poisonous plants and animals)	• What was the **Local economy** where your ancestor resided? • Is the **Wealth distribution** even? • What is the major basis for **Labor/occupation**? (e.g. urban, marine, agricultural, rural) • Is the area near a hub of transportation that had **Access to markets**
Social	**Technology**
• What was the **Lifestyle** of your ancestor and those around him/her? • What were the **Social networks?** (e.g. family, extended family, ethnic groups) • How did **Religion** play a role in your ancestors' life? • What were the **Demographics?** • What **Access to education** was available?	• How much **Access to technology** did your ancestor have? • What **Transportation** was prevalent? • What **Energy Resources** were utilized? • What **Type of Communication** was in use?
Legal	**Political**
• What **Laws** and **Regulations** influenced your ancestors' life? (e.g. marriage, military, taxes) • Was there a **Court** nearby? • Did the **Enforcement** level create/ hinder a safe environment?	• What **Type of government** did your ancestor live under? • How Stable was the society? • What Conflicts/ Wars occurred?

Environmental	Economic
Social	**Technology**
Legal	**Political**

(Here is a sample.)

Environmental	**Economic**
• Both Guinea Bissau and Georgia had coastal regions with tidal marshes ideal for growing rice. • The climate in Guinea Bissau is tropical, while the climate in Georgia was semi-tropical, both averaging over 45 inches of rain per year. • Mosquitoes and poisonous snakes infested the swamplands.	• The local economy was based on cultivating rice on large plantations. • The wealthy planters preferred to live in the city of Savannah, while enslaved Africans were agricultural laborers. • The rivers, streams, and waterways were used to transport the rice to the port at Savannah where it was shipped back to Britain.
Social	**Technology**
• The enslaved Africans had been taken from their extended family back in Africa. The planters did not split newly formed families during the colonial period. • Laws provided for Sunday's off with some possible religious instruction, but teaching reading and writing was not allowed. • The coast was sparsely populated with planters with enslaved Africans and small farms.	• The enslaved Africans brought with them the knowledge of how to build and maintain the dikes, canals, and gates used in tidal rice cultivation. • Rafts, boats, and ships were the most prevalent form of transportation.
Legal	**Political**
• Enslaved Africans were restricted by laws that kept them from reading and writing, playing drums, playing horns, or traveling in groups of more than eight without a white person. • The Colonial Slave Law of 1755 allowed enslaved Africans to work up to 16 hours per day while keeping them in subjection and obedience.	• Colonial Georgia was governed by a governor who represented the British. • Many of the wealthy planters were Loyalists who wanted to stay as part of Britain. When the Siege of Savannah ended, the British took many of the Loyalists back to Britain.

Appendix E
How History Impacted Your Ancestor's Life

Your ancestor lived through history that influenced his/her life. A thorough understanding of your ancestor's life includes knowing how history impacted it. Using the socioeconomic factors of occupation education, income, wealth, and place of residence, you can test whether or not a historical event impacted your ancestor's life. For example, in 1957, the Soviet Union launched the world's first artificial satellite, Sputnik I. On the one hand, this sparked the U.S-U.S.S.R. space race, but on the other hand, my father was swept up into the aerospace industry which specialized in aviation and space. He was employed by several of the fifteen largest aerospace companies located in Southern California, including one that was only fifteen minutes away from our house. Thus, that historical event affected his life in far-reaching ways, including his occupation, income, and place of residence.

Finding Historical Events

There are several ways to find the historical events that had connections to your ancestor's life. One of the easiest is by using the website <www.historylines.com>. You can upload your family tree or a gedcom file from most of the major genealogy websites. Or you can enter the data for your ancestor's information manually. The vast amount of information provided in the story about your ancestor includes all the important events, plus fascinating tidbits such as hygiene and holidays. You can create a free account with 2 free stories, otherwise, you will need a subscription for access to this great website.

Another way to locate some of those historical events is to research phrases such as; timeline of the 1770s, Early American History, what happened in the year 1770 or 1770s in Georgia.

Choosing and Analyzing those Events that Impacted your Ancestor's Life

You will most likely find more information than you need. First, make a list of possible historical events, then to whittle down the list, asks yourself did these events affect your ancestor's, occupation, education, income, wealth, or place of residence. Sometimes, you might have to do a little more research. For instance, I didn't think George Washington had much to do with Granvill. To check, I researched "Georgia and George Washington," which revealed that the president went to Georgia, but not to the interior. Finally, reflect on how that historical event affected or had connections to your ancestor's life.

Year	Historical Event	Affect or connection to your Ancestor's Life

Year	Historical Event	Affect or connection to your Ancestor's Life
1783	The end of the Revolutionary War	Enslaved African Americans such as Granvill were rounded up and possibly sold to new slaveholders
1784	Bounty Lands for service in the Revolutionary War	John Blair Gilmer received a 1,000-acre land grant most likely requiring the purchase of enslaved African Americans like Granvill
1787	Ratification of the Constitution	The three-fifths clause gave the South increased representation ensuring that slavery would thrive and the fugitive-slave provision made it harder for enslaved blacks to run away
1791	Haitian Revolution	This large and successful rebellion caused paranoia and laws were passed to tighten control of enslaved African Americans
1794	Patent of the cotton gin	The cotton gin led to the expansion of slavery to fuel the export of cotton
1803	Louisiana Purchase	The doubling of the size of the country of the United States provided more land for the explosion of cotton plantations
1804	Hurricane (From HistoryLines)	A massive hurricane struck South Carolina and Georgia killing more than 500 people, most of them enslaved. How did this affect Granvill?

Appendix F
Exploring What Economic Informs You about Your Ancestor

Early Life	Microeconomic- Personal Standard of Living	Macroeconomics- National Economic Events
Necessities	Describe whether your ancestor's shelter, food, and access to water was average, below, or above average for the times	Was it economically stable?
Material goods	Describe whether your ancestor's furniture, heating/lighting, clothing, access to healthcare, education, and toys was average, below, or above average for the times.	Was there a bust such as a recession or depression?
Comfort	Describe what your ancestor did during leisure time and what, if any, luxury items he or she had.	Was there a boom time?
Adult life	Microeconomic- Did the Personal Standard of Living change?	Macroeconomics- National Economic Events
Necessities	Describe whether your ancestor's shelter, food, and access to what was average, below, or above average for the times.	Was it economically stable?
Material goods	Describe whether your ancestor's furniture, heating/lighting, clothing, access to healthcare, education, and method of transportation was average, below, or above average for the times.	Was there a bust such as a recession or depression?
Comfort	Describe what your ancestor did during leisure time and what, if any, luxury items he or she had.	Was there a boom time?

Which economic information can you utilize to "resurrect" your ancestor's life

Early Life	Microeconomic- **Personal Standard of Living**	Macroeconomics- **National Economic Events**
Necessities		
Material goods		
Comfort		
Adult life	Microeconomic- **Did the Personal Standard of Living change?**	Macroeconomics- **National Economic Events**
Necessities		
Material goods		
Comfort		

Early Life	**Microeconomic-** *Personal Standard of Living*	**Macroeconomics-** *National Economic Events*
Necessities	Granvill and Eliza's son, Jack, was probably a typical enslaved African American child. His shelter was **below average** as multiple family members lived in one room. His access to food and water included the minimal amounts provided plus whatever could be grown or gathered.	When Jack was born in about 1814, things were **stable** after the War of 1812. There was an expansion in the young country as young men like the slaveholder, George O. Gilmer, moved out to the frontier.
Material goods	Jack had few material goods which included uncomfortable clothes, hand-made toys, some healthcare, and no access to education with walking his only mode of transportation, all of which were **below average** for the times	After being taken to Madison, Alabama, when Jack was a small boy, there was the first **depression** in the young country called the Panic of 1819.
Comfort	Jack very likely had **no luxury** items, and his leisure time was spent with family and friends playing games, listening to stories, and making needed items.	The economy was uncertain as many were moving West searching for opportunity.
Adult life	**Microeconomic-** *Did the Personal Standard of Living change?*	**Macroeconomics-** *National Economic Events*
Necessities	When he married, Jack may have been able to have a bed in his one-room cabin. The amount of food available increased, although it continued to be **below average** for the times.	By the time Jack's first child was born in 1844, the United States was **stable** and beginning its transformation into an industrial country, which included the textiles and clothing made from cotton.
Material goods	Jack and his wife could provide a few more material goods because they could sell produce to earn money for special clothes for church on Sundays, but it continued to be **below average**.	The Panic of 1837 was another **depression,** but George and his son James managed to buy more land, including 10,000 acres in Bossier Parish.
Comfort	Jack could probably obtain a **few luxury items** if he saved up his earnings. He could attend parties on Saturday nights.	When Jack and the rest of the family moved to Bossier, Louisiana, in 1840, the economics of cotton caused a **boon,** especially in the Southern states.

Appendix G
Discovering What Politics Tells You about Your Ancestor

Politics at the National Level		
	_____________Politics in__________ s (Country)　　　　(years)	How it affected my ancestor
Year	Major Events	

Politics at the Local (State, County, Province, etc.) Level		
	Code of law or Legal System in _____ in the _______ s	How it affected my ancestor

What politics impacted the life of your ancestor?

	_U.S._ Politics in _1830-1860s_ (Country)　　　(years)	How it affected my ancestor
Year	**Major Events**	
1837	Louisiana, Alabama, Mississippi and Arkansas joined the nation as slave states	Once Louisiana became a state, federal land auctions allowed the Gilmers to buy more land
1850	Fugitive Slave Law	This law made it more difficult to runaway because the law required everyone to return "slaves to their owners."

Politics at the Local (State, County, Province, etc.) Level

	Code of law or Legal System in _Louisiana_ in the _1800s_	How it affected my ancestor
1806	Black Code of Louisiana	Its 37 Sections, not only defined the nature of a slave, but the discipline and regulation of enslaved blacks
1825	Civil Code of Louisiana	Elaborated on the emancipation of formally enslaved blacks
1847	New laws and amendments to the Civil Codes	Added great detail

What politics impacted the life of your ancestor?

Typically, in genealogy, one investigates the lineage of their family. Examining all the members of a family all at once in a family timeline creates a new perspective. After you have

found the location of all your ancestor's children, list moments in their lives to discover patterns that help you to resurrect your ancestor?

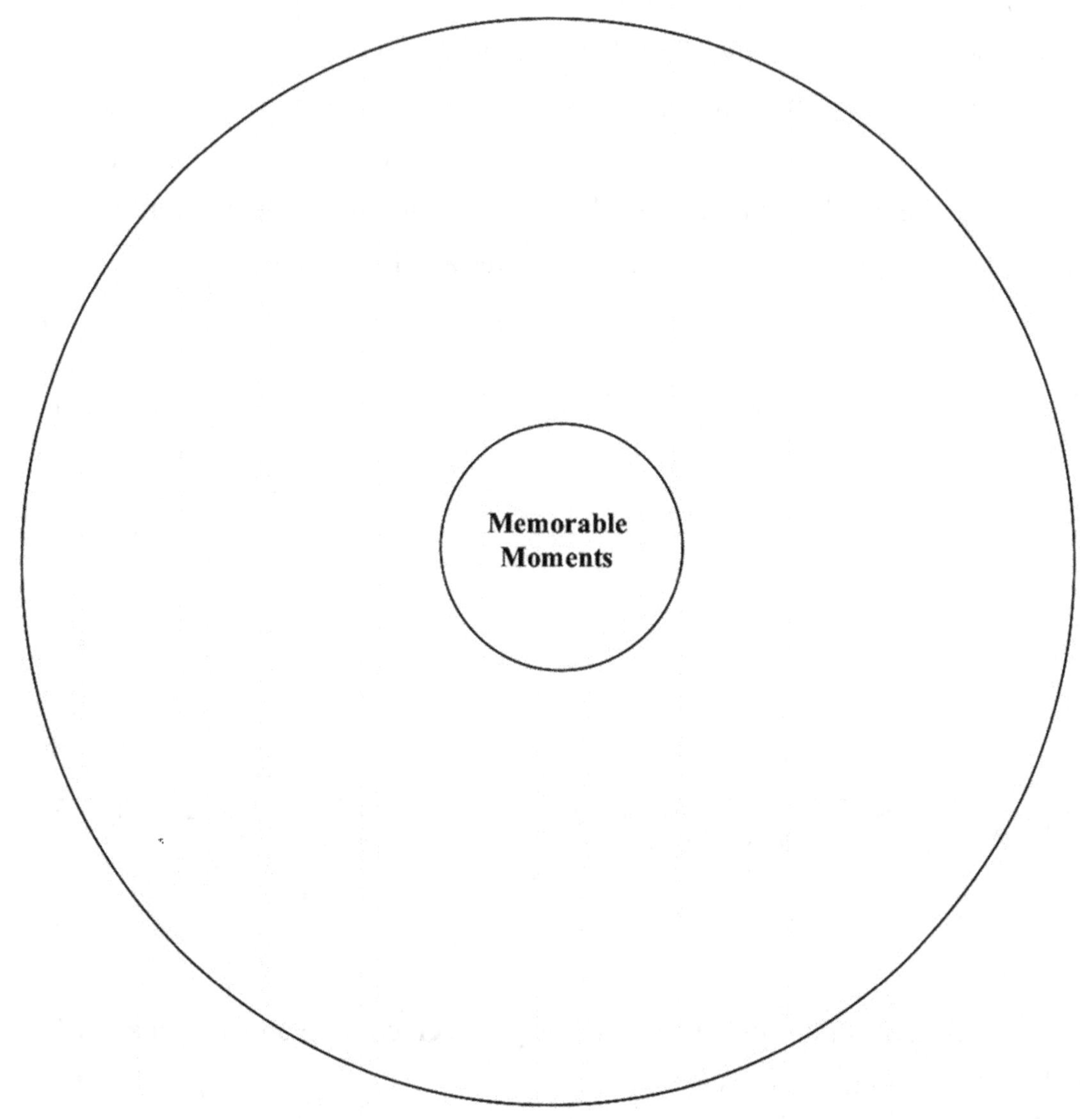

Appendix I
Shared Values

Values are the principles that guide people's lives and reflect what is important to them. Shalom Schwartz devised a scale that measures the degree to which each of us view the importance each of ten universal values.

To measure which values you share with other members of your extended family, you can have them take an online Schwartz Quiz at:

<.https://www.bbc.co.uk/taster/pilots/global-values-where-do-you-fit>or <https://www.visualdna.com/quizzes/> (Take the Success quiz)

You can also get a less sophisticated short paper version at:

<https://gosling.psy.utexas.edu/two-short-measures-of-values-tivi-and-twivi/>

Next, use the top 4 results from each family member to make a line plot.

(This is the beginning of a line plot with four X's for 2 people)

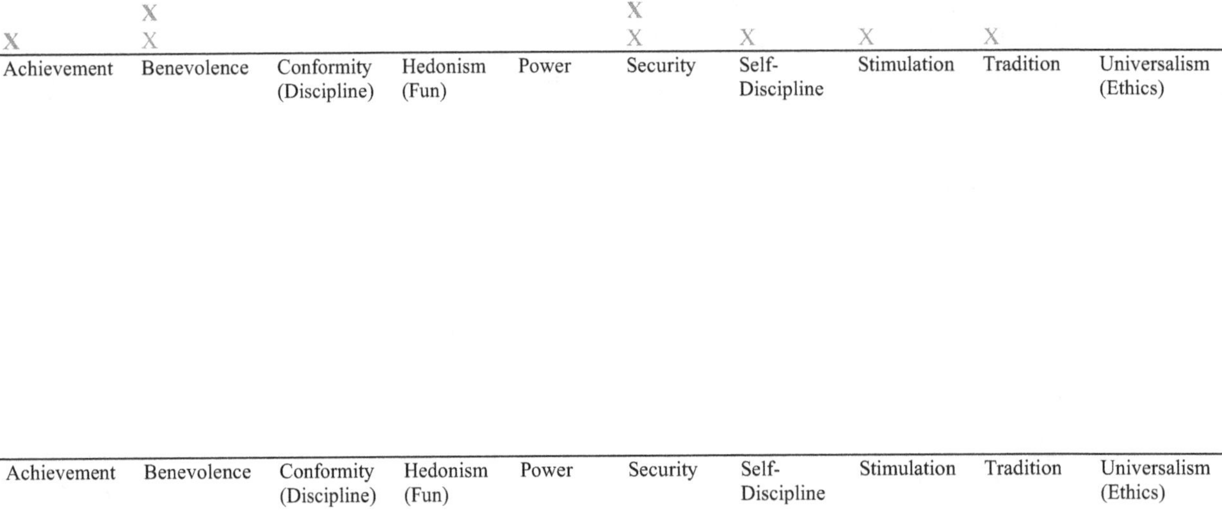

To find data on values in the census, analyze each column and also check what did or did not change over multiple censuses.

Defining goals for each value:

ACHIEVEMENT: Personal success through demonstrating competence according to social standards

BENEVOLENCE: Preservation and enhancement of the welfare of people with whom one is in frequent personal contact

CONFORMITY: Restraint of actions, inclinations, and impulses likely to upset or harm others and violate social expectations or norms

HEDONISM: Pleasure or sensuous gratification for oneself

POWER: Social status and prestige, control or dominance over people and resources

SECURITY: Safety, harmony, and stability of society, of relationships, and of self

SELF-DIRECTION: Independent thought and action - choosing, creating, exploring

STIMULATION: Excitement, novelty, and challenge in life

TRADITION: Respect, commitment, and acceptance of the customs and ideas that traditional culture or religion provide

UNIVERSALISM: Understanding, appreciation, tolerance, and protection for the welfare of all people and for nature

Subcategories for each value:

Achievement	Benevolence	Conformity	Hedonism	Power
Intelligent	Honest	Self-discipline	Enjoying life	Social power
Capable	Helpful	Honoring the	Self-indulgent	Wealth
Successful	Responsible	elders	Pleasure	Authority
Ambitious	Loyal	Politeness	Gratification for	Social recognition
Influential	Mature love	Obedient	oneself	Preserving my
	A spiritual life	Restraint of		public image
	Forgiving	actions		Prestige
	True friendship			
	Meaning in life			
Security	Self-Direction	Stimulation	Tradition	Universalism
Social order	Independent	Daring	Humble	Broadminded
Healthy	Curious	A varied life	Devout	Tolerance
Clean	Freedom	An exciting life	Respect for	Equality
Family security	Creativity	Novelty	tradition	Wisdom
National security	Choosing own goals	Challenge in life	Moderate	Social justice
Reciprocation of	Privacy		Accepting my	Inner harmony
favors	Self-respect		portion in life	Protecting the
Harmony			Detachment	environment
Safety				A world at peace
				A world of beauty

*Can you find evidence for the common shared values in your extended family? What values do you hypothesize your ancestor also had?

Appendix J
Patterns in the Data

To peer deeply into the lives of your ancestors' descendants, you will need to collect and analyze data. The most assessible place to find data on multiple line of the family is the original records of United States Federal Census. Other data-rich records are obituaries including those on the website Find A Grave and military records such as the Draft Registration Cards and Enlistment Records. Record the information using graph paper, then interpret any patterns that you discover.

Type of record	Topic	Possible topics to investigate
Census	age	What was the age at first marriage, the difference between the ages of the spouses*, the age of mother at birth of the youngest or oldest child?
	marriage	If mostly married, single, divorced or widowed, how many years married? Did your family members tend to stay married or did multiple members get divorced?
	residence	Are family members nearby*, are the birthplace of the parents and the children the same, which denotes stability or are there frequent changes in residence even within the children, which show an adventurous type or immigration?
	children	How many children and how many are living in 1900? How long did the children go to school? When did the children start working? How late did the children stay in the family?
	location	Examining the page your ancestor is on over several censuses, are most of the other people from the same place or not? What languages are spoken besides English? Are the occupations similar or is there a variety? Can you tell which type of neighborhood your family member lived in such as laborers or professionals?
	home	Is it rented, owned, mortgaged or owned free*?
	education	Can they read or write*? What was their level of education in 1940? Was there a gender gap in the amount of education the males received vs. the females?
	Other	Was there a pattern of illnesses, disabilities, blindness or deafness
	Wars	In 1910, there is a question on whether your ancestor was a survivor of the Union or Confederate Army or Navy?
Military	Physical description	About 98 percent of men born between 1872 and 1900 are covered in the U.S., World War Draft Registration Cards, 1917-1918, what was the hair and eye color, height, and build?*
		U.S, World War II Army Enlistment Records, 1938-1946 include height and weight, draft cards include complexion
Immigration records	Life details	Besides the name, age, gender, marital status and occupation, what was the physical description of your ancestors? Were they naturalized?
Marriage Records	Life details	Age at the time of the marriage, church, county, full names, occupation, witnesses
Death Records	Life details	Age at death, cause of death including health issues that run in the family, occupation, religious affiliation
Obituary	Life details	What was deemed important enough to describe in the obituary - schooling, religious activities*, hobbies, career, personality and most memorable trait?

*The patterns I found in the resurrection of my ancestor. What patterns can you find as you look at multiple families that descended from your ancestor?

Appendix K
Rating My Family's Tendencies

One of the ways you can describe a family is by what tendencies they have. You can characterize a family by what makes them unique as well as by their strengths. Perhaps the easiest way to determine how your family is unique is to follow the tendencies on your direct line of the family and then see if it is the same on other lines. In the worksheet below, please evaluate the characteristics to see which ones apply to your family.

Part 1: Possible tendencies or characteristics that may apply to your family:

I see evidence in my family to show my family is…

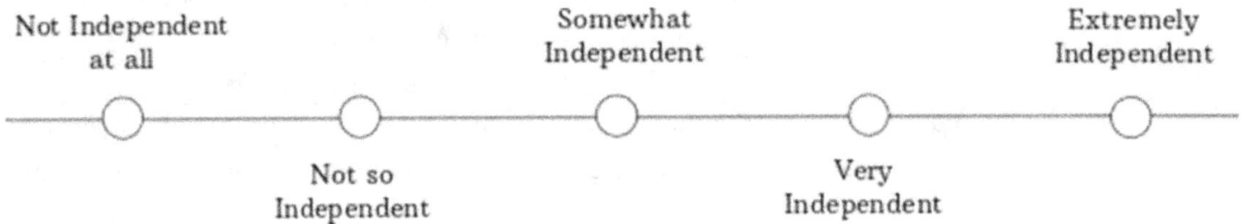

I see evidence in my family to show my family takes care of family and each other…

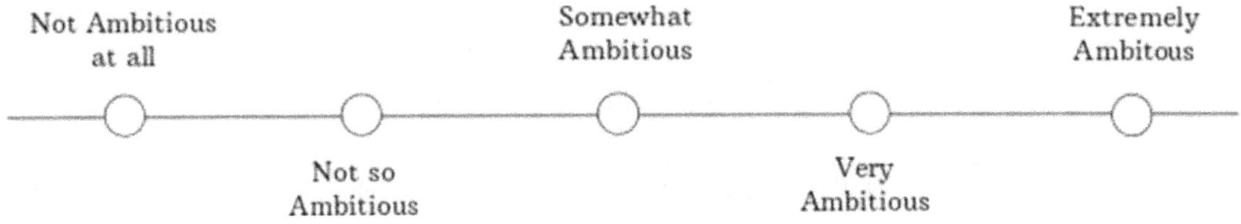

I see evidence in my family to show my family is committed to education…

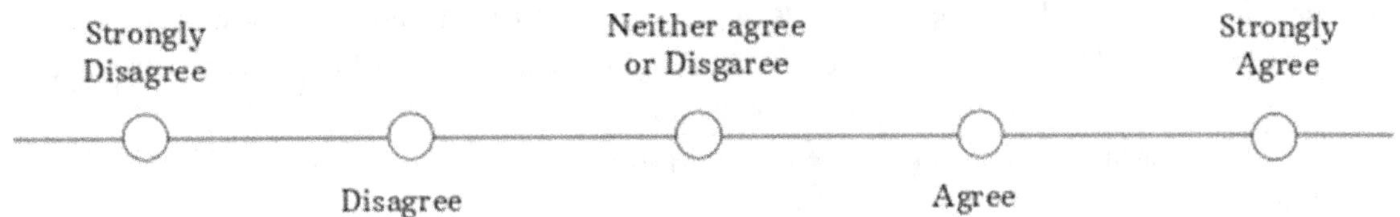

I see evidence in my family to show my family's religious conviction is…

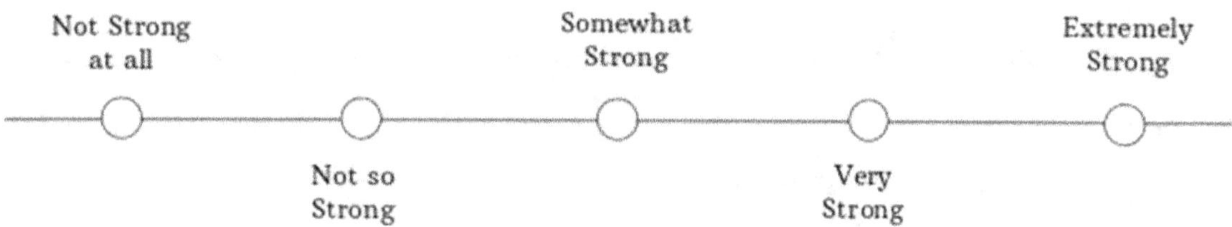

Part 2: Another way to rate your family is to utilize the characteristics of strong families to assess which strengths your whole family displays.

Possible Family strengths researchers say strong families have that might apply to your family.

I see evidence in my family that they show appreciation for each other…

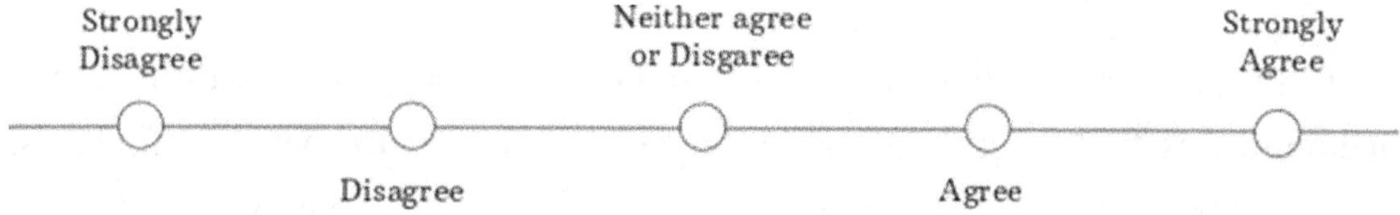

I see evidence in my family to show my family is…

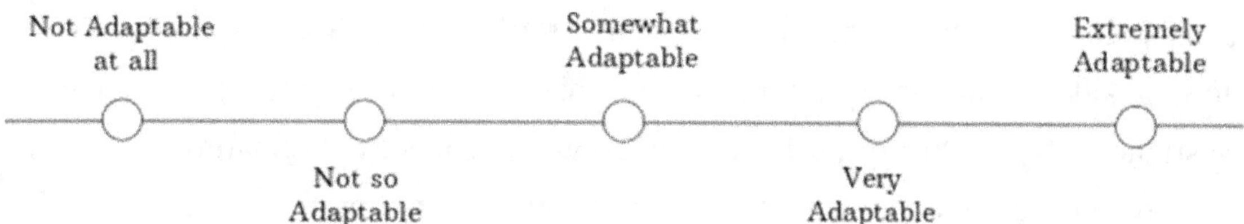

I see evidence my family engages in positive communication…

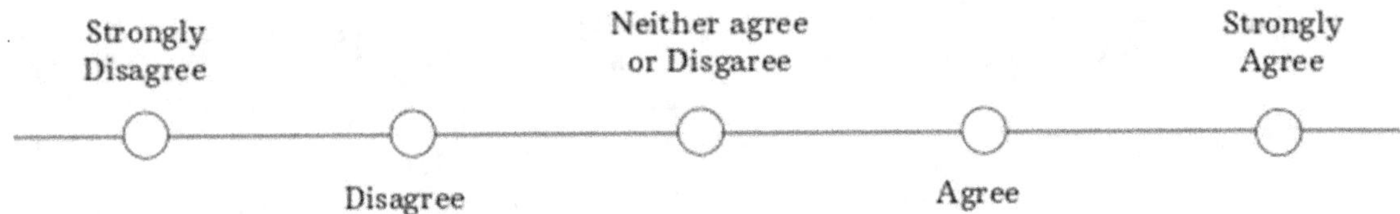

see evidence my family is engaged in the community…

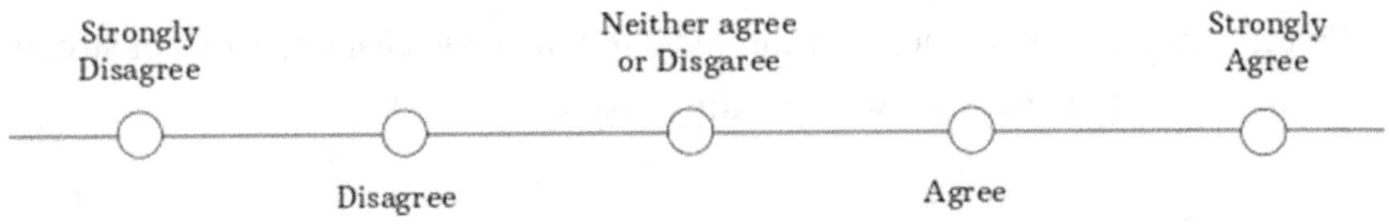

Appendix L
Finding Your Ancestor's Personality

Finding the occupations cluster under one interest

Use the "Interest" section of the database O*NET (Occupational Information Network) <onetonline.org/find/descriptor/browse/Interests/> to decide which of the six work environments to view first. Hint: Realistic (doers), Investigative (thinkers), Artistic (creators), Social (helpers), Enterprising (persuaders), and Conventional(organizers).

Or you can place the occupation in the Occupation Quick Search, but you have to scroll down the page to find the interest section. For example, my mother's maternal side had a dietary manager, teacher, and minister, which fell under the Social type. While my father's paternal side, contained carpenters, psychiatrist, and engineers that landed in the Investigative type. On my husband's paternal side, it was fascinating that a shopkeeper, judge, and education administrator were all under the Enterprising type.

Connecting the Occupation type to a Personality

Each of the Job Personality and Work Environments has its preferences and traits that will help you to get a rough idea of the personality of your ancestor.

Realistic	Your ancestor prefers physical, hand-on activities that need skill, strength and coordination and deal with things like plants or tools Traits include being honest, practical, stable, frank, conforming
Investigative	Your ancestor prefers working with information and ideas that require considerable amounts of thinking and problem solving Traits include being curious, independent, analytical, precise, introverted
Artistic	Your ancestor prefers creative, original activities without having to follow clear sets rules using artistic skill and a good imagination Trait include being imaginative, impulsive, complicated, emotional, nonconforming
Social	Your ancestor prefers activities that help, heal and develop others and are involved with working with or providing service to people Traits include being friendly, generous, sympathetic, warm, understanding
Enterprising	Your ancestor prefers competitive environments where their leadership skills are useful for selling, influencing people and seeking status Traits include being ambitious, self-confident, domineering, energetic, extroverted
Conventional	Your ancestor prefers activities that follow set procedures and routines that are orderly and efficient Traits include being careful, obedient, unimaginative, detailed, persistent

*You may have more than one type. What are your findings? Are there other genetic traits that help in "resurrecting" your ancestor's life?

Part 2

Another way to learn about your ancestor's possible personality and other traits is to dig into genetics. In particular, what runs in families and more specifically in your genes.

Fact or likeliness	Evidence
PERSONALITY TRAITS	Rate other family members, ethnic tendencies and tendencies from the genes of several descendants from high to low
Level of extroversion of sociability and friendliness	
Level of openness to new ideas and experiences	
Level of neuroticism anxiety or worry	
Level of agreeableness or kindness	
Level of conscientiousness or work ethic	
PHYSICAL TRAITS	Record information using photographs and oral evidence from family members of several lines of your ancestor's family
Skin pigmentation	
Hair type and color	
Hairline is straight or not	
Eye color	
Earlobe attached or not	
Lips full or not	
GENES	Upload your raw DNA data to <genomelink.io> to record your evidence from several lines
Food & Nutrition	
Personality	
Intelligence	
Physical traits	
Sports	
Health	

What DNA Evidence Shows Granvill and Eliza were My 3rd great-grandparents?

Understanding genetic versus genealogical relationships

Genealogists usually use records to reveal clues on how two people are related. The most important way to find this genealogical relationship is to determine which ancestor those two people have in common. When you have no clear records, how might DNA be useful?

By utilizing your DNA matches, you can try to uncover genetic relationships. The measure of your genetic relationship is the sum of DNA you share with a DNA match provided in centimorgans (cMs). The more centimorgans you share with another person, the closer you are related to them. According to Blaine T. Bettinger on *The Shared cM Project Version 3.0,* <www.thegeneticgenealogist.com>, if you share between 3,330-3,720 cM with someone older, they are a parent, and if they are younger, they are your child. Since I share 3,471 cM with my dad, that verifies he is my dad genetically, and my birth certificate provides that evidence genealogically.

The smaller the amount of centimorgans shared, the trickier it is to find out the genetic relationship. For example, my DNA cousin, Cheryl, and I share about 60 cM. That means she could be any of 26 different genetic relationships from half 3rd cousin to 5th cousin. Her genealogical relationship is 2nd cousin once removed because we have documents that prove Samuel and Caroline Smith are her great-grandparents and my second-great-grandparents. While the 30 cM my DNA cousin, James, and I share also could be multiple genetic relationships, genealogically, we are 4th cousins. We don't have a conclusive paper trail that shows Granvill and Eliza are our 3rd great-grandparents. Cheryl shares 17 cM with James, my father shares 182 cM with Cheryl, and 132 cM with James. He shares more centimorgans with them than I, because he is one generation closer to them.

Using genetics to provide evidence for relationships

If I had yDNA from all the sons of Granvill, ideally, a consistent signature would demonstrate they were all related. Absent that, I set out to use DNA matches. Although we have evidence that Granvill and Eliza had seven children, and Granvill had at least one daughter by another wife, we currently only have DNA matches for six of those children. To complete this investigation, I couldn't just use my data because those DNA matches only match to me. I needed access to the DNA matches for my father, Cheryl, and James. I googled, "how to share your DNA results," to find how to get them.

Next, I selected two DNA matches, which I called A and B, from each of Granvill's six children; Lucy, Jack, Austin, Marywether, Samuel, and Jane. Each of these 12 relatives is a DNA match to my father. Some of them did not match with Cheryl, James, and myself. I carefully recorded the centimorgans those matches shared with my father, Cheryl, James, and myself in a table. The ThruLines on Ancestry were very helpful in gathering this information.

	Lucy Ann		Jack		Austin		Marywether		Samuel		Jane	
Shared	cM		cM		cM		cM		cM		cM	
DNA cousins	A	B	A	B	A	B	A	B	A	B	A	b
My father	162	16	32	48	106	13	63	7	342	465	32	12
Me	25	17	7	49	22	22	31	0	121	281	22	12
Cheryl	50	10	27	34	8	17	0	0	172	35	76	42
James	15	21	7	49	1851	102	0	14	0	15	0	12

The Shared Centimorgans (cM) of Selected Granvill and Eliza's Descendants

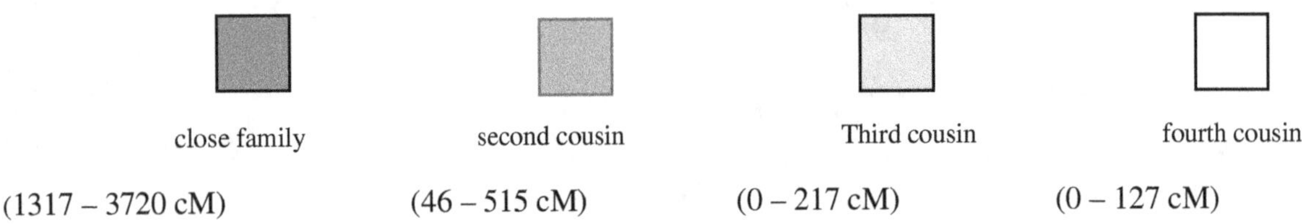

When I recorded all the data into a table, some expected patterns occurred. First, my father, Cheryl, and I all have the same common ancestors of Samuel and Caroline. So, if you look down Samuel's column, the number of centimorgans that we share with Samuel's DNA descendants A and B is higher. The ones who are second cousins have higher amounts than the third cousins. Also, you can see that my father is second cousins, while I am second and second cousin once removed. The same thing happens if you scan down Austin's column. James shares a very high number of centimorgans with a close family member, while the third cousin's number is lower.

Next, most of us DNA cousins are 4th cousins to everyone else except those in our direct lineage. That make sense, because 4th cousins share 3rd great-grandparents. Also, the data is in line with the range of 0 – 127 shared centimorgans for 4th cousins, with an average of 35 cM. Something interesting occurs glancing down the Lucy Ann column. She is a half-sibling, so she does not have centimorgans from Eliza. Her numbers are consistent with half relatives.

In conclusion, I wanted to find out if DNA could be used to find relationships. I used multiple DNA matches that are related to me and to each other. The findings were consistent, I was 4th cousins with everyone except those on my direct lineage. My DNA cousins were also 4th cousins to everyone else except the ones on their lines of descent. Thus, there is a very high probability that Granvill and Eliza were our common ancestors and my 3rd great-grandparents.

www.ingramcontent.com/pod-product-compliance
Lightning Source LLC
Chambersburg PA
CBHW081433250726
48662CB00009B/2769